The Life and Work of
MOTHER LOUISE MARGARET
CLARET DE LA TOUCHE
containing
A Message From Our Divine Lord
For The Clergy Of The World

Mother Louise Margaret

The Life and Work of
MOTHER
LOUISE MARGARET
CLARET DE LA TOUCHE

containing

A Message From Our Divine Lord
For The Clergy Of The World

Compiled from original sources
by
Fr. Patrick O'Connell, B.D.

Delegate of the Central Council of the Priests'
Universal Union of the Friends of the Sacred Heart

TAN BOOKS AND PUBLISHERS, INC.
Rockford, Illinois 61105

Nihil Obstat: Jacobus Browne
                  Censor Deputatus

Imprimatur: ✠ Jacobus
                  Episcopus Fernensis
                  die Ia Martii 1950

Originally published in 1950 by the Irish Members of the Priests' Universal Union of the Friends of the Sacred Heart and printed in the Republic of Ireland by John English & Co., Ltd., Wexford.

ISBN: 0-89555-311-2

Library of Congress Catalog Card Number: 86-51579

Printed and bound in the United States of America.

TAN BOOKS AND PUBLISHERS, INC.
P.O. Box 424
Rockford, Illinois 61105

1987

DECLARATION

When giving these pages to our venerated confreres in the Priesthood and to the public, we have no intention of pronouncing on the mystic communications which they contain ; we conform ourselves to the established discipline and declare that we submit filially and entirely to the judgment of our Holy Mother, the Church.

Dedicated by the Translator and his Brother to the memory of their dear Parents.

" I was not born to be a Religious, or to be a Superioress. In the designs of Providence, I was to be both, but that is not my raison d'etre. My raison d'etre is to be a nothing, a feather flying with the wind, a grain of sand heaved up by the sea, but this feather, this grain of sand, are **Messengers of Infinite Love.** Yes, my role here below is to publish the good news throughout the world, the good news that can never be repeated by enough people, the good news that has been repeated for the last twenty centuries without ceasing to be the news that all men have need to learn : It is **that God is Love, and that consequently He loves His creatures.** To know this would mean happiness for the individual, happiness for peoples, happiness for humanity : but people refuse to believe it, and thus refuse to be happy—for men's intellects for want of light remain in darkness, and men's hearts for want of this heat remain cold and sad."

From *Intimate Notes* of Mother Louise Margaret

TABLE OF CONTENTS

Contents

Contents

FOREWORD

In the foreword to *The Sacred Heart and the Priesthood*, we promised to publish a translation which was made in China of three volumes, under the title of " In the Service of Jesus Priest," containing a detailed account of the life and revelations of Mother Louise Margaret Claret de la Touche. The publication was delayed because the matter contained in these volumes was being rearranged so as to give her life and work, and her writings, in separate volumes. That work is now completed. The new edition consists of two volumes instead of three. Everything dealing with her life and mission—which was the establishment of the Priests' Universal Union of the Friends of the Sacred Heart and the foundation of a new Monastery of Sisters to serve as a spiritual support for it—is found in the first volume ; while in the second volume, her writings not included in *The Sacred Heart and the Priesthood* and *The Book of Infinite Love* are given in order of subjects.

The materials for this first volume are drawn from *The Messenger of Infinite Love*, which is a history of the life and work of Mother Louise Margaret written by a Visitation Sister, and from the three volumes of *In the Service of Jesus Priest*, which is a collection of her letters and writings arranged in chronological order and made to tell the story of her life.

The first part of the present work is a translation of the summary found in *The Messenger of Infinite Love*, but for the second part, which deals with the important questions of the establishment of the Priests' Universal Union, the foundation of Bethany of the Sacred Heart and the proceedings at Rome, we decided to give the original letters and documents, instead of the summary found in *The Messenger of Infinite Love*, and to allow the chief actors, Mother Louise Margaret, Monsignor Filipello, Father Charrier, and the Roman Authorities to tell the story in their own words.

In all her writings, and when questioned by her Director, Father Charrier, her Bishop, Monsignor Filipello, and the Cardinals at Rome, Mother Louise Margaret never varied in her statement that neither the establishment of The Priests' Universal Union, nor the foundation of the new monastery, nor her spiritual writings were the expression of her own ideas or the result of study and investigation ; but that the establishment of the Priests' Universal Union and the foundation of the new monastery were commanded by Our Lord, and her spiritual writings were communications received from Him to be transmitted to His priests. All her writings of every kind were examined at Rome by the Congregation of the Council and were found to be free from error ; the establishment of the Priests' Universal Union of the Friends of the Sacred Heart and its Statutes, which were drawn up by her, were sanctioned by the Congregation of the Council, and she was entrusted with the foundation of the new monastery by the Congregation for Religious.

INTRODUCTION.

Our Divine Lord is the absolute Master of His gifts. If He chooses to bestow special favours on any of His servants whom He selects to carry out His commands, it belongs to Him to mark out the limits of their mission. When St. Gertrude the Great asked St. John the Evangelist, on the occasion when he appeared to her, why he had not published to the world the secrets of the Sacred Heart of Jesus which were revealed to him when he reclined his head on Our Lord's breast at the Last Supper he replied that his mission to the early Church was to speak of the uncreated Word of the Father ; that the revelation of the secrets of the Sacred Heart was reserved for later ages, in order that the world, when grown cold in the service of God, might have its love for Him rekindled.

The revelations of the Sacred Heart made to St. Gertrude and many other Saints hundreds of years before the time of St. Margaret Mary Alacoque, and in essentials similar to those which she received, were indeed written down and found their way into all the Religious Orders and helped wonderfully to excite and conserve their fervour ; but they did not reach the ordinary faithful, because in the designs of Providence, the privilege of publishing them to the world was reserved for St. Margaret Mary Alacoque. When Our Lord selected her to propagate the devotion to His Sacred Heart, He prepared her for the work, not by making her study the lives and revelations of those Saints to whom He had spoken already—there is no indication in her life that she even heard of them— but by making her share in His own suffering life. After the lapse of two and a half centuries, when the world had sunk to depths of wickednes hitherto undreamt of, Christ selected a new instrument to deliver a new message of love. He prepared her as He had prepared St. Margaret Mary Alacoque and all His chosen messengers, by a life of suffering, and He marked out the limits of her work when, during the Octave of the Feast of the Sacred Heart in 1902, He said to her : " Margaret Mary has shown my Heart to the world ; do you show It to My priests."

Her mission bears a great similarity to that of St. Margaret Mary Alacoque, but it is not identical ; it does not consist in merely repeating the revelations made to her ; for these revelations she referred the clergy to the authorised works on the devotion to the Sacred Heart and urged them to study the devotion deeply in order that they might be able to explain it to the faithful.

A study of the evidence given in the present volume will show that the work given to her by Our Lord was the establishment of the Priests Universal Union of the Friends of the Sacred Heart and its branches, the principal of which is Bethany of the Sacred Heart ; and that the communications which she received on the dignity of the priesthood, the virtues which the priest should have, the sublime mysteries of Infinite Love, found in *The Sacred Heart and the Priesthood, The Book of Infinite Love* and in Volume II of the present series, are the food with which the new organization is to be nourished.

As there is a great similarity between the mission of St. Margaret Mary Alacoque and that of Mother Louise Margaret, there is also a great similarity in their lives. Both of them lost their father during their infancy, and both felt keenly the loss of a father's warm love ; both of them made vows of virginity in their infancy, before they were capable of understanding their full meaning ; both their mothers used every device to keep their daughters in the world and get them married. Both were under the special protection of the Blessed Virgin ; both were miraculously cured by Our Lady in answer to vows made to her, from maladies that were regarded as incurable ; when they recovered their health, both were allowed to experience how weak poor human nature is when unaided by grace. The account given by St. Margaret Mary of her struggle with nature is almost verbatim the same as that which we shall find in the life of Mother Louise Margaret.

St. Margaret Mary describes it for us in her autobiography as follows :—

" When I recovered my health, I thought only of seeking pleasure in the enjoyment of my liberty, without troubling much about carrying out my promise . . . ."

And later on, when they had grown up, the story of the two is again the same.

St. Margaret Mary writes : " The devil instigated several desirable suitors to seek my hand in marriage. This attracted much company . . . and my mother urged me with tears to remain in the world . . . The tender affection which I had for my mother began to get the upper hand; I thought that as I had made the vow of virginity when I was only a child and did not understand its meaning, I could get dispensed from it. I began to see visitors and to adorn myself to please them, and sought only to amuse myself as much as I could."

Both were pardoned by Our Lord and to the end of their lives, never ceased to weep for their resistance to grace and to sing the mercies of the Lord.

To prepare them for their mission Our Lord demanded a promise of abandonment to His will from St. Margaret Mary, and a vow of abandonment from Mother Louise Margaret. He sent both specially chosen directors to guide them and reassure them, and when the time came to act, He demanded from St. Margaret Mary and Blessed Claude de la Colombiere that they should consecrate themselves to His Sacred Heart, and from Mother Louise Margaret and Father Charrier that they should consecrate themselves and make a total donation of themselves to Infinite Love.

But the most remarkable similarity about these two, neither of whom had studied books on the devotion to the Sacred Heart, is the way in which they agree on points that many learned authors fail to explain satisfactorily. St. Margaret Mary strove with all her power to obtain honour for the Sacred Heart of Jesus, hypostatically united to the Divine Word ; but emphasised the fact that the Sacred Heart, though worthy of adoration, is not the principal object of the devotion, but the infinite love of that Heart which induced Him to undergo all the sufferings of His Passion.

Father Croiset, who wrote the first book on the public devotion during her lifetime and under her direction, writes :

" The devotion to the Sacred Heart cannot be reduced—as some people might think at seeing this title—to merely loving and honouring by special worship this Heart of flesh like ours, Which forms part of the adorable Body of Jesus Christ.

It is not that the Sacred Heart is not worthy of adoration . . . . ; if His Sacred Body and His precious Blood deserve our respect and homage, who does not see that His Sacred Heart has still more special claim to respect and homage. . . . What we wish to make clear is that the word " heart " is taken here only in its figurative sense, and that the Divine Heart, considered as a part of the adorable Body of Jesus Christ, is, properly speaking, only the sensible object of the devotion ; and that it is nothing less than the immense love which Jesus Christ bears us which is its principal motive." [1]

---

[1] See " The Devotion to the Sacred Heart of Our Lord Jesus Christ " by Father Croiset, page 50.

Mother Louise Margaret writes in *The Book of Infinite Love :* " This salutary devotion which has come so opportunely in these last ages to aid us in the fight against indifference, coldness and egoism, served marvellously to increase and enkindle divine love in souls by making them see in epitome in the Heart of Christ, ' the length and breadth, the height and depth of the Charity of God.' The devotion to the Sacred Heart, in order to be efficacious, should not be, as too often happens, a vague, superficial, sentimental devotion attached to the exterior object. **Although very justly we may and ought to adore this Heart of flesh, Which is the real tabernacle of divine Charity and most truly the Heart of God in virtue of the hypostatic union, we should not, however, stop there, but we should penetrate by the opening of the Heart into the most profound mysteries of Infinite Love.**

We should in particular apply ourselves to this by an assiduous study of the Holy Gospels, of the immortal Epistles of St. John and St. Paul, by the reading of the early Fathers and of the Catholic authors who have treated this admirable subject. We shall thus acquire a true and solid devotion to this divine Heart, and we shall be in a position to communicate it to the faithful who do not all yet understand the treasures of regeneration and grace which are found there."

We find also that there is complete agreement in the teaching found in the revelations made to St. Margaret Mary and that found in the writings of Mother Louise Margaret on the relations between the devotion to the Sacred Heart and devotion to the Blessed Sacrament. St. Margaret Mary makes the practice of the devotion to the Sacred Heart consist chiefly in acts of devotion to the Blessed Sacrament ; the First Friday Communion, visits to the Blessed Sacrament and the Holy Hour. Father Croiset in his *Devotion to the Sacred Heart of Our Lord Jesus Christ,* writes :—" The devotion to the Sacred Heart of Jesus is a more warm-hearted and ardent devotion towards Jesus Christ in the Blessed Sacrament, its principal motive being the extreme love which He shows us in this Sacrament, and its principal object, to make reparation for the contempt and outrages which He suffers in this same Sacrament."

On this question Mother Louise Margaret writes in *The Book of Infinite Love :* " The devotion to the Blessed Eucharist and the devotion to the Sacred Heart are not only two sister devotions, in reality, they are one and the same devotion. They complete each other and develop each other ; they blend so perfectly together that one cannot stand without the other, and their union is absolute. Not only can one of these devotions not be prejudicial to the other, but, because they complete each other and perfect each other, they also reciprocally increase each other.

If we have devotion to the Sacred Heart, we will wish to find It, to adore It, to love It, to offer It our adoration and praise, and where shall we look for It but in the Blessed Eucharist, where It is found eternally living?

If we love this adorable Heart, we will wish to unite ourselves to It, for love seeks union.   . . . .

The devotion to the Divine Heart infallibly brings souls to the Blessed Eucharist, and faith in and devotion to the Blessed Eucharist, necessarily lead souls to discover the mysteries of Infinite Love of which the Divine Heart is the organ and the symbol."

Finally, there is a close parallel between how the Holy See treated the revelations made to St. Margaret Mary Alacoque and the communications made to Mother Louise Margaret. The Holy See examined the revelations made to St. Margaret Mary and sanctioned all the details of the devotion to the Sacred Heart exactly as recommended by them. No further pronouncement was made on these revelations except that they contained nothing contrary to the teaching of the Church. The Holy See allowed the devotion to the Sacred Heart to grow gradually, indulgenced it as it grew, but did not force its growth. It was not until the time of Pope Pius XI that the Feast of the Sacred Heart was raised to the dignity of a double of the first class with an Octave. The cause of St. Margaret Mary was introduced soon after her death in 1690, but she was not beatified until 1864, and was not canonised until 1919.

The treatment accorded to the communications of Mother Louise Margaret is in all respects similar. All the details of the plan which she said she received from Our Lord were sanctioned exactly as she submitted them—the Priests' Universal Union of the Friends of the Sacred Heart and its Statutes, and the project of a new monastery of Sisters to act as a spiritual foundation for it. All her writings of every kind were submitted to the Holy See and examined, and were found to be free from error. Permission was given to publish them, and Pope Benedict XV ordered that they be published without change, exactly as she wrote them.

The three Popes who have succeeded Pius X, in whose reign the work of Infinite Love was sanctioned, have continued to bless and encourage it. His present Holiness, Pius XII, gave the translator and editor of her writings in English a special blessing for the publication of these writings and for the introduction of the Priests' Universal Union of the Friends of the Sacred Heart into Ireland, England and America. When the first English edition of *The Sacred Heart and the Priesthood* and *The Book of Infinite Love* were presented to him, he sent through Cardinal Montini a gracious message of encouragement for the propagation of the Work of Infinite Love and His Apostolic Benediction to the translator.

Formerly the impression was common that the devotion to the Sacred Heart of Jesus began with St. Margaret Mary Alacoque, and that impression exists still among many of the laity. The lessons of the second nocturn of the Breviary make it clear, however, that a form of the devotion goes back to Apostolic times and that the devotion itself, almost in the same form as we have it, without, however, the First Friday devotions, was practised in nearly all the Religious Orders from the Middle Ages onwards. Hundreds of years before the time of St. Margaret Mary Alacoque, Our Divine Lord appeared repeatedly to various Saints and His revelations to them were almost word for word the same as those made to St. Margaret Mary. Many of these privileged ones, for instance, St Mechtilde and St. Gertrude, were contemporaries. Father Croiset, the Director of St. Margaret Mary, mentions this fact in his book on the devotion to show that the devotion to the Sacred Heart of Jesus, then for the first time preached to the general body of the faithful, was no innovation in the Church.

It would be strange indeed if messages of love from the Sacred Heart of Jesus to the faithful, which had continued all through the ages down to the time of St. Margaret Mary, were to cease at her death. Such, however, is not the case. The present volume deals with a well-authenticated message from the Sacred Heart of Jesus in our own times, directed chiefly to the clergy of the world. And as in past times, Our Lord had given his loving messages to many holy souls, but reserved for one the work of publishing it to the whole world, so He has done again in our times. In the appendix to *The Sacred Heart and the Priesthood* (pages 216-217) we referred to one of these contemporary witnesses to the message conveyed by Mother Louise Margaret—Sister Josefa Menendez, who died in 1925—and we quoted from her writings. Since that time a new and more complete life of Sister Josefa, edited by two French Jesuits, has been published in France. An English translation of this life has just appeared under the title : " *The Way of Divine Love or The Message of the Sacred*

Heart to the World." There is a remarkable similarity between the Messages of Love and Mercy from Our Lord delivered by these two saintly Sisters. There is, however, a difference in their missions. It was Our Lord's design that Mother Louise Margaret should devote herself and sacrifice herself completely, both in her own person and in the Religious Community which she founded at His command, to the spiritual interests of the Pope, bishops and priests of His Church ; and she left an organisation consisting of four parts, sanctioned and blessed by the Holy See, to perpetuate her work.

Sister Josefa Menendez was also the bearer of a message from the Sacred Heart of Jesus to the world in general and to Priests and Religious in particular ; she prayed and suffered for priests and recited daily for them the following beautiful prayer taught to her by Our Lord :

" O Jesus, by Thy most loving Heart, I implore Thee to inflame with zeal for Thy love and glory all the priests of the world, all missionaries, and those whose office it is to preach Thy word, that, on fire with holy zeal, they may snatch souls from the devil and lead them into the shelter of Thy Heart where for ever they may glorify Thee."

She also urged priests to combine together in a League of Love and to make devotion to the Sacred Heart their bond of union, but it was not her mission to have this league founded. It was Mother Louise Margaret whom Our Divine Lord chose to bear His message for the founding of this League of Love—The Priests' Universal Union of the Sacred Heart—to Pope Pius X. As we shall see in the course of this volume, the Holy See, after careful consideration, sanctioned its foundation, and four successive Popes have given it their blessing and support.

To all these messengers of love of Our Divine Lord we may apply the words of Mother Louise Margaret : " Their role here below has been to publish the good news throughout the world, the good news that has been repeated for the past twenty centuries without ceasing to be the good news that all men have need to learn :

It is that God is Love and that consequently He loves His creatures."

May Our Divine Lord deign to bless this humble effort to make known the mysteries of Infinite Love.

PATRICK O'CONNELL.

January 1st, 1950.

xxi

FRANCE AND ITALY.

In the little district of Canavese, about forty kilometres from Turin, at Vische, on the 25th March, 1932, an intentionally simple but very touching ceremony took place. Monsignor Filipello Bishop of Ivrea, surrounded by twelve priests and the competent authorities, proceeded to verify and translate the remains of a French Sister who had died seventeen years previously. Her tomb, which up to then had been in the public cemetery, will be henceforward in the enclosure of the Sisters of Bethany of the Sacred Heart, but placed in such a position that all can view it from outside and pray near this sacred spot. A marble slab, also brought in from the public cemetery, leans against a wooden cross. On it is written this simple inscription :—

May Jesus ✠ be praised.
Sister Louise Margaret Claret de la Touche, Superioress of Visitation of Holy Mary, Monastery of Vische, died 14th May, 1915.
May God ✠ be blessed.

How came this daughter of France to find her last resting place under the skies of Piedmont? Why is the tomb of this daughter of St. Francis de Sales surrounded by Religious who bear neither the name nor the habit of the Visitation? By what prodigy do we see kneeling inside the enclosure by her humble tomb, Sisters speaking many different languages, and outside, lay folk and above all priests in great numbers, come from the different countries of Europe and indeed from more distant places?

These questions will be answered in the pages of this book. But first, let us listen to the lesson of this tomb. The Saints, the true disciples of Christ, alone are able to bring about union, to make unity a reality, to overcome the barriers of race and divergent interests. With the Apostle, they repeat : " There is neither Jew nor Greek : there is neither bond nor free : there is neither male nor female. For you are all one in Christ Jesus. (Galatians iii, 28)."

The Sister whose acquaintance we are about to make understood better than most people the meaning of these words : " That they may be one as we are one " (John XVII, 22), which issued from the Heart of the Word made Man on the last evening of His mortal life ; and if her prayers and sufferings demand that these words be made a reality, especially by priests, may her powerful intercession obtain this blessing of unity for all Christians especially for the two countries, one of which was her birthplace, while the other holds her tomb.

CHAPTER I.

EARLY YEARS.

THE MIRACULOUS PROTECTION BY MARY

Breton and Champagne blood mingled in the veins of Margaret Claret de la Touche. Her father, who belonged to an old aristocratic family from Vannes which suffered during the Revolution, had married at thirty-three a young girl of twenty-two, Mary Cousin, who came from the town of Troyes. Both were what the world calls people of distinction and were possessed of charming qualities. Both of them possessed something better : a solid Christian faith, and habits of virtue which exterior influence never changed.

When the second daughter was born on the 15th of March, 1868, at Saint Germain-en-Laye, where Mr. Claret de la Touche was Customs' Officer, she was welcomed with copious tears. Her parents wanted a son, especially her mother, who had prayed so fervently to the Blessed Virgin and lit so many candles at her altar that she believed she would certainly obtain her petition. Her disappointment was so great that it was feared that she would die. Her husband consoled her and her friends made the happiest predictions for the newly-born child. Health, beauty, happiness were to be for her whole life the lot of Margaret.

" Divine Goodness was indeed to favour me with great blessings," she wrote afterwards, " but they were not to be those which worldlings esteem. The cross was over my cradle ; suffering was to be my lot, and was the first mark of predilection given by Jesus to my soul."

Careless treatment by an incompetent nursery-maid ruined for ever the robust constitution of the child and brought her to death's door. A vow made by the distracted mother saved her. Up to the age of seven, Margaret wore the colours of Our Lady. But if the malady was cured, the source of the malady remained within. In the following year, at the new residence of the family at Angouleme, it appeared again in a painful and humiliating form : an eruption covered her face and her whole body. It was thought that the child was disfigured for life. Again her mother had recourse to Our Lady, again her prayer was answered.

2

" One day," Sister Louise Margaret relates, " my mother saw the terrible mask with which I was covered becoming gradually loosened. Then, under the scabs which fell off, there appeared a new skin formed by kind Providence of a delicate white colour without any trace of the former disfigurement. Ah ! how my mother loved this miraculous complexion ! Later on, it was sometimes to minister to my vanity. In order to expiate these faults I used often to try to tarnish this white colour, either by allowing the rays of the sun in summer to beat down on my face, or by exposing it all wet to the rigours of the winter ; then turning my thoughts away from myself in order to think only of Christ, I left to age and time the task of destroying this fleeting beauty."

But other maladies attacked the little girl. Successive attacks of bronchitis wore her out and again threatened her life. Her mother vowed to erect a votive tablet on Our Lady's altar in the Church of Obezine if she were cured. Perhaps it remains there still as a witness of the favour obtained. Had the end yet come of this struggle between death, which seemed to claim at all costs this future privileged one of Our Lord, and the Blessed Virgin, her heavenly Mother, whose tender love always intervened to save her ? No ! We again see M. and Madame de la Touche at Versailles prostrate in the deepest grief beside the bed of their child. She had lost her speech, she had scarcely any pulse and gave no sign of life. Her mother suddenly felt herself urged to pour a few drops of Lourdes water between the lips of her dying child. A minute afterwards, the eyes that were closed opened again joyfully and then closed again in tranquil sleep. Margaret was cured.

" The recollection of this incident is still very vivid in my mind," we read in her autobiography. " I remember very well this painful illness and the evening that I was so sick. I had lost consciousness : Suddenly I experienced a very pleasant sensation, something inexpressibly sweet ; it brought me back to myself again. Eighteen years later I felt this same infinitely sweet impression, and then I remembered that I had experienced it before, and that it was in 1874 when the miraculous water of Lourdes cured me."

It is sweet and instructive to see the Blessed Virgin bestow her very special protection on this child from her earliest years. In these incidents, Our Lady exercises her role of preparing for the work of God and of acting as sure guide to Jesus. And we are perhaps justified in regarding these tokens of love as presumptions in favour of the holiness and of the mission of Mother Louise Margaret.

HOME LIFE

" Our family life," she writes, " was calm and pleasant. I was very much loved by my father. When my childish sorrows made my tears flow and when from his office he heard me crying, he would open the door and then would take me in his arms, and to console me he would allow me to rummage in the drawers of his writing desk, a thing that he would not have allowed anyone else to do.

" In the evening, after a day spent working at his office, he loved to find himself in the peace and calm of his home with his wife at his side, his eldest daughter at his feet and the Benjamin of the family on his knees or in his arms. He would read for my mother some passage from a tragedy which he was composing in his leisure hours, or a saying of La Rochefoucauld which he had put in verse that day ; he explained to my sister some point of history or science for her instruction ; he answered my childish questions and amused himself listening to my prattle."

The atmosphere which surrounded these charming scenes was calculated to form the taste and to inspire a love for the beautiful. At that time also Margaret learned the *Credo* in Latin from her father.

" The big words of the symbol were a bit difficult for my little tongue, and so, in order to make a better effort to pronounce them, I would shut my eyes and apply myself with my whole heart, to the great joy of my father."

Margaret was very gay in spite of her habitual state of suffering. Her mother insisted on energy and self-mastery from her daughter, and this forgetfulness of oneself and one's troubles and of the inconveniences that arise from people, things and events, which both good education and virtue demand. Firmness was required to form the character of the younger sister, who was perhaps a little spoiled in her early childhood on account of her bad health. Her strength of will threatened to become obstinacy, the consciousness of her personality caused little angry scenes, her joyous temperament prompted her to play tricks and to tease. For the rest, she was gifted with a keen, clear intellect, perfect loyalty and a heart of gold.

The following quotation from her autobiography shows her love for the poor, even as a child :

" I had contracted the bad habit of awakening during the night and asking for a drink. My mother, who was indulgent towards me on account of my long illnesses, usually acceded to my request. My grandmother, however, thought it was time to cure me of this troublesome habit, and as she had noticed that I was fond of the poor and liked to have a well filled purse in order to be able to help them, she promised to give me a few pence every morning if I had asked for nothing during the preceding night. On the following nights I awoke as usual, but the tempting little piece of money which I would have lost next morning if I said a word, made me keep silence, and when I left Provins, where my grandmother lived, I was completely cured."

Even at that early age charity began to dominate this richly-gifted child.

FIRST CONTACT WITH MENTAL SUFFERING

In March, 1875, Mr. Claret de la Touche became ill from inflammation of the lungs. He displayed admirable Christian resignation ; he asked for and received the last Sacraments, put his affairs in order, recommended his daughters to their mother and endeavoured to console her and to make her accept the will of God. He retained consciousness to the last and died without agony at the age of forty-seven years.

" When he had just expired," writes Margaret, " my mother raised me up to the height of his face and said to me : ' embrace your dear father once more.' I placed my lips on his fine broad forehead, which I had loved to caress, and as he was still warm, I thought that my father was asleep. His face was calm and peaceful ; his half-open eyes were sightless, it is true, but I had never before seen death, and it was only several hours later that I learned the truth. I was then seven years old. On that day, I left off the virginal colours of Our Lady to put on a mourning suit. At first, I did not realise the loss which I had sustained, I did not understand what death was, it seemed to me that my father was going to return, and I suffered more from the grief of my mother and the sadness of the house than from my personal sorrow."

It was not long until the child felt her sorrow profoundly. The happy family life was broken up, the home was no longer the same ; the warm atmosphere in which paternal love had enveloped it had vanished.   Being too little to accompany her mother on visits, like her elder sister, she remained at home under the care of a governess. It became still more painful when, at the end of a year, Madame de la Touche manifested her intention of getting married again. Margaret, who was too respectful to allow her feelings to appear, suffered much.

" In my childish egoism," she writes, " I considered it quite natural that my mother, by remaining faithful to my father's memory, should devote herself entirely to his children.   My little eight-year-old heart, which was perhaps already dreaming of eternal love, had its first disillusionment.   I suffered profoundly and all the more because I did not wish to manifest my grief to anyone. I was afraid that my mother   should in   the end discover it and that she should in her turn become heartbroken."

Madame de la Touche never learned the secret of the tears of her delicate child, and it did not mar the joy of her marriage with Mr. de Chanberet in May, 1877.   The dear child understood that henceforward her mother would belong less to her two daughters.

" I had not yet learned to turn to God and seek from His infinitely loving Paternal Heart consolation in my sadness," she wrote, " but in His divine forethought for me, the good Master had endowed my soul with great strength of will as well as delicate sensibility of heart ; and although I was very young, I was able to bear the already heavy weight of my little troubles without being cast down."

By the new alliance of her mother, Margaret had found a brother, a friend, and companion to play with, in the son of M. de Chanberet, whose age was about the same as hers.   It was some compensation, but not without its disadvantages.   The little boy was gentle and affectionate, respectful and submissive, but he had not the qualities of order and refined politeness of Miss de la Touche. His stepmother, not wishing to correct him directly, pretended to be angry with Margaret when he deserved a scolding.   This way of acting offended against justice and wounded the heart of the little girl. Hermand, pained at seeing his sister scolded, did not understand that it was meant for himself, and Margaret, always tactful and able to control herself, never said a word that would make him suspect the truth.

FIRST COMMUNION

Margaret's mother, despite the fact that she had the faith, that she carried out the laws of God and the Church, and had devotion to the Blessed Virgin, did not trouble much about training her children in habits of piety. When Margaret was ten and a half years old, her mother thought it time to think about her first Communion ; she gave her a catechism and told her to prepare for the catechism class which was to begin in November.

" In the month of October, 1878," she writes, " I had just reached the age of ten and a half, and my mother thought that it was time to think of my first Communion. She went to enquire at the Cathedral when the catechism classes would begin ; she was told that it would be in the following month. On her way home she bought a catechism for fifty cents, and putting it into my hands she told me to begin and learn the first chapters. I had never yet learned any Christian Doctrine, and the amount of religious knowledge that I possessed was very slight. I had read a small Bible History, I knew the Our Father and Hail Mary in French, and, during vacation time, I had learned by heart two or three passages of the Gospels out of the prayer book ; that was all. I began to study the catechism and in November I was sent to the catechism classes."

Thanks to her natural gifts, she none the less distinguished herself at the catechism class conducted by a former military Chaplain, who had neither the time nor the inclination to give individual attention to each of his eighty young pupils. Jesus, the sweet Friend of children, was Himself at this time to become the Master and Director of Margaret. The following passage from her autobiography reveals at the same time the love of Jesus for her soul and her own absolute loyalty and simplicity :

" It was at this time, in December or January,—I don't remember exactly—that Jesus, the sweet Friend of children, was pleased to make His first sensible communication to me. One evening about five o'clock, I was alone in my mother's room, seated before a table, engaged in doing my home work. My sister had read to me during the day an episode of the great revolution, which I was to write out myself as an exercise in style. The rest of the members of the family had gone out : the cook was in the kitchen, and I, with my pen in my hand, was endeavouring to commence. After striving in vain for some time, what appeared to me to be a bright idea struck me. I knew where my sister had left the magazine in which the episode that I was to repeat was to be found. I would just give a glance at the beginning of the episode, of course not in order to copy it, but only just to get an idea how to commence. Besides, no one would know anything about it, and then I did not intend to read over the episode. I recalled it so well. I began to put my plan into effect immediately ; I got up and opened the door of my sister's room. By the light of the lamp which penetrated into the room, I could easily make out the little white magazine on a chair in the far end of the room and ran forward to get it. When I arrived at the middle of the room, I felt myself stopped by an obstacle ; something placed itself before me at the height of my breast, like an arm stretched out to bar the passage. I stood still in astonishment ; I saw nothing, but I heard the voice of a man, grave and sweet, saying to me : ' What you are going to do is wrong.' I raised my head to see who was speaking, but saw nothing and, without being either frightened or troubled, I said ' Oh, I will only look at one line, just the first line.' Immediately the obstacle disappeared ; I felt myself free to continue my way ; I had only two steps more to go, and my hand could lay hold of the magazine. Nevertheless, I remained motionless ; a thought occurred to me ; I said to myself : ' All the same, I have been told that it would be wrong . . . .!' and with this promptness of decision which is customary with me, I turned about and left the room. I sat down at the table again and, without any further searching, I began my exercise. Being then only a light-hearted child, I soon forgot completely all that I have just written ; never once in fifteen years did my memory recall this event. One day after my profession, as my divine Master was favouring me with His divine presence and making His voice heard within me, I remembered that I had heard it before, and immediately the whole scene which I have described above returned to my mind with extraordinary precision of detail and clearness, and Jesus then told me that He had wished on that day to make a first trial of my fidelity and that if I had failed in it, perhaps He would never have given me the graces with which He has since favoured me."

What a beautiful lesson we find in this incident ! How closely the Lord watches over His creature and offers him His light and grace, and how He respects the creature's liberty ! But was not the little girl very brave to reply to the invisible Being without faltering? Had she not a keen sense of duty to follow the first suggestion which pointed it out to her, and was not her will prompt and firm to come to a decision without hesitation?

The voice of the Master had spoken for the first time ; later on, when the time marked out by His wisdom and His Love had come, her fidelity to grace inclined Him to resume His secret intimate conversations with her.

" O my sweet Love," concluded Margaret, " O Jesus ! up to that time Thou didst seem to leave me entirely in the hands of Thy dear Mother Mary, as little children are left to the vigilant, tender hands of their mothers, but now that my childhood was finished, Thou Thyself didst wish to take care of me ; like a loving father, Thou didst deign to begin to instruct me and to speak to me Thyself."

She made her first Confession on the 29th March. When she had left the Confessional, she told her mother that she had forgotten something. Her mother called the priest back. " Father," said Margaret, " mother told me to take off my gloves before going to Confession and I forgot to do it. Must I begin my Confession again? "The priest reassured her and she went away rejoicing, to perform her penance.

The following day was the happy day of her first Communion. Of it she writes :

" March the 30th was to be the day of my first Communion. Jesus was going to give me His divine wealth ; to me who was poverty itself ! I brought to Jesus a heart still very innocent, it is true, and profound, genuine faith ; that was all. No movement of fervour carried me toward God ; none of these transports of ardent love, of these desires excited by love, made my soul exult. I went to accomplish this act, which was one of the greatest of my life, in a serious mood and with respect, but without any movement of the heart. Religion at our house was like that. My step-father was a practising Catholic. I never saw any member of the family miss Sunday Mass or the abstinence on Friday, except when they were really ill ; all approached the Sacraments four times a year, seriously, to fulfil a duty. My mother reminded us from time to time that we should make an act of contrition as often as possible before going to sleep, and say a Hail Mary in the morning ; she often had the Holy Sacrifice celebrated for my father and for our deceased friends ; she gave large alms, and urged us to practise charity, but for us, God was only a just Master whom we must serve strictly, respect for His greatness, and leave in the infinite heights of His Heaven amidst His Angels and Saints ! O my adorable Master, why hast Thou allowed me to be thus ignorant of Thee ? Why hast Thou permitted that, during the years of my innocence when I could have loved Thee so well, my heart should have remained so far from Thee. Thy designs are inscrutable, O my God, and all that Thou doest is just and good !"

May we be permitted to answer for the good Master and to say that His Wisdom made no mistake in keeping far away from His privileged one, in this early period of her life, everything that could excite the sensible faculties of her soul, even what was of a religious nature. The apostle of Infinite Love was to receive from Him directly the burning light and heat, and not by any roundabout way or from her natural disposition or temperament.

She continues : " No remembrance has remained of the moment when I received the Sacred Host, or of the moments which followed. What did I say to Jesus ? What did He reveal to me about Himself in this first embrace, in this close union between the Divine Master and His frail creature whom He was later on to bind so intimately to Himself ? My memory has kept no record of it." It was like a sleep from which her mother had to awaken her to make her take a biscuit after the long ceremony. One thing she knew : that she was very happy ; " happy with a calm, profound happiness. It was the peace of Jesus in the soul ; peace such as the world and its joys cannot give ; the superabundant peace of heaven, the foretaste of eternal happiness."

CONFIRMATION

Confirmation followed the same day. In the evening, at the renewal of the Baptismal vows, an incident occurred which after wards appeared to Margaret to be significant of her future mission. As she was going down the steps of the sanctuary after swearing fidelity on the Holy Gospels, she slipped and fell into the arms of a priest, that were opened out to save her. He bent down and whispered into the child's ear : " You are a little angel to-day, remain always so, won't you." He opened his arms again and the child resumed her place. Of this incident she wrote :

" Was not that, my most sweet Jesus, an indication of Thy designs over my soul ? When, on the solemn day of my first Communion,

Margaret at the age of three

Margaret at the age of eleven, when she made her vow of virginity

in the midst of the crowd that filled this church, on the very steps of the Sanctuary, Thou didst permit that I be pressed against the heart of one of Thy priests, was it not an indication that Thou hadst then given me to Thy priests ? Was it not the first sign of this mystical adoption, the first knot of these mysterious bonds which Thou wast to form one day between my soul and the souls of Thy priests ?"

HER VOW OF VIRGINITY

Three weeks after this great day, it pleased Our Lord to favour her with a very special grace. She did not remember the exact day and hour. In her autobiography she writes : " Soon after Easter, about three weeks after my first Communion, our divine Lord was pleased to favour me with a very special grace. I cannot recall either the day on which I received this favour, or the manner in which it was given to me ; I confess that I am astonished at having a clear remembrance of very many insignificant details of matters of no account and at being completely unable to recall facts so important for me. Jesus, the sweet Master of my soul, wished to bind me to Himself with indestructible bonds ; by His inspiration alone without my ever thinking of it beforehand, I made the vow of perpetual virginity. A mysterious veil, like that which covered me at the time of my first Sacramental union with Jesus-Victim, envelops this moment when I was bound by this vow to the sacred Spouse of souls. The only thing that I know is that I had really made this vow, that I was very happy over it ; and I renewed it whole-heartedly and with joy. Being still very innocent, I did not know the full meaning and obligations of this vow ; I only knew that I had promised not to marry.

When renewing this vow, I promised God in addition that I would become a Religious if He favoured me with a vocation. Divine Goodness at the same time gave me the inspiration to keep this grace hidden in the inner recesses of my soul ; although I am by nature frank and open, I never spoke of it to anyone. Besides, the thought never occurred to my mind that it was necessary to tell this to my confessor. I thought that we could not tell anything at confession but our sins.

One of the first effects of this grace was to give me an extreme aversion for, almost a horror of caresses of any kind. Up to then I liked very much to caress my mother and those around me ; from this time on, without my noticing it and by a sort of natural instinct, I changed completely."

The family noticed the change ; they were astonished, the child was reproved but she would not yield.   When Hermand, her step-brother, wanted to embrace her, she resisted by force, and the other members of the family had to tell him to let her alone or he would make her sick.

Christ had indeed put His seal on her soul, and being reserved for the Lord, she resisted all contact with human beings by a sort of natural instinct.   She was carrying out in advance the admonition that was to be addressed to her on the day of her profession : " This veil will be for your eyes in order that you may never receive any token of love from any other than Jesus Christ."

EDUCATION AND MORAL FORMATION

Margaret's education had been hitherto very elementary.   It was time to think more seriously about it.   In October, 1879, a mistress was hired to teach her ; it was the pious Miss Plantier.

" She might have done me much good," wrote Margaret, " but she had very little to do with me.   Her whole work was to come for some time every day to teach me grammar, geography, and arithmetic. We hardly ever talked together, and when we did, I gave her very little satisfaction."

Margaret's grandmother taught her history, her elder sister gave her lessons in drawing, literature and dancing.   Her step-father taught her German, and her mother took charge of her moral education.

" I had plenty of masters," she writes, " but the absence of regular life, worldly cares, my mother's fears for my weak health, and most of all my natural laziness, prevented me from making progress. Reading, conversation, the artistic and well-informed circle in which I lived, developed my intellect, but from the point of view of education in the strict sense of the word, I was very ignorant.   As for religious instruction, it was not even mentioned ; the reading of the abbreviated Bible History and four months' instruction on the Catechism during my youth were supposed to suffice for the rest of my life."

The Lord did not wish the work which He was to operate in her soul to be attributed to anyone but Himself alone.   In a mysterious and hidden way, He was soon to begin this work of directing her mind and affections to those lofty regions from which she could appreciate at their worth all human values, establish herself in the supernatural and become grounded and rooted in truth.

Of the political differences in the family she writes :

" I have said that my grandmother taught me history ; however, everyone took a hand at this subject. There was complete divergence of opinion in our family, and party questions often formed the subject-matter of interminable discussions. My step-father was a royalist by race and education. . . . .

" Now, each one tried to form me according to his or her own opinion ; my good grandmother made me read the life of Marie Amelie and all the history books that she could find treating of the family of Orleans ; my step-father gave me books which upheld the claims of the family of Charles X ; by way of antidote, my mother stigmatized the scandals at court. For my part, I listened to all they said to me, but did not side with either party ; I read all the books but kept silent. I saw that opinions in my family were very much influenced by party-spirit, partiality, or by considerations that were doubtless very creditable, but not sufficient to serve as basis for just and reasonable judgments. Later on when I had grown up, when political discussions were started in our family, I kept out of them and did not in any way get entangled in them. Sometimes the belligerents, nettled by my silence, turned towards me and said, ' But, Margaret, on which side are you ? What is your opinion ? ' All the more calm because I saw the others excited, I would answer with the greatest tranquillity, ' Oh, I am on the side of the Church.' What reply could they make ? They were all Catholics ; that usually finished the discussion."

The intimacy which grew up between Margaret and her grandmother caused little family troubles. Her mother, as a counter-measure against what she alleged to be spoiling the child, became more severe towards her. Her step-father, for some undefined reason, perhaps financial worries, also changed his attitude towards her ; during one of his absences, he gave a very dry reply to an affectionate letter from Margaret. She was very much hurt by it and confesses humbly that she allowed a sentiment of resentment to penetrate into her heart and that it rankled there for several months.

" This was, indeed," she writes, " very far from the spirit of Jesus. Ah ! if I had been taught to open my soul to a priest ! If I had had the grace of the Sacraments to raise me up after my fall! But I received Our Lord only three or four times a year, and I went to Confession the same number of times; I never examined my conscience, and my evening prayers consisted of a *Memorare* recited in bed when my eyes and mind were already heavy with sleep.

" From this time onwards, shadows began to descend on my soul, gradually dimming the serene lights which had illuminated it at the blessed time of my first Communion. I renewed my vow of virginity every evening, it is true, but it was only mechanically, without attention and without fervour. New ideas began to penetrate into my mind. I sometimes heard my sister and my cousins talking among themselves of what they called their ' beau-ideal.' This ' beau-ideal ' was some young man whom they had met at a ball, or seen when out walking, or perhaps some youthful friend. The poor ' ideal ' was himself, most probably, unconscious of the dreams of which he was the object. I thought that it was time for me to act like a young girl and I too resolved to adopt an ' ideal.' It was purely out of a spirit of imitation, without any personal attraction, I admit ; but since young girls do so, I thought that it was necessary for me to imitate them !"

She then gives an amusing account of her search after an ' ideal ' and of how her choice fell on a poor ugly-looking fellow who, having no one to love him, had excited her interest and compassion, and of how her efforts to think of him met with no success. She concludes :

" I acquired from this some useful knowledge which has since been of service to me : a person cannot love with the head, or by an effort of the will alone ; when the heart is not touched by love, the mind cannot give its attention."

And she explains :

" In order to be able to turn frequently towards Our Lord, instead of trying to use violence with our brain, we should rather empty our hearts of the love of creatures, and fill them with the knowledge and love of Jesus Christ. The heart will then set things in motion and draw everything after it."

Her mother gradually formed Margaret for the world, where she had already commenced to appear to advantage. In order to cure her of the headaches she made her take vigorous physical exercise. On the subject of her moral formation, she writes :

" Energy was the key-note of the education given me by my

mother. While taking good care of our health, this dear mother wished to make us strong, courageous women, elevated above all weakness and effeminacy, which she deemed unworthy of beings endowed with reason. It was not by considerations of Christian morality, such as the motive of pleasing God, that she sought to raise us up ; she did not think of that. She quoted for us the Sages of Greece, the constancy of the Stoics, the virtue of the Roman matrons, rather than the martyrs of the early Church and the heroism of the Christian virgins ; Socrates and his hemlock, Lucretia and her dagger were very much more familiar to me than St. Augustine and St. Cecilia.''

Margaret was allowed great liberty for her reading, and we shall see that she availed herself of it to great advantage. However, her mother limited her in the choice of religious books and forbade her to read the life of St. Teresa. Of this Margaret writes : '' Poor dear mother ! Perhaps at the time of my first Communion she had seen in me an inclination to Religious life : she had always a kind of natural fear of seeing me turn in that direction, and she made use of all opportunities to develop in me a taste for the world, and to close my soul to religious influences. God permitted it to be so in order that my vocation should be His work alone, and that no exterior human influence could claim any share in it.''

Margaret obeyed faithfully ; her mother's authority was firm and uncontested ; no thought of rebelling against it was ever allowed to enter her mind. Though her mother was liberal with her daughters in the matter of permissions, she kept a firm hand over them ; all their letters were read and their presses examined. Furthermore, they were trained to be good housekeepers and, in order that they might be capable to direct servants, they were made to learn to do everything for themselves. In a word, from a human point of view, their mother wanted them to be perfectly trained young girls.

LIFE IN THE WORLD

Margaret was now fifteen. Her parents were wealthy and enjoyed their wealth. They had their residence at Valence for the winter months, and a country house for the summer, and frequently spent the spring and autumn in Paris, or travelling abroad.

The house of the de Chamberets was a place of social gatherings for their wealthy friends. There were musical entertainments once a week, and in addition, there were dancing parties and concerts frequently. Later on, they turned to comedies ; and as each family offered one in their turn, there was a continuous round of these entertainments. Margaret enjoyed them very much and contributed her share to their success. She was, however, left very much to herself ; she had no friends among the young girls. Those who were brought up in old French style regarded her as too worldly and avoided her ; as to the others who were frivolous and affected, occupied with trifles when not backbiting their neighbours, it was Margaret who avoided them. She was just the opposite. In spite of her free and easy manner and her unconcern for the judgments of the world, she took care that what she did was free from sin, and when she was satisfied on that point, she did it simply, without troubling about what people said, but without taking sufficient care to guard against giving disedification or against leaving herself open to be misrepresented. Later on she confessed that she was wrong in this, and added—" Now I have come to know that if human respect is a great evil, wise reserve and Christian prudence are necessary to edify our neighbour."

In spite of this worldly and frivolous atmosphere, the thought of a religious life was still kept alive in the depth of her soul. She was very reserved and did not tolerate the least familiarity ; that was well known, she inspired respect and was treated with respect. In the little comedies in which she always took part, she carefully suppressed everything that would have broken the reserve with which she surrounded herself. " Kiss my hand if you wish," she would say, " it is all that I allow you." For all that, she was full of life ; her gaiety communicated itself to others, and her conversation and manner were charming.

For several years the family spent the summer at the castle of Arbods, near Crest. The castle was surrounded with woods and was far from any other country house. It was a place where they could find repose from the fatiguing worldly life they led. Their days were passed in reading, discussions and long walks. The family never missed Sunday Mass ; however cold or wet the weather might be they always attended.

Margaret enjoyed country life to the full. Nevertheless, all these innocent enjoyments failed to satisfy the longing of her heart. She experienced a new sensation, a hunger for something which she could not explain. From being a source of irritation, it became a torment.

This void in her soul became ever deeper during the seven years
that separated her from her entry into religious life.

" I was vainly seeking in earthly enjoyment the happiness that I
should find in God, and Jesus seemed to abandon me to myself. He
allowed me to walk down very dangerous slopes. The Divine Master
was however watching over me and arrested my steps on the brink
of the abyss. He enveloped me in His divine purity and, without
my being aware of it, led me on by many detours to the goal that He
wished me to attain."

The miscellaneous collection of books in the castle library offered a
counter-irritant to Margaret's inward feeling of uneasiness, but it
made her run new risks. Let us listen to her own account of the
contents of the library and how she used her liberty to read :

" Our house contained a considerable library composed of the
remains of several inherited collections ; in it works of the most
various kinds were found side by side. The works of Voltaire and
Rousseau were beside those of Arnaud and Sacy, while the massive
Encyclopaedia of the eighteenth century elbowed the great Classics,
Racine and Corneille, Moliere and La Fontaine ; the novels in vogue
under the first Empire were mixed up with the lives of St. Hugh
and St. Bruno.   I had complete liberty to choose as I wished from
this library ; I began to draw largely from it and I continued doing
so each year. Reading had always a great attraction for me. There
was one class of books which I abhorred, namely those which spoke
directly against the Church and God ; as for those I knew for certain
to be on the Index, I would not even open them. I never took down
any of the books of either Voltaire or Rousseau because I knew them
to be enemies of God.

Some years later when reading the *Revue des Deux Mondes*, I
commenced an article which by its title promised to be interesting.
I had scarcely read the first few lines when I felt myself seized by a
strange feeling of uneasiness ; I seemed to see between the lines the
traces of a mind opposed to the mind of the Church ; I tried to
continue in order to discover if were so, but as the feeling of uneasiness, the interior suffering of my soul, increased, I turned over
to the end of the article to find the signature of the author ; it was
Renan.   Then I could not bear even to look at those pages again.

Once the book was closed, I thought no more about it ; my sleep,
the sleep of a child, was profound and peaceful and never troubled
by the illusions of dream.

My reading caused no trouble in my imagination. . . . . Doubt-less, Jesus, seeing me so young and weak, did not permit the enemy to direct his furious assaults against me then ; I was to experience them later on when I was leaving the world."

Her natural uprightness of soul, her simplicity, the nobility of her thoughts and sentiments, and above all, the special love of her divine Master for her, guarded her in the midst of the hidden dangers through which she passed.

Her mother liked to see her play her part in the comedy dis-guised in a costume corresponding to the part, and had got a boy's suit of clothes made for her. She wore this suit during her stay at the country house for three years. She found it convenient for her cross-country walks over rough mountains. The village Curé did not like it. He did not absolutely forbid her to wear it, but refused to allow her to enter the church when she wore it. She obeyed but says :

" It caused me much pain, when we passed through the village on our walks, to see my mother and sister enter the church to make a visit to the Blessed Sacrament and to be obliged to remain at the door. I used to kneel down outside on the market-square and adore Jesus from a distance, like the poor Publican, unworthy to enter the temple of the Lord."

Later on she regretted bitterly that she had caused pain to the good Cure, and scandalised the honest country folk.

When at Paris, where they spent a few weeks every year, they visited the ancient monuments and the museums. Margaret was more interested in the artistic than the religious aspect of these monuments. She says :

" The old mosaics of the Sainte Chapelle and its delicate arch-itecture captivated my mind much more than the thought of Our Lord's Crown of Thorns which it was built to contain."

Of the masterpieces of painting and sculpture, she writes : " I sought the beautiful, I admired the grace of form, the brilliancy of colour, the marvellous imitation of nature, the breath of life that seemed to pass through the dead marble and colour the paintings which enchanted me. No evil impression troubled my senses or sullied my imagination ; it was the splendour of the beautiful alone that attracted me, and without my knowing (because all beauty is a reflection of the divine) it raised me above myself and made me ascend towards God."

It was still the beautiful which she found in the splendid landscape of Jura, Savoy and the Dauphine. Her eyes were filled with these wonders, though they had not yet learned to recognise God in His work, but her heart and soul found repose in all that bore the impress of His infinite power, wisdom and love. Even in worldly success, she perceived the noble and impersonal aspect that escapes to many others.

" I loved success," she writes, " as I love light, music, beautiful flowers, silks and all that is beautiful and joyous ; I loved all that for others as much as for myself. Jesus held possession of the interior of my heart, and all human enjoyment remained on the surface of my soul."

We get still another characteristic of this soul, that was exceptional by its gifts, and also by God's watchful care over her, in two incidents that occurred during a visit to Paris. Among the officials at the Louvre was a man of rare taste and knowledge, who had formerly been a Religious. He offered his arm to Margaret's mother to show her around. Her feeling was one of disgust and revulsion to be brought in contact with a faithless Religious.

"As for me," writes Margaret, " I felt only profound compassion. I do not know whether it was because I was a sinner myself, but sinners are objects of great pity to me ; I did not feel that disdainful revulsion and disgust for moral misery that I have sometimes seen in good Christian hearts."

In the spring of 1886, Margaret met in a Paris drawing-room the licentious novelist whose unsavoury writings were pouring poison into all ranks of society.. Several people reproached him amiably, as is the fashion in polite society, " but really why do you put such things in your books?" " Oh ! you know," he replied, " that is what sells them !"

" No one," writes Margaret, " protested against this infamy. With that lightness common to conversations in polite society, they passed on to other topics. These words had pierced my heart. Then, one must live ! one must fraternise with the world ! with people so mercenary, with beings fallen so low that they do not scruple for the sake of a little gold to poison thousands of other souls and to tarnish, in thousands of young hearts, this exquisite, divine flower of innocence that should be kept in all its freshness ! I left this house sick at heart ; I told my mother that I was tired, that I had enough of Paris, and begged her to take me to my grandmother. She yielded to my request and took me to Provins."

THE BEGINNING OF A NEW LIFE

Who, in Madam X's drawing-room could have suspected that the infamous words received without protest would have caused a revolution in the young girl's soul, and by the profound emotion which they stirred up there, contributed to her conversion? It was but the climax however of a struggle between nature and grace that had been long going on silently in her soul :

" It was," she writes, " the combat between nature and grace so marvellously described by the author of the *Imitation.* I had not been accustomed to observe it in myself, I was ignorant of its alternatives, I suspected neither its dangers nor its merits. I had never read pious books, not even the *Imitation,* except a few chapters that had been given to me as my penance, and my mind, spoiled by frivolous reading, had not been able to taste the charms of this heavenly book. At one time, I felt myself attracted towards God, at another, the world and its pleasures took possession of me.

" I tried to bring myself to consider marrying some of those whom I met in the world, and who by their assiduous and respectful attention showed the desires and hopes they formed about me. But my heart remained dumb ; then something from on high attracted me and I renewed my vow of chastity and asked God to give me help, light and strength ; one of these powerful graces which snatch souls from the world and deliver them up to God. I understood that some external help was necessary for me and I prayed to God to send me some priest who could speak to me in His name and guide me to Him. I asked my mother to permit me to change my confessor, but she would not consent. I yielded, and continued to pray. When I say that I prayed it is an exaggeration, I did not know how to pray. I had no taste for vocal prayer ; at most I said one or two decades of the Rosary every day. I hardly ever said morning prayers ; in the evening all my devotions consisted, as I have already said, in an act of contrition and a *Memorare.* During Mass on Sundays, I read the prayers from my book almost without attention. As for mental prayer, I had not the slightest idea of it. All my prayer consisted in representing my needs to God from time to time ; when I passed by a church, I went in and put little offerings into the boxes at the different shrines, always for the same intention. Very often it was at St. Joseph's shrine that I put in my offerings. Sometimes I put in five or ten shillings at a time, and I called that praying to St. Joseph."

She prayed oftener and better in her grand-mother's dear old house at Provins. Holy Cross Church was quite near, and perhaps the proximity of the Blessed Eucharist made itself felt, for in that atmosphere she found herself more inclined to prayer and to doing good. This year she found herself more sensibly attracted to God. Sometimes she retired to her room to pray ; she went to the church every evening to assist at the May devotions in honour of Our Lady ; then she went to the devotions during the month of the Sacred Heart, and there, in the recollection of the house of God, she found peace.

" I tried to make little sacrifices," she writes, " those which I offered to Jesus were indeed trivial, but I thought them heroic."

It is with a smile that she mentions some of them : not to curl her hair for dinner, not to change her costume for a more elegant one. Must not He Who regards the heart more than the gift offered have been pleased with these little loving efforts ? He who returns royally, or rather in a God-like manner, was going to recompense his little servant with a very special grace.

THE ILLNESS THAT TRANSFORMED HER SOUL

In July, 1886, the de Chamberet family was at the castle of Arbods. Early in August, Margaret was stricken down by a violent attack of angina followed by scarlatina. As an epidemic of typhoid fever was raging in the district, the family was doubly uneasy, and sent in haste for a nursing Sister. When Sister Dominic, summoned by telegram, arrived, Margaret was so ill that her mother asked her if she would like to go to confession for the Feast of the Assumption, which was on the following day. Margaret was reluctant to put the Curé to inconvenience, but when pressed she gladly accepted the offer. She made her confession and awaited death calmly, as if it was the simplest thing in the world.

" I had indeed many faults," she writes, " but the thought of appearing before God did not alarm me. As for life, I did not regret it : I had already found by experience that the sum of its sorrows is much greater than the sum of its joys." The good Curé left her and promised her Holy Communion for the Feast if her condition should grow worse. After recommending herself to the Blessed Virgin, Margaret, worn out by seven days of high fever and insomnia, fell asleep. What happened during that night of the Assumption ?

" Had Mary deigned to turn towards me her eyes of mercy," Margaret asked herself, " had she given a new proof of her maternal goodness, such as she had given many times during my infancy? All the circumstances incline me to believe that she had. My fever had left me, all danger was over, and I soon began to convalesce.

" Sister Dominic had been very much edified at seeing the whole family, with my step-father at their head, approach the Sacraments. She was less so in the afternoon when, searching in my press, she found a boy's suit beside my Sunday clothes. The good Sister was scandalised. She told me that I should not have worn it, that the Church forbade it. The Curé had not absolutely forbidden me to wear these clothes, but suffering, so salutary for my soul, had inclined me towards good, and I resolved there and then never to wear them again. On the following day I asked the Sister to gather them together and make a parcel of them, and soon after I gave them to some poor boys. I was sorry for going against the desires and sentiments of the Church in this matter ; I asked pardon of God and promised to be more faithful."

On account of the danger of contagion, Margaret had no other companion during her convalescence but Sister Dominic. She got on very well with the humble Sister, who was young and gay, pious and delicate. The Sister volunteered to read for her. Margaret sent her to the library for *The Journey from Paris to Jerusalem* which she had never read for fear of finding it tedious, but which she considered suitable and Christian. She listened to it with pleasure, but she preferred to talk with the Sister about God, and told her about her hopes to become a Religious. Sister Dominic encouraged her and advised her to enter the Visitation. She taught her prayers and the meditations on the mysteries of the Rosary. Margaret became very much attached to her companion in solitude, shared with her what was sent to her, and used to send her every day to breathe the invigorating air of the mountain, on the pretence of getting her to gather flowers. Now the good Sister was afraid, and God, as He had done for Don Bosco, found for her a dog that rivalled the fidelity of Don Bosco's *Il Grigio*. This dog became the servant of Sister Dominic as long as she remained, and afterwards of Margaret until the end of the summer.

CHAPTER II.

VOCATION.

Margaret had returned to God, and in the peace and calm which filled her soul, she experienced again the impressions which the grace of her first Communion had made on her.

" I had no doubt about the will of God," she writes, " and joyfully renewing my dear vow of virginity, I sought the means of responding to the interior voice which urged me to leave the world. I saw many difficulties against it. I was still subject to my mother and my guardian. I knew that they would never permit me to decide on entering religious life before I attained my twenty-first year. Three years of waiting spent in the kind of life that I had led up to then appeared to me to be impossible. If I were to tell my mother about my intention, would not there be a new danger for me? She would do all possible to shake my resolution and multiply around me the occasions of destroying my vocation. Should I say nothing? make no change in my life? But I felt myself weak; I prayed, I reflected."

An idea occurred to her one day when she found herself alone with her mother. She expressed her regret at having interrupted her studies so early in life, at being so ignorant of many things; she told her mother of the pleasure she would find in following the course of studies at Valence, either in the convent of the Trinity or of the Blessed Sacrament. Very many young girls took their diploma, it would be quite easy for her to do likewise. The benevolent attention of her mother was aroused by the word ' diploma.' The diploma was all right for those who are obliged to enter the teaching profession; she would never allow her daughter to pass examinations. Besides, had she not just suffered the anguish of almost losing her, and now she wanted to keep her in the world in order to enjoy her company. A few further questions showed Margaret that it was futile to insist. The poor child felt herself alone without support or counsel; she shut up her desires and aspiration in the depths of her soul and abandoned herself to the current.

" Alas," said she, " like a poor little bark without rudder, I was going to become the sport of the waves and having been tossed about by the billows of the great sea, I was going to end up a few months later by a painful shipwreck."

THE GREAT CRISIS

" I returned to Valence," she writes, " perfectly cured, grown up, stronger than ever, with a sort of renewal of life and of exuberance of gaiety. I began again to live with all the ardour of my eighteen years, and putting aside all grave thoughts and serious reflections, I thought only of enjoying present happiness."

In the Valence Society circles, due to a multiplicity of circumstances, mundane entertainments became much more frequent. Receptions, balls, rehearsals, theatrical performances occurred so often that they appeared to be dovetailed into each other. In a few months of the winter, Margaret learned twenty-six pieces and some of these were played several times.

" If my eagerness for pleasure," she writes, " found in all that plenty to satisfy it, my little vanity found in the success and applause a food very much to its taste. Happily, I was not much given to thinking about myself, and so I hardly ever dwelt on thoughts of self-complaisance.

" Very frequently this year when I was preparing for some social function, a rather remarkable thing would happen. When getting ready to place flowers in my hair, the thought of Our Lord crowned with thorns would occur to my mind, and often when the flowers were already fixed there, I would take them out, not being able to endure the pain which the contrast caused me, and would replace them by a ribbon or a jewel. My mother would ask me why I had not worn the little diadem of flowers which she herself had prepared. I would reply that it would not keep on my head, that it was an inconvenience to me. Twice, however, I resisted the inspiration of the good Master and put the flowers in my hair. However, the thought of Our Lord or of His Passion did not occur to me at other times."

In this worldly life, dangerous occasions were not wanting. Heavenly protection attended Margaret everywhere, sometimes in a manner so sensible that years later she was still astonished at it.

" Why did Jesus deign," she writes, " to favour me thus at a time when I thought so little of Him? These are mysteries of His incomparable Love.

" Surrounded with friends and very much loved as I was, I had however kept my heart free. Jesus, who had destined it to be His own, had up to then defended it and guarded it well. But the hour was at hand when the enemy would take possession of this last retreat in which the love of the Master was entrenched."

A young officer twenty-four years old who had just arrived at Valence was introduced to the de Chamberet family and soon became one of their most assiduous visitors. Of gentle disposition, intelligent, very well educated and perfectly reserved, he gained the good will of all, and aroused hopes in Madam de Chamberet when she saw him full of attention for her youngest daughter. She, delighted with the amiable qualities of Mr. X., with his perfectly respectful conduct towards her, with the noble and righteous ideas which he expressed, and with his fidelity to his Christian duties, felt sentiments corresponding to those of the young man arise in her heart. Nobody suspected it. Everyone, even her mother, believed her to be of cold, calm temperament with a heart not susceptible to passion. They had called her " the little rock." But this time human love had conquered her.

" I was loved," she writes, " and I loved, and I was happy. I felt that my heart was made for love, but taking the shadow for the reality, I sought my happiness in earthly love, while a love that was altogether heavenly and divine was alone to satisfy my soul and give it happiness. We were in the month of May, the charms of nature in spring were as an echo to the joy of my heart, for my heart also sang of spring. . . . .

" One evening when I had retired to my room, I was preparing to go to bed and was entertaining myself with these pleasant dreams. When I had gone to bed I began to recite, as was my custom, the act of contrition and the *Memorare*, and while I was mechanically murmuring the sweet prayer of St. Bernard with very little attention, a thought, an old memory, presented itself to my mind ; my vow of chastity !

" Little by little in the midst of the life of distraction during the winter, I had neglected to renew it in the evening ; other thoughts had come to occupy my mind ; I had entirely forgotten it.

" When the remembrance of it suddenly returned to me that evening, it was as a terrifying, icy spectre that it appeared to me, coming to destroy my present happiness and ruin my joyful prospects for the future. Then a great combat took place in my soul. God demanded His rights, human love also urged its claim. My tears flowed in abundance, my breast heaved with sighs and I wrapped my face in the sheets to smother the noise. The struggle was terrible and lasted the whole night ; nature and grace fought one of these merciless battles within me, one of these bloody duels which end only by death.

" When the first rays of the morning entered between my shutters, all was over. Jesus, my Redeemer and my Master, my divine Benefactor, Who had chosen me and drawn me to Himself with so much love, Jesus, the great Persecuted One of all time, had been on this night again the great vanquished one !

" Being forced to choose between the love of Christ and that of a vile creature, I had, after a whole night's consideration and struggle, very deliberately chosen the creature and rejected Christ ! Life had appeared to me to be impossible unless I shared it with him who had made himself master of my heart. I said to myself that God could not oblige me to make this sacrifice : since He had permitted our mutual love, could He wish me now to break my own heart and his ? Could I inflict torture and despair on this heart that loved me ? And then, the wish of my mother was that I should settle down in the world, could I resist her ? As for the vow, doubtless, I had made it lightly, without reflection and without advice ; besides, I was too young to understand its import. I would go and find our bishop, I would kneel down at his feet ; I would tell him all and beg him to obtain from Rome a dispensation from my vow. A few hours of sleep had effaced the traces of the struggle during the night from my face. No one suspected it. I did not wish to tell my mother about my vow and I resolved to wait for a favourable occasion to go to the bishop's residence without my family knowing about it. I had at this moment 1,400 francs in my desk which was waiting to be invested. I took a thousand francs, I would give five hundred to the bishop for his works of charity ; five hundred would be for the *St. Peter's Pence.* I could well give that to buy my liberty ! A thousand francs ! My heart was certainly worth that, it seemed to me. I would have given still more in order that my heart should belong to myself and to have the power to bestow it on whomsoever I pleased. I rolled up the thousand francs and put them in a drawer where I could conveniently find them when I was going to see the bishop."

No one but Margaret herself could have described for us this terrible combat. In spite of appearances, it was Margaret who was the conquered, as happens to all who resist the Lord. The following passage which expresses the depth of her sorrow for her culpable weakness is worthy of a St. Augustine. How few there are found of the multitude who have been guilty not merely of the resolve but of the deed, who have imitated Margaret in her life-long atonement for her one weakness !

" O Master Divine, can it be that I have done thee this wrong? Can it be that I have gone so far? From my infancy, Thou hast loved me so much ! Thou hast anticipated my needs with Thy choicest graces ! And I ! How could I have been so unfaithful as to think of breaking this bond of love which Thou hast formed between Thy Heart and mine? O divine Heart of My Jesus, I have despised Thy love. I have dared to put Thee in the scale against a carnal and corrupted heart. Have I not in some way renewed Thy Passion the day that I committed this offence. After a whole night's deliberation, by an unjust judgment, I have condemned Thee to death by comparing Thee with an unworthy creature ; I have cried out with the Jews : ' Away with Him !' ' give us Barabbas !' ' Crucify Jesus !' O Jesus-Love, how hast Thou pardoned me? Could the total gift of my poor, faithless heart which I subsequently offered to Thee make up for the sufferings and humiliations with which I have afflicted Thy divine Heart? Would a whole life spent in the cloister, the sufferings caused by long illnesses, the agonies of heart and sorrowful abandonment of soul be sufficient to expiate so great a fault? Certainly not ; nothing, nothing in existence could have washed me from this stain except, O my Jesus, Thy infinite Love and Mercy. Thy Mercy ! how sweet it is to the despicable, faithless heart ! Thy Mercy ! It is the salvation and life of the sinful soul. Thy Mercy ! It is, O Jesus, my refuge and my hope ; it is Thy open Heart ; it is Thy Love, creating again and giving new life : it is Thyself, Saviour and Redeemer. O Jesus, sweet Mercy, make me love Thee unto Death !'

Would this merciful Jesus-Love allow her whom He had never ceased to love to break the link that bound her to Him? He does not so easily abandon those whom He loves.

Four days passed. It was Sunday, the 12th of June, 1887. News altogether unexpected, which rendered the project of a union completely impossible, came to the knowledge of Margaret that evening in a most unlooked for manner.

" At the first words which were pronounced," she writes, " I felt as if a thunderbolt had struck me right in the heart. I staggered ; there happened to be a chair near me ; I fell into it rather than sat down on it. By a violent effort of my will, I remained calm and impassive. But under this mask of impassibility, what a ruin ! Everything within me had been overturned and destroyed, everything swallowed up. Did I feel pain ? No, I suffered too much to perceive my suffering, but it seemed to me that everything within me was dead. For two days I came and went, I laughed and talked, I acted as before, but I was like a machine which causes movement without being aware of it. I was no longer conscious of anything within me, neither of my heart or my soul. On the second evening, I knelt down to say my prayers, and tears, the first that I had shed, commenced to fall from my eyes. They flowed slowly down my cheek without a sob, without a complaint, without a conscious thought to cause them. They were the only ones that I shed over this heart-break. I suffered to the very depths of my being, and all the more because I had no one to whom I could uncover my wound. For to whom could I have opened my heart ? Ah ! if a holy priest had been at hand to sustain and console me ! to teach me to turn the aspirations of my heart that had suffered deception, towards Infinite Love ! I did not deserve this grace, and I was to suffer alone and in silence under the divine hand which struck me down so justly."

CALM IS RESTORED—DIVINE VISIT

Towards the end of September, Margaret and the family came to spend a few weeks at Provins with her grand-mother. The old house had no longer the same charm for her ; for the first time she felt dull. She took no interest in work, the books which she used to read only caused her disgust. One day in November, when searching in a cupboard that was rarely opened, in the midst of old fashion journals and novelettes, she found a book bound in sheep-skin that appeared to have been very seldom read. On the first page an angelic looking figure attracted her attention ; she looked for the title, it was *The Life of Saint Aloysius of Gonzaga* by Father Cepari.

" St, Aloysius of Gonzaga was almost completely unknown to me," she writes ; " if in my youth I had heard of him, I have absolutely no recollection of the fact. But the heavenly purity of his countenance charmed me. I had read only a few pages when I felt a sudden transformation taking place in me. A celestial light was diffused through my soul, while a sweet unction penetrated my heart and healed all its wounds. By the rays of this divine light I saw, as in an open book, the loving designs of God over my soul. He had chosen me from my infancy and had separated me from the multitude by marking me with the sign of virginity. He had watched over my youth with incomparable vigilance ; at the moment when I was attempting to escape from His divine hand, He had mercifully broken my heart rather than lose the sovereign possession of it.

I remained long with my head bent over the book, without seeing the marks of handwriting which were on it, my soul lost in a supernatural brightness, and my heart quenching its thirst from this new fountain.

That evening, with the fulness of my will, I renewed my dear vow of chastity ; I asked pardon from God for my great infidelity, and, as I had sad experience of my weakness, I besought Him to defend and guard Himself this miserable heart which He had deigned to choose for His heritage and His domain. Sixteen months still separated me from my twenty-first year ; I resolved to employ this time to prepare myself by the practice of virtue for the religious life which I had irrevocably decided to embrace."

A NEW LIFE

With her soul in peace and her heart free, Margaret received what she called " the light of sacrifice," and henceforth she would refuse nothing to Our Lord. She who loved so much rare furniture and every convenience for her room, condemned herself to the bare necessities. She had to appear in society, but it was no longer with the same spirit, even if, exteriorly, it was with the same vivacity. No one could divine her inward thoughts which now all tended to bring her to God, Whose will she determined to do, whatever it might cost.

During the vacations of this year of 1888, which were spent at Saint Maurice d'Hostun, Margaret's reading, to the amazement of her mother, was taken from *The Imitation*, and from Bossuet and Massillon.

On September the 24th, the Feast of Our Lady of Mercy—Mary still continued to watch over her—a confession which she made to a visiting priest was a source of great grace to her. An irresistible interior impulse urged her to speak to him of her aspirations towards religious life. This confessor declared to her in a tone of authority that she must have a spiritual director, and at the same time indicated the Curé of Valence as the priest to whom she should address herself. When she told him of the difficulties that she would meet from her family, he said in conclusion : " Do your best, but it is absolutely necessary that you go and consult Father Raymond ; it is the will of God." And he sent his penitent to receive Holy Communion at a Mass that was being said at Our Lady's altar.

" During my thanksgiving," she writes, " I begged Our Lady to help me, to give me the means to carry out obediently what I had just been told, to take care of my vocation herself, and to break the chains which bound me to the world."

Margaret had unquestioning respect for authority, she would do nothing without the consent of her mother before she came of age. She decided to wait patiently during the five months that remained until she reached her majority and then to speak of her projects, and with the help of divine grace to surmount whatever obstacles might be put in her path.

During the following winter, by a combination of Providential circumstances, there were fewer social engagements and these were not so noisy. Margaret occupied the time with *The Exercises of St. Ignatius Loyola.*

Her mother did not like to see her reading such a serious book as *The Exercises,* but let her have her way.

She reached the age of twenty-one on March 15th, 1889. During the preceding months she had rejected firmly several offers of marriage that were advantageous from every view-point. She belonged to God ; she wanted no one but Him. Before acquainting her mother of her decision, she wished to steel her courage by exciting in herself the blessed sentiments of her first Communion. The ceremony fell on April 7th in her parish that year. She attended all the exercises and lived again the holy emotions of her first meeting with her divine Master.

" I cast into Infinite Mercy," she writes, " these ten years that were filled with so many infidelities, miseries and sins. I joined up my life to those days of innocence and peace which had been too long strangers to me. New graces were given to me. I felt myself stronger. I envisaged without fear the combats to come. I resolved to seize the first opportunity to declare my vocation to my family, to solicit respectfully the consent of my mother, and, if she should refuse, to use the liberty which my majority gave me to leave the the world and to give myself to God."

Eight days afterwards, it was Palm Sunday, Margaret found herself alone with her Mother and step-father. She felt that the time had come to speak. But having a presentiment of the tears that were to be shed, her courage failed her ; and an indescribable pain pierced her heart. She grasped her rosary beads, as she would have grasped the hand of a friend. Her mother left the room ; Margaret then reproaching herself for her cowardice addressed her step-father.

" I have something to say to mother," said she, " and I have not the courage to say it ; I am afraid it will cause her pain."

" What is it ?" said he, continuing to write.

" I wish to announce to her my resolution to become a Religious."

" A Religious ! " said he, bursting out laughing, but it was a laugh that sounded hollow. " You a Religious ! But it must be a joke."

Margaret was silent. The words affected her like a cut of a whip. She got up and sought her mother.

" Dear mother," said she, " please come here, I want to speak to you."

" My voice betrayed my emotion," she continues, " my mother appeared to be alarmed ; she turned round her head quickly, looked at me straight in the face, and taking hold of my two hands, said to me : ' What do you wish ? What is the matter ?' ' Mother,' I replied gently, though my heart was beating very strongly, ' I wish to speak to you of the resolution I have taken to enter a convent and to ask your consent.' Hardly had I finished these words when my mother seized me in her arms and burst into tears. Then there were caresses and sobbing which broke my heart. Oh ! how painful it is to make one's mother weep ! God gave me the courage to remain firm. After a moment, my mother cried out in the midst of her sobs, ' I cannot oppose the will of God ; I cannot refuse my consent !' How consoling these words were ! I had never before heard my mother speak of the will of God, and it was at this hour, at the moment that this divine will was breaking her heart, that she recognised it, that she submitted to it, that she adored it. What strength that gave to me ! Certainly I had no doubt about the will of God ; but what a consolation was it not in this sorrowful moment to hear my mother herself confess that my call to the religious life came from God, despite the repugnance of her whole nature and her motherly heart ; to see her discern this heavenly feature the very first time that I told her of my vocation ; to feel her so persuaded at this moment that she was not able to face the possibility of refusing her consent. Later on, in the days of darkness and violent temptations, the remembrance of these first words of my mother were to be to me a source of help, support and light."

The Christian had spoken first, the mother added : " No, I cannot refuse my consent, but I want you to delay your entry ; I want a delay of two years." It was a very long time for a soul eager to give herself to God. The best course for Margaret was, however, to accept the condition. Her mother begged her not to enter a cloistered order. Margaret told her that nothing had been decided on that point, that she needed advice, and that she asked her permission to change her confessor. " Oh !" said her mother, " you are free now, do as you wish."

Mr. and Mrs. de Chamberet met to discuss the matter ; Margaret, who had retired to the end of the room, heard only scraps of the conversation.

" I presume you did not consent," said Mr. de Chamberet.

" I could not refuse," replied her mother.

" Oh ! we will see," said Mr. de Chamberet, " it is just a young girl's whim ; in a few days she will think of it no more."

" No," said the mother, " I am quite convinced that it is serious ; it is the will of God."

STORM BEFORE ARRIVING AT PORT

In the De Chamberet's home nature gradually endeavoured to get back its rights. Margaret's mother, without withdrawing her consent that was given spontaneously, began a long-drawn out struggle against her vocation ; there were painful scenes, entreaties, assaults of all kinds that lasted up to the day that Margaret entered the Visitation Monastery. Bodily sufferings were added and sufferings of soul that she had to endure in the most complete spiritual isolation.

Margaret, remembering the order which she had received in the name of God six months previously, went to consult Father Raymond, the Curé of Saint-Jean de Valence. The reception which she received was capable of discouraging anyone of less firm determination and tenacity than Margaret's. But before leaving, she received excellent advice at this first interview and carried with her a clear idea of the help which she would find in this good priest, who was firm, prudent and spiritual. " Yes," he assured her, " the Visitation is the order for you ; but allow me to find for you the monastery you will enter. Think of nothing except of preparing yourself in a general way for the grace that awaits you."

Important affairs obliged the family to spend six months in the Jura. The damp climate and an incipient attack of asthma reacted adversely on Margaret's health. Her mother insisted on complete rest; rest from the long walks which she used to take, and rest from all social engagements.

When she was in this state of physical suffering and moral isolation, the enemy of all good assaulted her with the most violent temptations ; he seemed to have obtained permission from God to torment cruelly this soul that, in his infernal cunning, he foresaw to be destined for some special work.

" I was too far away from the Church," writes Margaret, " to be able to go there alone to receive the strengthening Bread of Life, and I suffered cruelly from horrible temptations.

" Up to then, I had of course believed in all that the Church teaches about hell and the demon ; but I confess that I did not believe at all in the exterior and sensible action of the evil spirit. I had never read the lives of the Saints, where the action of the devil sometimes appears so clearly side by side with the action of God, and my turn of mind prevented me from giving credence to what I had sometimes heard related.

" One day, soon after our arrival at Proby Castle, I managed to direct our walk so as to pass through the village. It was Saturday, and I wished to go to confession. We were passing along a by-path ; I was in front preparing for confession, when I suddenly heard beside me a strange, dry, harsh voice that sounded like metal, which said to me : ' Confession ! What use is it? It is nothing ! Jesus Christ never spoke of it ; it is an invention of the Church.' This strange voice, which was quite audible, astounded me. By the words that were spoken, I understood that it could be no one else but the devil. At first, I experienced a sensation of fear, then, raising my mind to God, I said firmly, in an undertone : ' I believe in all that the Church teaches.' From that moment, my soul was tormented with temptations of all kinds, so terrible and so violent that without special help from Our Lord and His blessed Mother I could not have been able to overcome them. . . . . I placed all my hope in God, and I walked alone, without help, in the midst of these terrible storms.   It was then that I commenced to seek support in Our Lord Jesus Christ, from Whose divine Person I had still kept far away.   Contrary to what happens for certain people who arrive by way of the sensible and exterior mysteries of the Humanity of Jesus Christ at the knowledge of His Divinity, I had first been attracted by His Divinity and it was by It that I was going to arrive at a knowledge of His Humanity.   But most usually at these times, I had recourse to the Blessed Virgin Mary, whom I called to my help in these moments of peril.

" I was tempted about all the mysteries of the Faith, and the devil proposed such subtle arguments that, later on, when I told some of them to Father Raymond under obedience, he forbade me to speak of them to anyone."

She would have liked to receive Holy Communion frequently, but the church was far away and the Mass on Sundays was late ; however, she often fasted till the late Mass in order to receive her divine Saviour.

Early in November, the family returned for just a few days to Valence before setting out for Paris.   A marriage had been arranged between Margaret's eldest sister and a Mr. Clavier, whom she had met at Jura, and this visit to Paris was to make the final preparations. At Valence, Margaret saw Father Raymond again and told him of her six months of suffering and trials, of the torments which the devil made her endure, and of the way in which she had repelled his attacks.   The good priest encouraged her, but told her that her time of trial was not yet over.   Then, seeing her so firm in her resolution to become a religious, he promised to tell her immediately after her sister's marriage the convent where he had decided that she should enter.

At Paris, she made a pilgrimage in the evening to the Basilica of the Sacred Heart at Montmartre, which was then in the course of construction.   It was still without roof, but there was a wooden altar surmounted by a statue of the Sacred Heart.   Mr. Clavier, her future brother-in-law, who was with the party and who had been informed of her intention to enter a convent, saw her prostrate herself in prayer before the statue of the Sacred Heart. He little suspected that while she prayed for her family, her vocation, for

France and the Church, that she prayed in particular for himself who had given up the practice of religion, and that he was to owe his conversion later on to her prayers and sacrifices.

"While I prayed for this soul," Sister Louise Margaret tells us later on, "I felt that God gave it to me, that, in some mysterious way, He put it into my hands in order that I might give it back to Him. I understood also that, for its conversion, I should not only contribute by labour and my efforts, but that I should above all suffer. The value which the suffering of the creature acquires when it is united to the suffering of Christ was shown to me. I understood that if prayer can be of much avail to move the Heart of God, sacrifice, united to the Sacrifice of Jesus, is still more powerful. All that was shown me in an instant."

The marriage of Margaret's eldest sister, Matilda, took place on January the 6th, 1890. Margaret appeared at it with her usual grace and vivacity, endeavouring by her gaiety to counteract the sombre impression which the approach of her own departure, now known to all her friends, cast on the nuptial festivity.

MARGARET DECIDES TO ENTER THE CONVENT OF THE VISITATION AT ROMANS

"Some days later," she writes, "I went to see Father Raymond. After Confession he said to me : ' You are to go to the Convent of the Visitation at Romans. I know this house, there are saintly souls there, it is the place for you.' I bowed to the will of him who spoke to me in the name of God. I did not know either Romans or the Visitation. I told my mother of the decision which had been made for me, she wept much and told me that she would not take me there. My step-father also refused to take me and so I asked my brother-in-law to do me this service.

"We set out on February 6th. The Rev. Mother then in charge, being informed of my coming by a letter from Father Raymond, was expecting me and came immediately to the parlour accompanied by our dear Mother ——, then Mistress of Novices. They welcomed me cordially but on seeing my slender frame and delicate countenance they did not hide from me their fears that my delicate health might be an obstacle. As the presence of my brother-in-law made it difficult for me to speak of my vocation to these good Sisters, I proposed to him that he should go and see the town and leave me some time to speak to them ; but I believe he must have received orders from my mother not to leave me for a moment ; he refused to do as I asked him, and so I was obliged to confine myself to vague, purely exterior questions.

Knowing that this was not sufficient, on the following day I wrote a long letter to the Rev. Mother in which I opened my heart to her in all confidence and simplicity. She was pleased with it, and wrote to me to encourage me and to propose to me that I should make a little retreat.

From this time on we carried on a correspondence.

My mother did not permit me to go to make this retreat before Easter, and during the days of the Carnival and the week of torchlight processions, I had to go into mundane society and play the comedy as usual.''

The following is the letter which she wrote to the Mother Superior :

Feb. 11th, 1890.

" Dear Rev. Superioress,

During the visit which I paid you last Saturday, I have been able to make myself known to you only very imperfectly ; the presence of my brother-in-law, who indeed is very good to me, prevented me from speaking freely, and I have not been able, as I would have wished, to tell you about my vocation, my tastes, and my inclinations, and thus put you in a position to judge me. I do not wish to wait until the month of May to do that ; I therefore take the liberty of writing to you, and trust that you will kindly pardon me for causing you so much trouble.

My mother, who was unable to accompany me, is very much grieved over my entry into religious life ; however she consented to it on seeing my desire for this life and because she recognises in me a special vocation.

I have, dear Mother, been brought up in a Christian manner, but in a very worldly atmosphere. I received my first Communion at the age of eleven, after attending the course of religious instruction at the Cathedral school, and about a year afterwards, the desire for a religious life came to me for the first time. I even made a promise to God to consecrate myself to Him, if He granted me several graces which I asked for at this time, among others, better health for myself. In the course of the six years which followed, I finished my studies, and made my entrance into the world. My studies were directed towards a worldly career; the state of my health prevented me from completing them. I made my entry into society when very young, but in spite of all this, during these six years I thought often on the promise I had made, and almost every day at my prayers, I asked of God the grace to carry it out; in the meantime I abandoned myself to the pleasures of the world and relegated the thought of convent life to the distant future.

In 1886, when I was eighteen years old, I became very ill with scarlet fever and was very near dying; I had the happiness of being nursed by a Bon Secours Sister.

My illness made me reflect, I spoke of my projects to the dear Sister, she encouraged me and strengthened me in my resolution. . . . . . . By the time winter came, I was completely conquered by the world again.

When people recover from serious illness they are so happy to be back to health again that they feel in themselves, as it were, the sap of life coursing through their veins; they are, in a certain manner, intoxicated and dazzled by the joy of being restored to life. This has been my experience; I threw myself with all the ardour of my eighteen years into the whirlwind of worldly distractions.

I forgot my good resolutions of the summer and my former promises, I thought seriously of marriage and as I did not wish to perjure myself by breaking my vow, I thought of getting dispensed from it.

I was cruelly punished for having consented to abandon my God; in the spring, I had great grief of heart; everything around me seemed to be crumbling, and I suffered from this, all the more because I confided my trouble to no one; even my mother was ignorant of it. I threw myself at the feet of God and asked His pardon for having abandoned Him, but I was so totally crushed by this blow that I did not think immediately of religious life; prayer and the profound calm in which I passed the summer appeased my sorrow. I was consoled, when, in autumn, a book fell by chance into my hands; it was the life of St. Aloysius of Gonzaga. The beautiful vocation, the angelic purity and marvellous detachment of this young Saint, made a profound impression on me; I returned to God anew and promised Him to belong to Him." It was only after Easter that Margaret, accompanied by her mother, went to make the retreat which the Mother Superior had advised her to make. Of this retreat she speaks as follows : " After three days my mother returned home leaving me to make my little retreat.

" I did not go through the holy exercises of the retreat to seek for light, for I had no doubt about my vocation, but rather to bring myself near to God, from Whom I still felt myself very far away, and in order to know Him better.

" The Preacher gave me my dear Manresa (a retreat according to the method of St. Ignatius), and I remembered that I relished particularly, and got several lights from the meditations of the first part especially on these three subjects : ' I am from God, I belong to God, and I am for God.' Almost the whole retreat centered round these thoughts."

When she returned to Valence a last desperate effort was made to settle her in the world. She never for a moment thought of yielding.

However, her temptations continued to be as violent as before, but there were times of consolation.

" Yesterday, and to-day again," she writes, " my poor soul, buffeted in a thousand ways, could not even utter an appeal to Thee. Why, O Lord, dost Thou overwhelm me with so much confusion and affliction ? Why dost Thou allow such horrible images to pass often before my eyes ? . . . .

The winds were blowing and the waves were surging within me even to the holy Table ; in my trouble and anxiety I awakened thee : ' Lord, save me,' I cried, I opened my mouth and received Thee.

" Then Thou didst arise and looking upon me with pity, say to me : ' O creature of little faith, why dost thou fear.' (Matt. viii, 26). And suddenly Thou didst command the storm and there came a great calm ; peace, refreshing and sweet, inundated my soul."

Margaret tried several times unsuccessfully to obtain a reduction of the two years' delay imposed on her by her mother. However on July the 16th, the feast of Our Lady of Mount Carmel, after placing the matter in the hands of St. Joseph, she advanced such reasons that her mother was obliged to consent. The day of departure, arranged after consulting the Rev. Mother at Romans, was fixed for the 21st November.

In the interval which elapsed she made a pilgrimage to Paray le Monial, where she renewed her consecration to the Sacred Heart.

The following is the formula of consecration, composed by herself, which she used :

" O adorable Heart of my divine Saviour, I offer and consecrate myself entirely to Thee : my soul which Thou has created to Thy image ; my intellect which Thou has enlightened with the lights of Thy faith ; my heart which, after loving creatures, now wishes to love only Thee and to beat for Thee alone ; my body which has contributed to, and shared in the wandering of my soul, but which wishes by penance to sustain and contribute to its uplifting ; all the higher powers of my soul and the lower powers of my body, I give and abandon entirely to Thee. For the future I wish to have no other will but Thine, no other desire but that of pleasing Thee, no other love but Thy pure love. Amen."

A final temptation awaited her when she arrived home.

" When returning from our pilgrimage to Paray le Monial, I was assailed by a very violent temptation on our arrival home. Miss X (her teacher) who had accompanied me related the incidents of the journey to my mother. Being absent at the time, I was ignorant of what the dear lady had told my mother with reference to a young lawyer who had made the journey with us ; at any rate, my mother began again to speak of marriage to me, and to beg me to marry this young man if he pleased me, and endeavoured to persuade me that I should remain in the world to do good and to convert my brother-in-law. I refuted the arguments with vigour and defended my vocation ; but a little later when I had retired to my room, all the old thoughts against my vocation returned to me ; I asked myself if I should not follow my mother's wishes ; if this was not the will of God ; if this young man had not been put providentially on my path ; finally the devil, making use of the most specious pretexts, so enveloped my mind that I was perhaps going to give way, when a vague thought of all that Our Lord had done to have me for Himself dawned on my soul. Being pressed on the one side by the temptation, and on the other, seeing a little light in the depths of my soul attracting me to God, not knowing which way to turn, in the extreme trouble of my heart, I threw myself on my knees, and, in the middle of the room, with my arms extended in the form of a cross, I uttered a cry of desperate appeal to our Lord. Then I got the inspiration to renew my vow of chastity ; I did so, and immediately all trouble ceased. I felt my soul inundated with the purest and sweetest consolations. A heavenly peace succeeded to this frightful storm.

I remained for some time on my knees inundated with divine joys, and more than ever determined to belong to God alone.

This was my last temptation in the world. In less than two months, I entered the Monastery."

CHAPTER III.

THE CLOISTER.

" Let nothing of me remain, but a humble
servant of Jesus, always ready to do
His will."

Margaret went back to her mother after a visit to the convent, having definitely decided to return there as soon as she should be free. Of this visit she writes :

" I did not seek to learn much about the rule and the kind of life ; I knew that God wished me to belong to Him ; I felt the need of a life hidden and completely separated from the world. Father Raymond had said to me in the name of God : ' It is this convent that you are to enter ' ; wishing only to do the will of God, I counted on His grace, and I accepted in advance in a general way, all the sacrifices which religious life involved.

The sacrifice involved in religious life which I desired by my faith, which I wished because I knew God wished it from me, was shown to me in all its rigour, and God allowed me to taste its bitterness."

Nine days afterwards, on the evening of Nov. 20th, 1890, she entered the Monastery of the Visitation, at Romans in the South of France.

" The heavy door opened before me," she writes, " I stepped in, it closed again ; all was finished ; I knelt down before the Mother-Superior, she blessed me.

" What did I do then ? What took place around me ? I do not know. I have a vague memory that I dined, and then was brought to the chapel ; the rest is lost, I do not remember any more. I do not know what happened during the hours which followed. I presume that I did as I was told. Later on when I retired to the cell that had been prepared for me, I knelt down before the crucifix and wept for a long time and without restraint. These tears which were shed in peace at the feet of Jesus comforted me. It was neither regret, nor fear, nor uncertainty of the future that made me shed them ; it was my heart, grievously bruised and wounded by the separation from everything which I had loved on earth, that was bleeding slowly through my eyes. . . . .

I had hoped to enter the Novitiate after a few days. . . . . They were not in a hurry to admit me. However, it had pleased my divine Master to relieve me from my head-aches and the fainting-fits from which I had suffered previously. The emphysema of the lungs remained and made me cough frequently ; but that was an infirmity, not a malady.

In spite of the cold fogs which surrounded me, at the bottom of my soul, I was aware of a sweet feeling of joy. I felt that I had done the will of God.

" I will not write anything more on this copy book. God alone and the holy women who will take care of my soul will be my confidants for the future ; I will hide nothing from them. In order that a physician may cure my wounds, I must show them to him and not conceal from him the pains which they make me suffer ; I must act in like manner with the venerable nurses of my soul.

" I have given myself irrevocably to Jesus, my sweet Master ; by continual care I will root out my faults and my evil inclinations one by one ; I will unite myself with all my strength to Him Who, in order to be united to me, did not disdain to hide Himself under the material species of bread.

In order to combat my pride I will accept humiliations with joy and even seek for them. Finally, I will not allow myself to be discouraged by anything, I will put all my confidence in God alone, I will drive every desire from my mind and follow holy obedience in everything.

" Let nothing of me remain, but a humble servant of Jesus Christ always ready to obey His divine will."

A rather unfavourable reputation had preceded her at the Monastery. The Vicar General of the diocese, who was also spiritual Father to the monastery, only laughed when he was told of her request to be admitted to the novitiate ; he did not believe that she had any vocation to the religious life. A pious lady from Valence laughed too when she heard the news and said to the Rev. Mother : " If you want a subject who is a good actor in comedies,

Miss de la Touche is just the person for you ; she is an excellent comedienne."

She was received cordially by the Rev. Mother and the Sisters ; if the stories of the gossipers had given rise to any mistrust on their part, it was not apparent in their conduct towards her. However, her superiors prudently decided to make her wait two months before admitting her to the novitiate. That two months' wait was indeed calculated to try her vocation. The greater part of the day was spent in her cell, from which there was no view ; she was afraid of giving trouble, of being where she ought not to be ; she knew that her mother was broken-hearted and had not courage to reply to her letters.

" I remained for two months," she writes, " like a stranger in the house. How long these two months appeared to me !

" A vast field of sufferings and abnegation opened before me at the outset, and my cowardly nature would, doubtless, have been wanting in generosity to embrace them, were it not for the help of this great thought (a conversion which she wished to obtain ; and which she obtained some months later). Indeed, mortifications came to me in throngs. All that however seemed trifling to me, and the ardent desire which I had to save souls and especially the soul of X—— urged me to add other little sufferings to those which I encountered."

Life in the Convent was indeed very different from what Margaret had been accustomed to in her luxurious home. Margaret, like all brave young souls who take God for their portion, accepted the conditions of life in the Cloister without a murmur ; in fact she added austerities of her own ; she put a plank under her in her bed until she was ordered by her Mistress of Novices to remove it. And her divine Master, on His part, did not wait long until He made her feel that, even in this life, He is able to give back a hundred fold, by bestowing peace and happiness which the world cannot give.

" For all that," she writes, " I was happy, yes, truly happy ! and Jesus, in order to help me and encourage me, commenced to make me feel at times during prayer inward consolations which I had never hitherto experienced. Often when I commenced my meditation, the point which I had prepared disappeared from my mind, an indescribable feeling of satisfaction and peace filled my soul, an indefinable divine influence surrounded me, and I felt my heart filled with an ardent desire to love God and suffer for souls."

On January 17th, 1891, Margaret was allowed to enter the novitiate ; she took the name in religion of Sister Louise Margaret. The following is her account of her first experience of religious life :

" Religious life was revealed to me with its rules, its observances, its obedience ; strengthened by grace, I entered into it with resolution and joy. At the very beginning, Our Lord was pleased to grant me a grace of which I was not aware then, but which I recognised later on. I cannot otherwise explain it except by saying that I became a little child again. I seemed to have forgotten everything ; the timidity and awkwardness of early infancy replaced the assurance, and I may even say, the cheekiness of the years of my worldly life. I had either forgotten or I could not make use of what I had known up to then ; I showed my ignorance in everything, and I had to learn everything over again.

" I admitted very sincerely that I was inferior to all my companions, and indeed, I did everything I was given to do very badly. I was told so, and I had no difficulty in believing it, for I saw it myself. If there was question of reading, I did it very badly, for my poor congested lungs refused their co-operation ; and then, I was afraid to read as I had been taught in the world, and that paralysed me."

Her delicate health was a source not only of physical, but of keen moral suffering to her.

" In the world," she writes, " ill-health had often caused me painful bodily suffering, but I had never been prevented by it from following my worldly life, and I had never to suffer morally from the great delicacy of my temperament. In the Monastery it was to be otherwise, and from the time of my entrance, I found in these things an abundant source of suffering and self-sacrifice. It was one of the greatest causes of suffering during my first years of religious life to see myself unable to take a hand at the common occupations like the other Sisters ; incapable of stretching out the linen that had been washed, of doing the sweeping and other such little tasks as are usually performed by novices and young professed Sisters.

" My self-love, no doubt, being responsible, it caused me real pain of soul when, on my volunteering for some work to be done, I heard this phrase, always the same : ' Oh ! not you. Sister !' This : ' Not you, Sister ' pierced my heart, and it was only by fervent prayer at the feet of my good Master, and the help of His grace, that I brought myself to accept this inferiority of weakness and this abjection of infirmity. It required implacable handling of myself, and meditation on Jesus suffering and humiliated, to succeed in conquering my self-love on this point, and to love this state so humiliating in the eyes of creatures, but so precious in the eyes of Jesus."

Obedience is the daughter of humility. Sister Margaret was not long in learning it. She saw in her book of rules that no private penances may be undertaken without permission. What was she to do about the plank which she had put in her bed? Simply take it out? She thought it more perfect to ask her confessor and do as he told her.

" A little perplexed," she writes, " I resolved to consult our chaplain, Father Toupin. He told me immediately that I must tell the Mistress of Novices. That would cost me a great effort. I went to see her and told her all. She did not permit me to continue the practice and even refused me the discipline that I asked her to give me. I bowed before her will, but regretted the little discipline which I had made with cords (after a picture she had seen in *The Life of St. Aloysius*) the last year of my life in the world and which I had thrown in the fire on the day of my entry, thinking that I would get a better one at the Monastery."

That she was not gifted with an ear for music soon became evident to the Mistress of novices, who, on observing that she recited the Office in a low tune, ordered her to raise her voice. The result was so unhappy that she was not permitted to recite the Office in choir any more, and was placed in the ranks of Associate Sisters. This was a very hard sacrifice for her. She had a great attraction for singing the praises of God and loved the divine poetry in the psalms and hymns and canticles.

Another trial which affected her more intimately awaited her. From her first day in the Monastery, Our Lord had given her an attraction for a very simple form of meditation on the mysteries of His love, intermingled with familiar colloquies with Him. Her prudent Mistress of Novices had taught her the ordinary method of mental prayer. When Sister Louise Margaret timidly remarked that this method of meditation kept her soul in constraint, her instructress replied : " No, no, this method is excellent, you must follow it faithfully." She obeyed and derived great advantage from it, as she afterwards ascertained.

" All this," she writes, " was by the special permission of Our Lord. This constraint of soul was a good penance for me ; the intellectual effort which I forced myself to make was salutary for me. It helped to rid my mind of the profane thoughts which had up to then occupied it ; it developed in it a facility to apply myself to the study of divine things ; by the struggle and effort which it involved, it caused the holy thoughts, which too often remain on the surface, to penetrate into my soul."

On the morning of the Feast of the Assumption, Our Blessed Lady gave her privileged child a great joy. A letter from Mr. Clavier, her brother-in-law, announced to her that on the day before he had been fully reconciled with God and that he had been to Holy Communion. This was for her both an occasion for expressing her heart-felt gratitude to God, and an encouragement to continue her life of sacrifices, which cost her human nature so much. With the permission of her superiors, she carried out the vow which she had made at Paray-le-Monial when she consecrated to the Sacred Heart the soul that she wished to convert. She painted on parchment to be placed in the Basilica a votive tablet representing the Good Shepherd carrying His sheep on His shoulders with the sweet words : " Rejoice with Me, because I have found the sheep that I had lost." (Luke, XV. 6).

THE CLOTHING CEREMONY

The months of her first trial were finished. Sister Louise Margaret was admitted by the Chapter on September 1st to put on the holy habit ; she commenced the preparatory retreat in the early days of October. In order to strengthen her for the long road of trials which was opening before her, the divine Master made the sweet rays of His love and consolation penetrate into her soul. The past was receding more and more and already appeared to be only a distant dream, now very confused. She left the future to God, and in the present, she saw only Jesus bending down lovingly towards her and drawing her to Himself. The ceremony took place on October 7th. Her whole family were there and were indescribably touched.

" . . . . . My God," she writes, " how happy I was on leaving the livery of the world, this lace, these jewels, this coloured dust which dazzles so many eyes and deceives so many hearts ! How happy I was to put on this blessed habit ! My white veil, especially, delighted me ; all white and pure, it enveloped me and rustled in the wind like the wings of a dove. During the whole time of my noviciate I had a real devotion to my dear veil ; at night I folded it with respect ; in the morning I kissed it lovingly ; I took care of it in order that it might remain spotlessly white. I would have liked to keep it always. After my clothing, I continued my noviciate with new courage. Besides, since the time of my entry, I had accustomed myself not to stop at difficulties, and to pass resolutely over them without giving them too much consideration ; that seemed to me to be the easiest and the surest way."

So far, God had marvellously sustained Margaret's weak health. But in January of 1892, she had an attack of congestion of the lungs from which she nearly died. She realised that she was seriously ill, and as she said, to put everyone at their ease, she made her will and received Holy Viaticum and Extreme Unction. She gladly and gratefully accepted the offer of the Rev. Mother to pronounce her religious vows conditionally.

" . . . . . And there in the presence of Jesus and His priest, surrounded by our Sisters, I pronounced the abridged formula of our vows.

" In return for this promise, which for the Community was conditional, but which I made for myself without condition, Jesus gave Himself to me. Scarcely had I received the sacred Body of my Divine Master when everything vanished from my eyes. I completely lost consciousness of everything around me . . . . and I found myself transported—where, I cannot really tell in a place of repose and peace, alone with Jesus ! What took place ? I do not know ; but I felt myself penetrated with infinite sweetness which not only filled my soul and all its faculties, but which, flowing down to my members, brought to them a feeling of general well-being, a kind of relief from strain and such excessive pleasantness that I finally returned to myself.

On the following day, the doctors found me much improved and on the way to recovery, and were astonished at the sudden change which had taken place.

" My return to normal health was very rapid. . . . .

" I remember having previously experienced the intimate, penetrating sweetness which a visit from my Divine Master had brought. It was, as I have recorded in a previous manuscript, when, at the age of six, miraculous water from Lourdes had cured me just when I had come to my last moments. A fortnight after, I

was up and about and resumed the ordinary course of my Noviciate.
I felt myself more closely united to Jesus and more truly His, and
my soul, shaking off the excessive timidity which oppressed me,
expanded more freely in a warmer atmosphere. I knew that the
Community might send me away ; several times I believed that the
moment had arrived. I saw myself so utterly helpless and so use-
less ! But at this moment I belonged to Jesus, and Jesus belonged
to me, what did the rest matter !"

However, when, under a misapprehension about the real reasons
of the attitude of her superiors towards her, she became persuaded that
she was to be sent back to her family, her soul was broken with grief.

" I wished only the will of God," she afterwards wrote, " but I
suffered at the thought of taking off our dear habit, of being thrown
back in the midst of the world, rejected by Jesus, union with Whom
was the subject of all my dreams."

Her tears flowed abundantly. She knelt before the Blessed
Sacrament and said to Jesus :

" My God, I wish only Thy will. If it pleases Thee that I be
sent away, I wish it also. I know that Thy will was that I should
come here, I do not know if Thy will be that I should remain. I
do not wish to have any wish or desire ; do Thou inspire the Chapter
to do with me what will be most for Thy glory. I accept in advance
all the sufferings of the religious life, all the sorrows of a spoiled
vocation and of an uncertain life ; I make myself entirely indifferent
while waiting to know Thy will, and I promise to carry it out lovingly
and courageously whatever it may be."

The decision of the Chapter was favourable. Her profession was
fixed for October 17th, 1892.

" On the day of the decision of the Chapter," she writes, " my
profession was complete, for only the sanction of the Chapter was
wanting to my vows which had been pronounced seven months
previously."

In the time that intervened, she was assailed by violent temptations of the devil and she got a glimpse of the sufferings that were
in store for her in the carrying out of her mission.

She had to endure another trial also. The Mistress of Novices
to whom she had confided the secrets of her soul became ill. In
spite of the repugnance which she felt, from the outset, she gave the
same simple confidence and submission to the new directress as to
her Mistress of Novices.

During the preparatory retreat she was made aware that God had special designs over her soul and that they would entail much suffering on her part.

" During these holy exercises," she writes, " I understood that God had special designs over my soul. What were these designs? I knew not. I was troubled by the thought of what these hidden designs might be, and I went forward trembling. However, I abandoned myself to Jesus, and I offered myself for all the sufferings and trials which He had destined for me."

PROFESSION

Of the happy day of her Profession, she writes :

" . . . . . The morning sun of October 17th arose. It was a day of blessings and grace. I was happy to give myself to God, to unite myself to our Lord by indestructible bonds ; but I felt also the greatness of the act that I was going to perform, and a profoundly serious and grave sentiment reigned in my soul. Kneeling at the altar-rails, I pronounced slowly the formula of our vows, so majestic and yet so beautiful. I saw neither the celebrant nor his assistant nor those who were in the church and who filled the choir ; I felt myself alone before God and I paid attention to nothing else. When I had received the black veil, I went and prostrated myself in the middle of the choir, just where the coffin of our dead Sisters is placed ; the pall was stretched over me, and while one Sister chanted slowly the lesson of the Office for the Dead : " *Homo natus, etc.*" and while the choir sang the " *De Profundis,*" I remained there with my face against the ground, plunged in darkness, all alone before God, annihilated in the presence of His divine Majesty. I gave myself to Him with my whole will while I repeated these words : ' All for Thee, O my God, all for Thee ; I give Thee all, do with me and in me all that Thou wishest.' Lost in adoration, I heard neither the holy water falling on the pall which covered me, nor the grave strong voice of the celebrant uttering this appeal : ' You who sleep, arise from among the dead.' "

There was a moment of intense emotion among those present, for they saw no movement responding to these words of resurrection. Was the sacrifice already consummated ? No, it was only commencing, and the victim, placed on the altar of holocausts, was, without ever descending from it, to expire on it twenty-three years later.

" Finally," she continues, " I returned to consciousness of the things around me and got up. A heavenly peace filled my soul ; I went over to the grating, and in all the joy of my heart I intoned the two verses of the psalm : ' The Lord is my light and my salvation, what shall I fear. . . . .' All my fears had vanished. I was happy to belong to God ; a divine peace filled my soul, and during the whole day I felt my soul more in heaven than on earth. In the evening before retiring to our cell, I went to the Noviciate ; I deposited the crown of roses which I had worn since morning on the altar at the feet of the Virgin, and I prayed this Mother of Goodness to be the guardian of the promises which I had made to Jesus. It was done for ever, I was consecrated to God, united to the divine Master ; time, which destroys everything, would not break my bonds. I was dead to the world ; I had left my family ; I had given up to Jesus all that I possessed, my heart, my soul, my liberty, my life, ... but how small all that was compared to what the divine Master was going to give me in giving Himself."

FIRST YEARS OF [HER RELIGIOUS LIFE

Sister Louise Margaret, though now professed, still remained in the Noviciate. For several years she continued to form herself in it to the spirit and the rules of the Order of the Visitation.

Two kinds of work occupied the time not spent in prayer. In order to make herself useful to the Community, with the permission of her Superiors, she had learned embroidery in gold and silk, and became very expert in it. She turned her skill in drawing and painting to good account, and it was a great source of joy to her to see the most varied and delicate designs, mostly of her own composition, adorning the vestments destined for the Holy Sacrifice.

At other times, her Superiors availed themselves of her great literary ability. She was given as assistant to an old Sister who was engaged in going through the various documents of the Monastery and in compiling a history from them, an occupation which increased her love for her dear Visitation.

Whether at embroidery or in the Archives, her prayer continued almost without interruption. While engaged in embroidery, she was mostly alone, and while the Choir Sisters were chanting the Divine Office, she composed and sang beautiful poems expressing her love and devotion to her Beloved Spouse, who from this time on began to favour her with His sensible presence.

SHE COMPOSES BEAUTIFUL POETRY

" During the first months that followed my profession," she writes : " I was almost exclusively employed in works of embroidery with gold and silk for the sacristy. I worked in the Noviciate in silence and peace for a part of the day. From that time Jesus commenced to make His presence felt to me in an ineffable manner, and my heart opened out to His love with ardent avidity.   I did not hear Him or see Him but I felt Him present as if He were standing before me, motionless and silent, hidden by a light tapestry ; I felt Him there in life beside me, and His divine amiable qualities manifested themselves to my soul, and my soul went out to Him, drawn by an invisible attraction.   I had always a taste for fine poetry, but never was my soul so profoundly moved or so strongly impelled as to burst into song.   Nature and its enchantment which had always delighted me had never been sufficient to produce such an effect, and even at the time when human love had occupied my heart, this chord had not vibrated.   Up to that time, my pen had never produced a line of poetry except a few comic verses, or some humorous epigrams.

Jesus, on taking possession of my soul, was to cause this spark to issue from it.   In the long hours of silent work at the Noviciate during which my divine Master used to come to me, my soul went forth to Him and my thoughts, in an endeavour to raise themselves up to His divine Majesty, enveloped themselves in poetry.

Doubtless, my verses were of little value and I did not even write them down ; it sufficed for me that Jesus heard them and that His love accepted them."

VOW OF ABANDONMENT

St. Margaret Mary Alacoque tells us in her autobiography that early in her religious life, Our Lord demanded of her the sacrifice of her liberty and her whole being, and that she made it to Him. Later on He demanded that this sacrifice be made in the form of a vow to do always what was most perfect ; this vow she made in greatest detail, after consulting her Superiors. He made similar demands from Sister Louise Margaret ; first He demanded of her a vow of total abandonment to His will, and later on, He demanded a donation of her whole being to Infinite Love.

She made the vow of abandonment on the First Friday of August, 1895, with the consent of her confessor and her superiors, according to the following formula :

" O my God, prostrate in Thy presence, I adore Thy infinite perfection, I adore Thy sovereign dominion over all Thy creatures and, in order to recognise Thy dominion over me, I make a vow of total abandonment of my whole being into Thy hands, allowing Thee to dispose of me according to Thy good pleasure, for time and eternity.

" O Jesus, I abandon myself without reserve to Thy divine Heart, giving Thy love entire liberty of action in me and around me, wishing to see only Thy action in all things and to adore every disposition of Thy will."

SHE IS ALLOWED TO SHARE IN CHRIST'S SUFFERINGS

" *I fill up those things that are wanting of the sufferings of Christ in my flesh, for His body, which is the Church.*" (Coloss. I, 24).

In inviting Mother Louise Margaret to share in His suffering life, Our Lord said to her as He says to His special friends : " I make you the same present as My heavenly Father made to Me." The present was the cross and He encouraged her to bear her sufferings joyfully :

" Jesus, strengthened me," she writes, " with the divine balm which flows from the cross. He showed me His divine countenance. It was crowned with thorns and covered with blood but a divine smile lit up His face.

" I understood that I am to receive with great joy from the hands of my Saviour the pains that He will send me."

He explained to her the mysterious efficacy of His sufferings and allowed her to share in them :

" My divine Saviour has given me to understand that He chooses souls to continue His passion in them, but as a single human soul cannot endure all His sufferings, He gives to each one a little share. He wishes to make me share in His state of painful crucifixion ; His hands and feet were bound fast ; He was suspended so that He could not move, suffering a slow and silent agony, and no longer active. He wishes me to remain like this under His action, being disposed to suffer everything.

" When Our Lord showed me His will in my regard, He did not mingle in it any sweetness or consolation ; I felt all the bitterness of the sacrifice, and I saw that He exacted from me an uninterrupted immolation of every minute of my existence.

" On the following day at about three o'clock in the morning, I awoke suffering inexpressible pains, and for more than an hour our Lord made me again share in His suffering.

" I suffered excruciating pains in all my members, especially my feet, and there remained with me for a long time after the impression of burning heat accompanied with sharp pangs.

" Yesterday, September 17th, during the six o'clock Mass, I offered myself to God to accomplish His will, and to allow myself to be destroyed and annihilated for His pure love."

SHE SUFFERED ALSO MENTALLY

" I was assailed with the most humiliating temptations," she writes, " and particularly with attacks against the Faith ; I felt them to be absolutely independent of my will and—in some way that I am unable to explain—exterior to me.   It was as if someone beside me, but not in me, had uttered blasphemies against the Faith, against Holy Communion.   I suffered horribly.   What caused me the greatest pain was that I still at times received graces from Our Lord. Sometimes, when I had been shaken by these temptations, when I had fought for several hours, crying to heaven for help, everything would finally cease at prayer or at Holy Communion.   It seemed to me that it was impossible that Our Lord should deign to approach me, and I did not know what to think.   I got no help, either from the Chaplain, who kept silent, or from the Mistress of Novices, who did not appear to understand.   I felt an imperative need of counsel, of support, of a light to guide me in this way of suffering and combat.

" My character is not naturally inclined to believe easily in the supernatural, and in spite of the numerous graces which I had received from Jesus, human nature within me still resisted, and my mind, which is naturally opposed to the uncertain and the mysterious, struggled against the invasion of the supernatural and divine action. At the beginning of May I suffered so much that I began to recite daily the Thirty Days Prayer to obtain from the Blessed Virgin her protection and her help, and a little light for myself or for those who

were directing me. I made this prayer with all possible fervour."
The prayer was completed only four days when it was answered.

FATHER ALFRED CHARRIER, S.J.

St. Jane de Chantal had suffered, wept, and prayed for a long
time before Providence sent to her St. Francis de Sales, who, after
calming her soul, led her so far towards the heights of sanctity.
St. Margaret Mary Alacoque, by her tears and mental anguish,
had paid dearly for the grace of being reassured and encouraged by
Blessed Claude de la Colombière. The spiritual daughter of the
one and Sister of the other, destined like them for great things, was
going to receive a similar favour for the good of her own soul and
for the accomplishment of the divine designs, and she also was to
suffer much.

Father Alfred Charrier, S.J., the priest given by Our Lord to
Sister Louise Margaret to guide her and to establish the truth of
her mission, though comparatively young—he was thirty-nine—had
already acquired a reputation for prudence and firmness in the
direction of souls. In dealing with Sister Louise Margaret he took
nothing for granted. What St. Gregory says about St. Thomas
the Apostle, in his homily on the gospel of his feast, may well be
applied to Father Charrier. Thanks to his long years of minute
examination of everything in the life of Sister Louise Margaret
that could throw light on her mission, and to his insistence that she
put down in writing all the lights that she received, when later on
the Holy See examined her at Rome, there was available a written
account, covering her whole religious life, of everything connected
with her case.

If, as we are justified in believing, Our Lord chose Father Charrier
to direct the spiritual life of Mother Louise Margaret in extraordinary circumstances, we are justified in believing also that Father
Charrier, without his knowing it perhaps, acted under His divine
guidance ; and that what might appear to us to be excessive caution,
humility carried too far, and undue hesitancy in giving a decision,
were part of a divine plan. At any rate, during the long years that
he was her Director, there was no precaution against error that he
did not take, nor was there the slightest trace of partiality towards
her in his dealing with her communications. Hence, while he
prudently left to the Holy See the duty of deciding on the origin of

her communications, his own personal opinion, clearly expressed after long years of investigation, that they were from God, carries all the more weight.

On the evening of June 4th, 1896, the Feast of the Blessed Sacrament, Father Charrier preached for the first time in the Chapel of the Visitation at Romans. As he had taken no refreshment since morning, his voice was weak and he could scarcely be heard by the Sisters in the choir. Sister Louise Margaret, not being able to hear him, spent the time adoring Our Lord in the tabernacle. When the sermon was over, just at the time of Benediction, a voice which spoke within her, which she knew,and which she had reason to believe was the voice of Our Lord, said to her, designating Father Charrier : " Go and open your heart to Him." The suggestion appeared to her to be so strange, that she rejected it as a distracting thought and began to pray. A little later, when serving the Sisters at supper, having occasion to cross the refectory, she made a profound bow to the crucifix, the same interior voice repeated : " I wish you to open your heart completely to My servant." She felt the greatest repugnance to going to confession to this unknown priest. She reasoned with herself that her rules left her perfectly free not to ask for or make this confession. When going to sleep that night she recommended herself to Blessed Claude de la Colombière, to whom she had a great devotion since her pilgrimage to Paray le Monial, and asked him to aid her in ascertaining the will of God. On the following day, the Rev. Mother announced that the preacher (Father Charrier) was to replace the extraordinary confessor, who was unable to come. There was no further hesitation possible for Sister Louise Margaret, but her repugnance to going to confession to him had not diminished. It happened providentially that it was on June 6th, 1896, the anniversary of the foundation of the Order of the Visitation, that the first spiritual meeting between these two souls took place.

" After the simple weekly confession," she writes, " at the very first words spoken by Father Charrier, all my repugnance vanished completely, and I resisted no longer. I revealed to him the secrets of my soul not only with facility, but with a joy, a peace, a contentment that I had never before tasted. I told him everything ; my most horrible temptations, the graces of the good Master, my sufferings and anguish, just as I would have done with Our Lord Himself. The Father did not say much to me the first time. However, after three-quarters of an hour, I went out from him, my soul inundated with peace, and with the inward assurance that I had done the will of God."

And she added, showing herself to be a true Sister of St. Margaret Mary in her fidelity to her rule and acceptance of suffering from the hand of God :

" I felt that a firm hand had taken hold of my soul and was preventing it from falling, and I understood that this prudent direction, enlightened by the very spirit of Jesus, would not make me depart from the way of filial submission and respect in which I earnestly wished to walk courageously.

" Our Lord in sending me His servant did not wish by that to put an end to my sufferings and trials ; on the contrary, they went on increasing. The cross was going to weigh down more heavily on me ; all kinds of pain of body and heart and soul were going to come upon me and envelop me in their waves. But a mysterious power was to sustain me, and peace, the peace which the world cannot give, and which is the gift of Jesus, was going to radiate its joy in my soul in the midst of furious tempests, and Infinite Love, like a shining beacon light, was to guide me to port."

CHAPTER IV

THE MESSAGE FROM OUR DIVINE LORD FOR THE CLERGY OF THE WORLD

In the year 1913, now nearly forty years ago, Mother Louise Margaret herself and all her writings—*The Sacred Heart and the Priesthood*, published three years previously, all her letters, and her Intimate Notes containing the communications which she received from Our Lord—were examined at Rome by the Sacred Congregation of the Council and the Congregation for Religious. The substance of the communications which are recorded in these Intimate Notes was a message of love from Our Divine Lord for the bishops and priests of the world ; a command to have an organisation established binding the bishops and priests of the world together for the purpose of promoting devotion to the Sacred Heart ; and a command to establish a new monastery of the Visitation to act as a spiritual support for that organisation.

All her writings were pronounced to be in conformity with the teaching of the Church; the new organisation demanded by Our Lord for the bishops and priests of the world and its Statutes (drawn up under obedience by Mother Louise Margaret) were sanctioned by the Congregation of the Council; she received a commission from the Congregation for Religious to found the new monastery, and she left Rome with a special blessing for the work from His Holiness Pius X, written with his own hand. During the years which have elapsed since then, almost all her writings have been published, and have been translated into most of the languages of the world, and the organisation for bishops and priests and the monastery which she founded have continued to grow and develop with the approval and blessing of the Popes who have reigned since then.

Of her mission, she herself writes :

" I was not born to be a Religious, or to be a Superioress. In the designs of Providence, I was to be both, but that is not my *raison d'etre.* My *raison d'etre* is to be a nothing, a feather flying with the wind, a grain of sand heaved up by the sea, *but this feather, this grain of sand are messengers of Infinite Love.* Yes, my rôle here below is to publish the good news throughout the world, the good news that can never be repeated by enough people, the good news that had been repeated for the last twenty centuries without ceasing to be *the news* that all men have need to learn : *It is that God is Love, and that consequently, He loves His creatures.* To know this would mean happiness for the individual, happiness for peoples, happiness for humanity. But people refuse to believe it and thus refuse to be happy—for men's intellects, for want of this light, remain in darkness ; men's hearts, for want of this heat, remain cold and sad."

The " Messenger of Infinite Love " would, doubtless, have wished to make this good news heard by every human ear ; however, in obedience to an inspiration from on high, and to a supernatural logic, she directed it to the clergy. The priest is the voice of God for the people ; he is their spiritual father and the director of their souls. He fashions them after his own pattern and leads them where he is going himself. If he knows the good news and lives by it, the whole body of Christians will be penetrated with it."

PREPARATION FOR HER MISSION

" I had been brought up with great respect for priests," she writes. " I had never heard any one of my family speak lightly of any member of the clergy. Whenever a rumour of one of these sorrowful scandals which make the tears of Our Mother the Church flow, reached us, we never talked about it among ourselves and we endeavoured to cast a veil over these human weaknesses. When the servants took the liberty of laughing at the rustic manners of the good country Curé, or of criticising in any way whatever the sacred person of a priest, my mother would reprove them so severely, and impose silence so effectively on them, that it would not happen a second time."

What a salutary lesson for all Catholic families ! God gave her in addition an instinctive love for the Church and respect for all its decisions. We have seen that while she used freely her permission to read other books without anxiety, she would never touch a book which contained anything against faith or morals. When she went to pray in the privileged sanctuaries of Mont Martre and Paray le Monial, one of the principal intentions for which she prayed was for the Church. On her return from Paray le Monial, in an account of her pilgrimage which she wrote for her family and friends, she speaks as follows of a chance meeting with the Bishop of Valence :

" I was burning with eagerness to get his blessing and kiss his ring, but I did not dare to approach him. The exalted dignity of bishops has always inspired in me a respectful fear ; I seem to see in them one of Our Lord's Apostles. The power which they have of creating priests, of clothing them with the dignity of the priesthood, seems to me to be so divine that I tremble when approaching."

Even while she was in the world, the Lord had deposited in her soul and fostered these precious germs. He had then brought her into the solitude of the cloister to speak to her heart. He purified her by sufferings of many kinds and, by making her pass through the fire of temptation, He gradually fashioned her after His own Heart. He favoured her with supernatural communications ; and when the time came to reveal to her His special secret and His divine plan, He entrusted her to the care of a sure and prudent guide who would guard her against error and prevent her from being unfaithful.

LIGHTS RECEIVED ON THE MYSTERY OF INFINITE LOVE

As we have seen, Sister Louise Margaret, from her youth, continued to receive very special favours from God. Some of these, such as her vow of virginity at the tender age of eleven, her vocation to the religious life, her fidelity to it in spite of her mother's opposition, visits from St. Francis de Sales and from Our Lord Himself, might be called the remote preparation for her mission. Other favours which she received, such as lights on the nature of God— that He is Love, Infinite Love—were intimately connected with her mission of making Him known under that aspect. These, we shall endeavour to gather together from her Intimate Notes, and give in order.

" Oct. 4th, 1896.

" For some time past, God has been bringing me close to Him in a new way ; it seems to me that my soul is completely bathed in very pure light and that it sinks down with very great peace and tranquility into the incomprehensible depths of light and love which are in God.

" This impels me to sacrifice more and more every desire and every exercise of my own will, for the least exercise of my natural will, would be like a hard body in my soul which the divine substance could not penetrate and which would impede it in its action. All this is taking place in great repose."

" Oct. 8th, 1899.

" I saw the immense desire which God has for union with man, a desire which proceeds solely from His love for him ; and this Infinite Love, so strong since man's sin has not been able to weaken it, so ardent, since it has made Him go out of Himself, so disinterested, since it has made Him sacrifice Himself for us, this Love which is God, this bottomless, endless, boundless sea of Love, which is the divine Essence, as It causes Its waves to descend on me, submerges my soul and leaves it without speech and without any other movement except a sort of ardent, incessant aspiration towards a union becoming ever more complete. I would wish to be able to convey to all creatures how great this desire of God is ; I would wish to open my arms and take hold of the whole world, to clasp it to my breast and to throw myself with it into the ocean of Infinite Love in order thus to satisfy the desire of God.

" God is Love, and Love wishes to be loved. In vain do I open my heart in order to receive the overflow of love from the Heart of God ; my heart is too small, and besides, it is only one heart.

" What God looks for and demands are hearts which love Him even to the contempt of everything else, hearts so given up to Him, so stripped of their own interest that He can find His pleasure in them."

" April 13th, 1900.

" Yesterday, after Holy Communion, being intimately united to Jesus, *I saw in His Sacred Heart His desires as God : He wishes that Love be diffused, that It inflame the world and renew it ;* it is no longer by the waters of a new deluge that God wishes to purify and re-generate the earth, but by fire.

" The minds and wills of people have been led astray ; the world which needs purification is, above all, the world of intellects and souls ; that is why the fire which God wishes to employ is a purely spiritual fire. Love and mercy must be preached to every creature, for the Heart of God has an immense desire to pardon ; if He sees even a little love in a heart in response to His, He pardons. But my soul suffers strange sorrows at the sight of the indifference and cold-ness of the greater part of Christians, and the little correspondence which the love of God finds in the hearts of His creatures ; but how it suffers also at being able to love only so little what it sees to be so amiable and so desirous of love !"

" 1901.

" If anyone could say that some attribute had precedence in God, in Whom everything is eternal, I would say that before being power-ful, before being wise, before being just and good, God was already Love. And doubtless one can say so ; because before acting on nothingness, God had not shown the fullness of His power ; before creating angels and men and forming the worlds, He had not revealed His marvellous wisdom ; before He had created inferior creatures towards whom He could incline, He had not manifested all the grandeur of His goodness ; before evil existed, He had not exercised the plentitude of His Justice and . . . He was already Love, nothing in God was before Love ; Love was before everything."

" 1901 (Autumn Retreat).

" I saw before me an immense abyss, so vast that no human eye could sound its depths ; it was Love-Creator. . . . Then I saw another abyss : man had sinned, he had transgressed God's command, and this rebellious creature was to be punished. Infinite sanctity demanded its rights, and Justice was about to annihilate this being that had responded to the liberality of Love-Creator only by dis-obedience and pride.

" But Love-Mediator, placing Itself between man, the sinner, and God, Whom he had outraged, formed a profound abyss and Justice could no longer reach man. . . . .

" A third abyss of Love is now shown to me, so vast, so profound, so incomprehensible, that an incomprehensible Love alone could explain it. It was Love-Redeemer. The Word had become incarnate ; He had revealed to man the hidden mysteries of salvation ; He had given all His Blood. .. . .

" Love-Priest had offered Love-Victim ; the world was redeemed, divine Justice was disarmed.

" A new abyss of Love was shown to me; it was Love-Illuminator ! The Holy Spirit had descended on the Church to fertilise it.

" A fifth abyss was shown to me ; the times were accomplished ; new heavens and a new earth had appeared, and Love-Glorifier was going to crown the elect. An immense abyss, It contains all beings ; like a torrent of divine delights, It inundates the elect, and like a consuming and avenging fire, It devours the accursed. Love reigns as sovereign and undisputed Master.

" And I perceived yet another abyss, the proportions which no human words can express nor can any created intellect measure. It was Love without form, Love without exterior manifestations ; it was God Himself.

" Prostrate on the edge of this unfathomable abyss, my soul adored in silence, and I seemed to hear a voice saying to me : Infinite Love envelops, penetrates and fills all things. It is the only source of life and fertility ; It is the eternal principle of all beings and their eternal end. If you wish to possess life and not be sterile, break the bonds that bind you to yourself and to creatures and plunge into this abyss."

THE PRELUDE TO THE GREAT MESSAGE

" March, 1902.

" My Jesus, tell me what are the desires of Thy Heart ? ' The world is becoming frozen ; egoism is contracting men's hearts ; they have turned away from the source of Love, and they think they are very far from God ; nevertheless, I, Infinite Love, am quite near, and the bosom of divine Charity, all swollen with love, must needs open. Allow Me to love you and, through you, to descend to the world.' "

" Allow Me to love you, and through you, to descend to the

world." This was the heavenly prelude to the eternal decree which marked out the soul of Sister Louise Margaret as the Messenger of Infinite Love. It has a distant resemblance to the divine scene of the Annunciation, which was being commemorated those days. Like our Blessed Lady, Margaret formulated her difficulties in carrying out the divine behest : " My Jesus, what can I do for the world, since I am separated from it ?" And Jesus deigned to reply : " I will explain to you this mystery which is beyond your power to comprehend. I became incarnate in order to unite Myself to men ; I died to save men ; My sacrifice was of sufficient efficacy to redeem the whole human race, and infinitely more ; but because man is endowed with free will, he must co-operate in the work of his own salvation. The superabundance of My merits obtains for him sufficient grace for that ; however, there are many who reject My graces. **Then, I take souls, I invest them with myself ; I continue My passion in them, I separate them from others for My work ; I unveil to them the mysteries of My Love and Mercy, and making them like purified channels, I pour out on the world a new abundance of grace and pardons.**"

At this annunciation of the mysterious work which Our Lord wished to operate through her, the humble Religious pronounced her *fiat :*

" My Saviour, I belong to Thee, do with me according to Thy will."

" Yes, I take possession of you, I will make your soul the channel of My Infinite Love. Although it is hidden and obscure, it will do My work. All the love which I shall pour into it will go to the world, but retain none of it, nor ever seek your own interest, but always seek Mine. Be faithful and cherish suffering."

THE MESSAGE FROM OUR DIVINE LORD FOR THE CLERGY OF THE WORLD

On June 6th, 1902, the Feast of the Sacred Heart, which that year was also the anniversary of the foundation of the order of the Visitation, Our divine Lord overwhelmed His beloved one with favours. Beginning on the first Vespers of that great feast, He declared to her her special function in the transmission of love and shows to her what royal posterity He had reserved for her.

" June 6th, 1902.

" Yesterday, I was alone before the Blessed Sacrament. I was suffering, and was in that weary and painful state in which I had been for some weeks, when He made His presence felt by my soul.

" I adored Him, being sweetly consoled by His presence, and began to pray to Him for our little noviciate ; I asked Him to give me some souls that I might form for Him. Then, He replied to me : ' I will give you souls of men.' Being profoundly astonished by these words, the sense of which I did not understand, I remained silent, endeavouring to find an explanation. Jesus spoke again : ' I will give you souls of priests.'

" Being still more astonished, I said to Him :

" ' My Jesus, how wilt Thou do that ? I live here hidden from the world, and besides,' she added in her humility, ' I do not wish to become another Mother Mary de Sales.[1]

" ' No,' He replied to me. ' It is for My clergy that *you* will immolate yourself.' "

On each day, during what has now become the Octave of the Sacred Heart, Our divine Lord spoke to her of the dignity of priests, of His love for them, of the return of love which He expected from them and of the new bond of union which He wished to form between them. He ordered her to write down the instructions which He gave her during this Octave.

That evening Our Lord continued : " My priest is my other Self. I love him, but he must be holy. Nineteen centuries ago, twelve men changed the world, they were not mere men, they were priests ! **Now once more twelve priests could change the world."**

On June 7th Our Lord continued : " The heart of my priest ought to be a burning flame, warming and purifying souls. If the priest only knew the treasures of love which My Heart contains for him ! Let him come to My Heart, let him draw from It, let him fill himself with love until it overflows from his heart and spreads itself over the world !

Margaret Mary has shown My Heart to the world, do you show It to My priests, and draw them all to My Heart."

Sister Louise Margaret told her confessor of the visit of Our Lord, and of the very great suffering which she was enduring. He told her that this exceptional suffering was a sign that Our Lord had some special grace to give her ; that He would tell her something definite.

---

[1] Mother Mary de Sales, Superioress of the Visitation of Troyes, died in the odour of Sanctity 1875. With the co-operation of Father Bresson, S.J., she founded the Oblates of St. Francis de Sales. In her humility, Mother Louise Margaret, who wished to remain unknown, asked Our Lord not to give her an honour of that kind.

On that evening she wrote down what she had received from Him that day : " That evening He showed me the greatness of the priest. Chosen from among men, the priest ascends even to God ; he is placed between man and God, a mediator like Jesus, and with Jesus. He has been, so to speak, transubstantiated into Jesus, and he enters into all His divine roles and His divine prerogatives. He is with Jesus offering, expiation, victim. From this state of special union with Jesus, all the acts of the priest acquire an incomprehensible excellence."

Three days later, on June 10th, she wrote down as directed by Our Lord :

" After Communion, I said to Jesus : ' My Saviour, when our Blessed Sister (Margaret Mary) showed Thy divine Heart to the world, did not priests see It ? Does not that suffice ? '

" Jesus replied : ' I wish now to make a special manifestation of It to them.'

" Then he showed me that He had a special work to do : to enkindle the fire of love in the world ; and that He wished to make use of His priests to do that. He said this to me with such touching and tender expression that tears came to my eyes :

" ' I have need of them to do My work.'

" In order that they may be able to extend the reign of love, they must be full of it themselves, and it is from the Heart of Jesus that they must draw it. ' My Heart is the Chalice of My Blood,' said He to me again ; ' If anyone has the right and the duty to drink from It, is it not My priest who each day brings the Chalice of the altar to his lips ; let him come to My Heart and let him drink.' "

Sister Louise Margaret wished, as it were, to hide behind St. Margaret Mary, whom she loved so much, and to repeat her message. But her divine Master decided otherwise when He said :

" I wish now to make a special manifestation of My Heart to My priests."

She was not to become the echo of St. Margaret Mary or merely to explain her teaching ; nor was St. Margaret Mary the mere echo of St. Gertrude the Great, or of any of the other Saints to whom Our Lord manifested His Sacred Heart. Our Lord spoke to all these ; they listened submissively, and humbly transmitted His divine behests. Sister Louise Margaret was also to transmit His behest and on the condition that He had already laid down for her :

that she should surrender herself completely to Him for a life of suffering and immolation.

THE NEW UNION TO GROUP THE PRIESTS OF THE WORLD AROUND THE SACRED HEART OF JESUS

On June 11th she received from Our Lord the first details of the divine plan ; her confessor had expected that this was to come. She wrote on the following day :

" All day yesterday I had a vision of a special grouping of priests around the Heart of Jesus, of a work exclusively for them ; I do not know if I am mistaken. Oh ! how greatly I need light and help ! I am suffering, nevertheless my soul is in great peace ; all within me is calm. I have neither temptations, nor painful or fatiguing thoughts. The depths of my soul are sweetly rapt up in Jesus.

" When by myself, I wish to think out any of these things which He has communicated to me, I cannot do so ; nothing clear or precise occurs to my mind ; on the contrary, as soon as He speaks or touches my soul with His divine impression, everything is clear, luminous and definite."

On June 13th, Our Lord again spoke to her and explained to her that the organisation which he desired was not one like The Guard of Honour, which is a work of devotion only, but an active organisation.

" This morning, when reflecting within myself, I thought that perhaps a special branch of *The Guard of Honour* might be formed for priests. Jesus said to me : ' No.' He gave me to understand that He did not wish His priests to be merely adorers of His Heart, but that He wished to form a body of knights who would fight for the triumph of His love.

" Those who would form part of this body of knights of His divine Heart would engage, among other things, to preach Infinite Love and Mercy, to be united among themselves, having but one heart and one soul in their campaign for the triumph of what is good, and never to obstruct one another in their activities."

Then Jesus became silent.

On June 17th, Sister Louise Margaret wrote :

" Jesus has given me no more. Perhaps He will not tell me anything more. I asked Him to tell the rest to one of His priests. As for me, what can I do except suffer for Him and offer myself as a victim for His glory and for the triumph of His love ? Oh ! I offer myself to Jesus for this intention with all the power of my heart ; and for active work also if He wishes it, but it seems to me that I have more capacity for suffering than for action."

In truth, everything had been said. In the divine communications given during this Octave, we have the outline of all that Our Lord wanted done, and of all that He would do through His servant. In the years which followed, further light was given on the execution of the divine plan. Our Lord insisted many times that a beginning be made to put it into execution, but nothing essential remained to be added.

THE SECOND PART OF THE WORK OF INFINITE LOVE :

BETHANY OF THE SACRED HEART

Already, on October 29th, 1899, Sister Louise Margaret had received an intimation (the full explanation of which was not to be given to her until her visit to Rome, fifteen years later) of the special part which was reserved for herself and her spiritual daughters in this work.

" At prayer," she writes, " I found myself suddenly transported into an unknown place. I saw a street, bordered on one side by a row of houses, on the other, by little low walls, and one of these houses was pointed out to me as a Monastery of the Visitation,[1] and while I was considering it, everything disappeared, and I found myself very intimately united to God in great repose and simplicity."

The following year, on the first Friday of May, 1900, Our Lord spoke again to Sister Louise Margaret :

" This afternoon," she writes, " when kneeling in adoration before the Blessed Sacrament, my most Sweet Jesus favoured me with His divine presence and said : ' I am seeking for a stone on which to rest My head.' I replied to Him : ' I have nothing to offer Thee, my sweet Jesus, I possess nothing in the world, not even an inch of ground, I am poor like Thyself, come and repose on my heart ; doubtless, it is hard and cold like a stone, but Thy divine presence will soften it.'

---

[1] This house is now the Monastery of Bethany of the Sacred Heart, at Vische Canavese, near Turin.

" Jesus said to me again, at least so it seems to me :

' I wish to build a dwelling-place in which the virtues dear to My Heart, humility, poverty, simplicity and charity, will reign,'

" Then I said to Him : ' My sweet Mercy, do as Thou willest ; I do not see in what way I can aid Thee, but if Thou shouldst need cement for Thy building, pulverise my bones, knead them with my blood and my tears and make use of them.   I can only give Thee myself, take me entirely and do as Thou willest,' "

She did not understand, but she felt that the divine words should be taken in the material as well as the spiritual sense, so much so that in May, 1901, she was a little disconcerted by the events[1] which seemed to be an obstacle to the realisation of the divine promises :

" My Jesus," she writes, " have I been deceived ?   Thou hast shown me a new house, small and having its beginning in poor and humble circumstances, but blessed by Thy divine Heart ; and now our house at X is going to ruin, and the persecution is upon us which will perhaps scatter and annihilate all that is standing.   What have I seen then, My Master, and what am I to believe ?   And Jesus, the divine Consoler, invisibly but sensibly present to my soul, replied to me :

" ' Fear nothing, I am faithful.'

" That was all, and my soul, filled with peace wanted to know no more.   It relied on Jesus.   And offering myself to Him, I said to Him: ' Do Thy divine work ; make me suffer, and annihilate me; and if it be Thy will, let me never see the effect of Thy promises, let me die before Thou hast put them into effect ; provided that Thy will be done and that Thou be recognised as faithful, that is enough for me.' "

This indeed was genuine, disinterested love :

Twice, in July and August, 1904, she saw again the little house coming into being, a very humble, very poor house.

" My God," she says in her humility, " what is it then ?   Is it an illusion ?   It must be, for everything around is crumbling and being scattered.   Is it a figure, an image of something, the sense of which I do not understand ?"

Time and obstacles count for nothing with God, and Jesus could say to her in her doubt : " The work is accomplished, come and repose on My Heart."

---

[1] The reference is to the persecution of Religious Orders then raging in France.

THE ROLE OF FATHER CHARRIER IN THE WORK

Our Divine Lord had waited to manifest His designs to Sister Louise Margaret for the hour when He gave her as Director, the priest who was not only to guide her and instruct her how to make use of His special graces, but to co-operate with her in the Work demanded by Infinite Love. She liked to think that through Father Charrier and herself Our Lord was uniting in His Heart the Company of Jesus and the Visitation. In a very eloquent passage, she shows how these two Orders complete one another, and between them reproduce the life of Our Lord on earth.

" The Company of Jesus," she writes, " lives the day of Jesus ; always calumniated, always persecuted ; it goes on instructing, enlightening, healing souls, doing good in charity, zeal and absolute devotedness by the active, fervent gift of the members themselves. Under the impulse of the Spirit of God, it enters into combat against the spirit of evil and disarms him ; sometimes, like Jesus, it must render itself invisible in order to escape from the blows of its enemies, but it is without fear ; and if need be, it goes fearlessly from prison to the Pretorium, and from the Pretorium to the Cross.

" The Visitation lives the night of Jesus ; like Him, it withdraws to the mountain to pray in solitude, obscurity, and silence. In it everything is hidden and obscure. It has received from Jesus, not the Cross of violent persecutions, but that of contempt and abjection, for no one among worldlings knows the perfection of its spirit.

" The Company has sometimes the triumphs of Jesus and sometimes His Calvary. The Visitation has the abandoned sleep of Jesus in the bark, and the silent agony of Gethsemani.

" The Visitation, on its knees, draws from the Heart of Jesus the treasures of love ; and the Company, standing, takes these divine treasures and distributes them to the world.

" Thus, when Jesus makes us repose on His Sacred breast, it is not us, poor creatures of nothingness, that He considers, but these two Institutes dear to His Heart which He wishes to unite in His incomparable love."

However, neither Father Charrier nor any Order or Congregation was to control the exterior organisation of the Work ; it was to belong to the Church, and all bishops and priests, irrespective of the fact whether they were Religious or Secular, were to be free to become members on equal terms.

Father Charrier was to be for Sister Louise Margaret what Blessed Claude de la Colombière was for St. Margaret Mary Alacoque ; and in addition, he was to be " the soul of the Work."

After events proved how accurate Sister Louise Margaret was in interpreting these words when she wrote :

" I asked Jesus what my Director was to be in this work." He replied to me : ' He is to be its soul.'

" When I reflected on these words, this explanation occurred to me : the soul gives life to the whole body without being visible : it makes itself known by its action and not by its form. I do not know whether this thought is my own, but it has quite astonished me, and every time that I recall the words of Jesus to my memory, this explanation also occurs to me."

Though the hesitation of Father Charrier to undertake the publication of what she believed to be the designs of Jesus, was a source of suffering for her, yet she loved and appreciated him for his great qualities and his labours for the Divine Master. She expresses her regret when she learns definitely that he is not to be the director of the Work, but bows to the will of the Master.

" I said to my Saviour," she writes, " that it caused me pain to conclude from what had been revealed to me on September 10th that Father Charrier would not be the official director of the Work.

" Jesus replied to me : ' He will be its founder.'

" It seemed to me, though I may be mistaken, that Our Lord wishes this in order that the Work may meet with fewer obstacles in its development."

On September 12th, 1904, she had written :

" This morning, He said to me : ' Have confidence.' Yes, I have confidence : confidence in Thy love, my Jesus, my beloved Christ ; I suffer inexpressibly, but I abandon myself to Thee in expectation and peace. I have, it seems to me, in the depths of my soul the inward, profound, living belief that it is really Thou ; that Thou hast given me for Thy priests ; that Thou wishest this work ; that it is Father who is to found it. Thou hast marked out Father for that. When Thou hast instilled into his soul this first sentiment of devotedness to Thy Priesthood ; when Thou hast shown him that this was his vocation ; when, each time that he has been able to devote himself to Thy priests, Thou hast communicated to his heart ineffable transports of joy ; when, receiving my soul from Thy divine hand, he thought that it was not without mysterious designs that Thou hast confided it to him ; when, at the foot of the tabernacle one day, Thou hast filled his soul with indescribable emotion when giving him a glimpse of Thy adorable designs, was it not, O my Master, that Thou hast destined him for this work ?"

FATHER CHARRIER'S PRUDENT SPIRITUAL DIRECTION

When Father Charrier found himself confronted with exceptional graces and alleged communications from Our Lord about a work in which he himself was to play a part, he adopted a policy of extreme prudence. He waited long years without giving any decision, and finally came to the conclusion that the case was one for the Holy See. During all these years Sister Louise Margaret felt herself urged by Our Lord to make known His designs of love.

Father Charrier's first care was to guide this soul entrusted to his charge safely on the road to perfection ; it was in reality the surest way of realising the designs of God. The foundations of holiness for every Religious are humility and obedience, which involve fidelity to their Rule. This was Our Lord's teaching to St. Margaret Mary Alacoque. Father Charrier then insisted on humility and obedience in her case. Next, he proceeded to study the communications which she alleged that she had received from Our Lord. To enable him to do so, he ordered Sister Louise Margaret to write down in minute detail the story of her whole life and of the graces which she received. As it is well known that the devil uses all his wiles against the special friends of God, Father Charrier ordered her to write down in a separate copybook an account of all her temptations. In his spiritual direction it could hardly be said that he took no notice of the communications which she told him she received from Our Lord, for he subjected her to greater trials and humiliations than he would otherwise have done, but he ordered her to act just as if she had never any communications from our Lord. He reproved her severely for anything that had the appearance of credulity.

The following letter, written on December 17th, 1902, from Sister Louise Margaret to him and his reply will serve to make this clear :

" Since September 15th, occasions for suffering have not been wanting to me, and I bless God for them. Is not this the only co-operation, and a very feeble one, that I can give to the designs of Jesus ?

" My pains and anxieties have been mixed with consolations also. On the day after your departure, my mother came to visit me and to confide a certain matter to me. I advised her to have recourse to the Sacred Heart of Jesus in order to find help and solace. . . . .

" Six weeks later, on the feast of All Saints, my mother sent me a hundred francs with these words : ' For the Sacred Heart for Margaret.'

" Oh, Father, a cheque has never caused me any joy, but this one, this first gift given to Jesus for the intentions of His Heart delighted me.

" Do you not see, Father, in this gift, in all this, adorable smiles of Jesus on the work of His Heart. . . . ."

In his reply, written on December 30th, 1902, Father Charrier said :

" You will continue to note down what you consider to be lights, and then you are never willingly to occupy your mind with them, that is to say, that you are never to attach any real importance to these lights. You are even to treat them with a certain amount of distrust, being very much afraid of being deceived by the evil spirit. And without judging whether what you believe to be a light comes from God or the devil, you are not to be troubled about them any more as soon as you have noted them down.

" Why do you wish me to see in those things which you tell me ' adorable smiles of Jesus on the Work of His Heart ?' I am far from believing that your lights do not contain darkness. I have not yet seen the will of the divine Heart, and I find you very positive when you speak of this Work, as if it were certainly willed by God.

" For myself, I suspend my judgment ; I am too much frightened by your unworthiness, and especially by my own, to dwell without trembling on your views.

" Labour then, my dear child, to make yourself very humble in order that Our Lord, attracted by your humility, may come into your soul, that He may shed His full light upon it, dispel possible darkness, and drive away all error."

In another letter, which Father Charrier wrote to her in May, 1908, he said to her :—

" Go down to the depths of your abjection and say to yourself that you will not be fully pleasing to Our Divine Master, that you will not be a true disciple of His Sacred Heart, until by His grace, you have arrived at true humility."

And in his own humility he added :

" I had a thousand difficulties in admitting that Our Lord could make use of a most unworthy and miserable instrument for so noble a work. If you knew my terrible unworthiness, you would understand my objection."

To which Sister Louise Margaret replied :

" The wretchedness of the instrument renders more brilliant the glory of the Worker."

Again, in February, 1904, Father Charrier wrote to her on the subject of humility :

" Are you sufficiently humble : sufficiently despicable in your own eyes ?

" I fear you have not a sufficiently clear view of your worthlessness in the eyes of Him Who is infinite purity, Who is Sanctity itself.

" I beg of you, dear child, to ask Our Lord to give you light and courage ; light to see how despicable you are, courage to make yourself despised and to rejoice at it with the view to acquiring humility.

" So long as you do not consider yourself the last of all, you will not be truly humble, you will never be truly holy. Now, your love for your divine Spouse should urge you to arrive at true sanctity in order to do Him honour.

" My daughter, I put more value on one degree of humility than on ten degrees of love. Not that ten degrees of love are not of much more value in themselves than ten degrees of humility. But one may fall from the summits of love. From the depths of humility the soul can only ascend. ' He who humbles himself shall be exalted, he who exalts himself shall be humbled.' These words are true even with regard to the heights of love. . . . ."

Again, in May, 1905, he wrote to her :

" If you descend to the lowest depths of your being by humility, Our Lord, Who is Infinite Love and Power, will certainly raise you up to true sanctity. The foundations of your sanctity cannot rest on any other foundations than the depths of humility."

Quotations could be multiplied ; those which we have given are sufficient to show the care which he employed to preserve the gifts of God from all human defilement. And indeed the soul of Sister

Louise Margaret felt itself at ease in this atmosphere of truth. Besides, Our Lord Himself had taken care to establish her in humility, not only by showing her the vanity of earthly glory, but by special lights on herself.

" I saw," she writes, " a picture of my wretchedness, complete, absolute wretchedness, and Our Lord said to me :

" ' You see that I have left in you sufficient to prevent you from ever being proud or elated on account of My graces.' "

At the same time He taught her not to dwell on herself :

" Too much introspection," she writes, " might impede the action of Love upon me. It seems to me that Our Lord wishes that I be nothing at all and that He Himself should do everything. That is why we should not pay heed to what is nothing, we should not dwell on what is only a valueless accident."

Formed by the Sacred Heart of Jesus and His representative, humiliations were to become sweet to her, because she regarded them as due to her.

In reply to the severe letter which Father Charrier had written to her on December 30th, 1902, she wrote :

" It is Our Lord Himself who has inspired that good, salutary letter which you have written to me. It is quite true that I have no real humility. I hide under the appearance of a few, more or less natural virtues, great depths of pride and many weaknesses and miseries unworthy of the soul of a Religious. However, I sincerely desire this virtue (of humility) which Jesus loves so much."

Father Charrier could be at ease, the soul of his spiritual daughter had all the marks of true humility. However, he hesitated about giving her an assurance about the origin of the communications which she had received.

" **I know well," he wrote to her, " that everything which you have told me or which has been communicated to you by Our Lord has the seal of sincerity, of the divine supernatural, which almost compels assent ;** but I cannot pretend not to know that, even in this case, something personal may unconsciously have slipped in, so that what seems to come from Our Lord may have come from yourself."

Then, as the Superiors of St. Margaret Mary had done, he demanded tangible proofs. And when under obedience, Sister Louise Margaret gave his message to Our Lord, that, as a sign that the communications were from Him, He would reveal to her some sin of his past life. And Our Lord deigned to reply :

" I have already given him so many : As for his sins, I no longer remember them, but I do remember that one day he made himself My slave by engraving on his flesh the mark of his servitude."

The good Jesuit must have been startled to the depths of his soul, but he never admitted to her that he had done so, probably because she asked his permission to do the same. It was only after her death that the confession was extracted from him that he had actually done so, and that the revelation made to her was exact.

What caused him to hesitate was, doubtless, the consciousness of his own incompetence in these exalted matters, but it was especially, as he confessed, the thought of his unworthiness to take part in these divine projects, for he regarded himself as a miserable sinner.

God permitted all this for the sanctification of His two instruments for His work. We cannot wonder that Sister Louise Margaret was sometimes alarmed at the thought that she might be deceived herself, or might be deceiving her Director and dragging him into error.

" However," she writes, " at the time when I receive this inspiration, or when it seems to me that Thou showest me Thy will, O Jesus, I have no doubt ; on the contrary, I feel a marvellous assurance that it is really Thy ideas and Thy divine wishes that have been communicated. Tell all this, I beseech Thee, to my Director, or have it told to him by his Superiors in order that he may believe it. I am so miserable that if I say anything it is enough to make people cast doubt upon it, and they are right, O Jesus, I am nothing but sin, but it seems to me, nevertheless, that it is Thou."

Another time she wrote :

" Oh, how I have suffered. I begged Jesus with entreaties, with tears, to enlighten Father, to dispel his doubts, to manifest His will clearly to him. I annihilated myself at the feet of my Divine Master. Prostrate, with my face against the ground, I said to Him : ' I am nothingness, misery, sin ; humiliate me, break me if Thou wilt, I deserve nothing else ; but enlighten him, help him.'

" I reflected for a moment ; since Father says that I am deceived, perhaps I have always been deceived ; perhaps what I have believed about Thee was not true. If it be so, do not permit that I should deceive others ; rather, let all creatures abandon me, let Father himself abandon me, but do not Thou, my Master, my divine Jesus, abandon me !

What martyrdom ! And at the same time I felt an ever increasing assurance in the depths of my soul that Jesus wished this Work, that He wishes it accomplished by means of Father. This interior assurance, this impression of a will which seemed to me to be that of God redoubled my suffering. I was crushed beneath the weight of this knowledge, of this light, feeling myself bearing it alone. Yes, my martyrdom was, to have such a strong impression of the Will of God for this Work and to see my absolute powerlessness in making Father feel it."

If such accents do not reveal the real depths of the soul, never has human pen written the truth !

CHAPTER V.

EXILE.

According to the law passed in France in 1904 against Religious Congregations, all property of teaching Orders was liable to confiscation and the members were to be disbanded. The Religious belonging to these Orders or Congregations had the option either of being secularised and returning to the world, or of transferring their Community to a foreign country, if they could find a bishop to accept them. The order of the Visitation, being a contemplative Order, did not properly come under the Law. It had a boarding-school for girls, because after the French Revolution, Religious Communities that wanted to re-open their convents were obliged to open boarding schools in order to get permission from the Government to do so. The Monastery of the Visitation at Romans, where Sister Louise Margaret, was, because it had a boarding-school, appeared on the official list of February, 1904, for liquidation. In an endeavour to avoid liquidation, the Sisters closed their boarding-school, to the great grief of the pupils and their families. Though it was a heart-break for the Sisters to see themselves compelled by an unjust law to abandon their active apostolate among the young generation in France, Sister Louise Margaret saw in it the designs of God and could not prevent herself from rejoicing over the return to the full, interior, hidden life of a contemplative, which was the real end of this order founded by St. Francis de Sales. And it is remarkable that at the very time when the pupils were taken away from the Visitation Sisters, Our Lord said to His privileged one:

" I will not leave you like one forsaken or like a mother without children, but I will make you so fertile that your sons will be counted by the thousands."

What hidden power there is in sacrifice, hidden immolation and prayer !

" My sons !" cried the happy privileged one, " many souls to give to Jesus ! But perhaps that is only an illusion of my heart ; however, these words have been spoken to the ear of my soul, and besides, I feel in my heart such ardour and material tenderness for souls. Would God have made it so, if He had not the intention to satisfy it one day ? Yes, I bear these unknown souls within me in pain ; I give them the blood of my heart and the best of my life. Happy would I be if, by my death, I could bring them forth to life."

The prayer of the humble sister has been heard, the divine promise has been realised, for already her children, who, through her prayers and sufferings and her inspiring writings, have received " the life of love, of devotedness, of zeal, the plentitude of the life of Jesus in themselves," are counted by thousands.

ITALY

The closing down of their boarding-school did not disarm persecution, and it soon became evident that their choice lay between taking the road for exile or being disbanded by force.

The Sisters were dispensed from their vows by the Holy See and were free to return to their families ; but on no account would Sister Louise Margaret consent to do this ; she would save her vocation at all costs, she would remain faithful to God, to her Order and to her Rule. Indeed, her firmness on this point inspired the other Sisters to do likewise. While there was still but little prospect of finding a place of refuge for the Community, she refused her mother's invitation to return home and had written to Monasteries of her Order in Belgium and Germany, asking to be admitted.

At last the Rev. Mother, Mother Mary Emmanuel, got a glimmer of hope that she would find asylum in Italy for her children. In spite of her advanced age and failing health, she set out herself and took as companions Sister Louise Margaret and another Sister. This was Sister Louise Margaret's first contact with the land that was to become her second homeland, the scene of great graces and indescribable sufferings, the cradle of the Work of Infinite Love and the place of her own tomb.

On August 19th, 1904, she wrote to Father Charrier :

" Our dear Rev. Mother will leave for Italy on Monday ; she will be accompanied by Sister X and myself. Our own Sisters of X Monastery and many others are already on the road for exile. Perhaps it will soon be our turn. If these sufferings and heart-breaks can contribute to the salvation of our poor France, and lift her up from the mire, we shall not regret them."

We give here in full her very beautiful and touching account of this voyage of exploration.

" During this voyage," she writes on September 4th, 1904, " I went very simply from one thing to another with the sweet and tranquil interior feeling of union with Jesus. I had no time to pray much ; my ordinary exercises had almost always to be suppressed by business necessities or the duties of charity and friendship.

" At La Consolate, the Holy Shroud, and Corpus Domini, during the too short moments that I could spend at these places, I gave my heart completely to Jesus, to Mary Our Immaculate Mother, and in a few ardent outbursts I recommended to them my priests, the Work, Father and his labours, the Community, etc. For the rest of the time I did not speak to Jesus, I kept silence with Him, but I felt Him there taking charge of everything, watching over everything.

" Our Rev. Mother had told me to notice everything, to observe carefully, to practise no mortification during this voyage. Renouncing my own desire to offer my divine Master some little mortifications for my priests by not looking at anything along the road except what was indispensable, I entered very simply into the views of my Superioress. I blessed God for this little moment of relief given to my poor enfeebled body. I accepted it from His adorable hand and profited by it with consolation and thanks.

" The beauty of the places, the marvellous grandeur of the Alpine landscape, the lofty summits covered with snow and sparkling under the rays of the August sun, the cascades bounding from rock to rock, the narrow gorges through which the torrents roared, the gigantic works executed by the industry of man, then these wide plains of the Po Valley, these rice-fields where the ripe ears waved to and fro as far as eye could reach ; all this raised my heart to God, the divine Creator of these splendours, and my soul chanted without words, canticles of adoration and praise to the divine power and to Infinite Love.

" At Moncestino, the magnificent view which extended before my eyes delighted me. The chain of the Alps crowned with its white glaciers shone in the morning sun ; green hills rose in the distance, tier upon tier, and went gently downward to vanish on the banks of a stream which, like a silver ribbon, rolled down into the plain. In my free moments, I went to the park all alone to sketch the old turret, or to stroll along the walks without doing anything, breathing freely this lively, pure air which blew vigorously, and I felt that a new life was penetrating into me and was regenerating my blood.

" I sometimes said to Jesus : I take these few days of liberty since in Thy goodness Thou givest them to me, besides, they will but serve to make me feel the more, the daily sacrifices which Thou permittest me to offer to Thee.

" People remarked that my face had a better colour and that my step was lighter. Well ! doubtless, nature needs liberty and pure air ; the body lives on all these legitimate enjoyments which form the matter of our daily sacrifices. On the contrary, privations, continual action contrary to natural impulses and instincts, the slow martyrdom of life in the cloister, make the body pine away and lead it to death. But what matter, it is not nature that should prevail in us ; it is destined, sooner or later, to disappear. What matter if the body grow feeble and the blood impoverished as long as the soul becomes purified and ennobled, and Jesus, the divine Martyr of Calvary, finds people to console Him in His Way, and humble ones to continue His work of redemption.

" We had taken the road back to our dear France, far away from which, we would be forced to go to seek a little security and peace. I was happy to go and pray beside the tombs of our dear Founders ; but from a natural view point it cost me much to enter this blessed monastery. I was not ignorant of the fact that I had been preceded there by a reputation not to my advantage.

" Scarcely had I entered the monastery when I felt great peace of soul, with a feeling of tranquil assurance, of safe repose, such as I have sometimes tasted after Holy Communion, or when I see Father, or at the time of receiving some special favour from Jesus. The fixed, profound, interrogating looks of Mother de V—— which hardly ever left me did not trouble me in the least ; an indefinable, sweet impression filled my soul ; I was at ease in this dear house, I felt something like a paternal blessing hovering over me ; beside the holy reliquaries this sentiment was intense. I prayed for my priests, for the Work ; I entrusted to the venerable hands and pure hearts of our Saint-Founders this spiritual bond so strong, so close, and so truly formed by Our Lord which unites the soul of Father to my poor soul. Scarcely had I remained ten minutes beside these blessed relics when we had to leave (a telegram had informed them of the death of a Sister), but although I had not the leisure to see so many holy souvenirs dear to the heart of a Visitandine, nevertheless I set out without regret. I carried away in my heart something like an assurance given by our holy Founders that I had not departed from the way traced out by them, and an encouragement to work for my priests in a union holy, confident and pure, with him whom Jesus had given me. I felt myself protected and blessed, and when on the threshold of the door, Mother de V—— while clasping me in her arms murmured in my ear in a voice full of emotion : ' Won't you pray for us,' I felt that I was pardoned."

PREPARATIONS FOR DEPARTURE

There was a short period of calm after the return from Italy ; the calm before the storm. Suddenly and without any warning, a liquidator appointed for the Monastery of Romans, visited the Monastery.

In a letter to Father Charrier, dated September 15th, 1904, Sister Louise Margaret described his visit :

" Our dear Rev. Mother, being extremely pressed by work, entrusts me with the task of writing to you to give you the latest news about our actual position. Although we have not yet received any decree of suppression, by a judgment of the tribunal, a liquidator has just been appointed for us. For the present, he will not have the mission of liquidating the goods of the Community since it is not dissolved, but of making an inventory, of cataloguing and of superintending these goods.

" This man presented himself at our door, without the Authorities giving us any notification whatever, at least officially. He read for Rev. Mother the text of the judgment and declared his powers ; but as there were two errors in the text, first because he called us a head-house and second, because he designated us as a teaching congregation and not as a mixed congregation, Rev. Mother said that she wished to bring the case to court, which would gain a few days for us.

" Just now, we have excessive work, the effect of which the Sisters are beginning to feel and perhaps will feel more later on. But, after all, it is Jesus who permits all this ! For dear Rev. Mother, this is a very painful time ; she asks the help of your prayers. She does not think that we ought to change the date of our retreat on account of the uncertainty of what may happen to us in October or December."

There was no hope of winning the law-suit, and there was no knowing how soon the blow might fall, though actually this law-suit itself and an appeal gave them a year and six months respite. Accordingly, the Sisters in the Monastery began to prepare for eviction : they hurriedly packed up their little goods and chattels, though they had not yet secured a place to which they could transfer them.

" Pray for us, Father," Sister Louise Margaret wrote to Father Charrier, " for our dear Rev. Mother, who has such heavy responsibility, for our poor Bursar and our Sisters who are exhausted by the work of packing up, and for your child, who abandons herself to Jesus in all simplicity, but who, nevertheless, often commits faults against humility and obedience."

She joined the other Sisters in the hard manual labour involved in the preparations for removal, and it was a cause of great pain to her that her strength gave out completely under the strain. She was also Secretary to Rev. Mother and by her tact and courage sustained her in this crisis. Then there was the question of the daily wants of the Sisters. The little revenue which was derived from the boarding-school was gone and they had to devise other means of livelihood. Sister Louise Margaret put her artistic talents at the service of the community ; she painted, designed post-cards, etc., and produced little master-pieces which found a ready sale.

Amidst these distracting occupations and painful trials, her union with God remained uninterrupted. She retained her calmness and good humour ; she had a smile always on her lips to console and encourage the Sisters.

" She is an angel," said her Rev. Mother to a Visitation Sister who was on a visit.

Our Divine Lord continued to favour her with His communications just as if the Community had been enjoying perfect peace.

" The Good Master," she writes, " took possession of my soul so completely that it seemed to me that it was no longer in my body but that it had gone and become united to God, and my heart, wishing to rejoin it, made, as it were, leaps to get out of my breast and go and unite itself to the Sacred Heart of Jesus.   It seemed to me that I loved this adorable Saviour, that I would have wished to die of this love and that I would no longer belong to this world.

" Since morning, I have not had a moment to recollect myself. From time to time, in the midst of all this bustle and of many vexatious occurrences, I entrusted my heart to Jesus : I endeavoured to do everything for His love and not to be wanting in meekness and patience.   Well ! my adorable Master saw all that : His Heart took pleasure in seeing me so busy with work ; and these few heartfelt prayers sent up to Him in the midst of this whirl of activity were perhaps, more pleasing to Him than more complete recollection in a calmer life.   That is why He attracted me to Himself in the evening with so much love."

In addition to all this work, mental and physical, by the orders of her Director and Superiors, she had to continue the writing of her autobiography, and this in spite of repeated illnesses and almost continuous suffering.

" I allow nothing to appear in the exterior," she writes, " in order that all may be for Jesus, for my priests.   It is good to suffer in body and soul without anyone being aware of it."

To add to all her other troubles, Father Charrier became so seriously ill in February, 1905, that his death was expected.

His illness affected her very keenly ; and she considered that his death would be, humanly speaking, a catastrophy for her.   Nevertheless she offered the sacrifice to Jesus.

" If Thou wishest to take him from me," she writes " I give him to Thee ; but it seems to me that I have need of him still, that Thy work of love has need of him, but Thou knowest best.   If Thou takest him from me, how I shall suffer, but it will be for the best, I know that everything which Thou dost is good."

She was willing to make a still greater sacrifice, because she thought Jesus demanded it from her.

" It seemed to me," she writes, " that Jesus wished to do something of which I had no knowledge, and to do this it was necessary to find my soul entirely humiliated before Him and stripped of all things.   I thought of making the sacrifice of all the sentiments which, it seems to me, He Himself has placed in my heart for His priests. I said to Him, ' My Jesus . . . . If Thou wishest more sacrifices still, I will endeavour to think no more of these priests whom, it seems to me, Thou hast given to me ! I will endeavour no longer to love these sacerdotal souls whom Thou dost love so much.'

" I have said what I believed Thou didst order me to say, now if it be Thy wish, take another intermediary. I am unworthy to help Thy servant in this work of Love, unworthy even to suffer for it ; if Thou dost wish that my prayers, that my sufferings be of no use for this work ; if Thou dost wish that I even renounce the consolation and the joy of being a victim for Thy priests, ordain that it be so, Jesus, my Lord and Master, and strip me of all these things. Thou art the absolute Master of Thy gifts ; I adore Thee when Thou dost give and when Thou dost take away ; and when Thou shalt have withdrawn from me all Thy blessings, I wish, with the help of Thy Grace, which I believe Thou wilt always give me, to be always more faithful, always more loving and devoted."

Sacrifice made by the creature draws down new gifts from the Creator. When the annual retreat came, Sister Louise Margaret continued to receive lights from her divine Master on the Work. He showed her that exile would be no hindrance to the execution of His designs.

On the contrary, His Work was to commence and develop outside France. Sister Louise Margaret repeated several times that they would have to leave France ; that it was necessary in order that the desires of the Sacred Heart of Jesus be realised.

THE REV. MOTHER RENTS A HOUSE NEAR TURIN

In October, 1904, Mother Mary Emmanuel went again to Italy to make definite arrangements. Her absence for several months, due chiefly to an accident, with which she had met, greatly alarmed the Sisters, she succeeded however in renting a castle at Revigliasco, to the South of Turin. It was indeed necessary ; for the Sisters lost the law-suit, as indeed they had expected ; they were pronounced to be a purely teaching Community. In order to gain more time they appealed the case. The court of appeal at Grenoble confirmed the first judgment and the Monastery of Romans appeared on the next official list of convents to be liquidated. The Sisters appealed to the Council of State ; there was still a faint hope, but they suffered from the painful state of suspense.

The good Rev. Mother, in spite of her seventy-five years and a recent illness, insisted on going in person to Italy to make arrangements for the transfer of the Sisters.

While they welcomed the Cross, it was none the less the Cross, and there was no one among the Sisters who suffered so much as Sister Louise Margaret. She understood now what Our Lord said to her years before : " I will perfect in your heart the faculty of loving and the faculty of suffering, in order that you may be able to understand and feel the sufferings of Mine." Her sufferings were her own secret. The Sisters, judging by her calm exterior and the smile on her lips, used to say : " Oh ! for Sister Louise Margaret, everything is easy ! nothing costs her anything."

While the horizon was becoming every day more overcast for the Sisters, they received another cruel blow. The saintly bishop of the diocese, Monsignor Cotton, who had been a great friend and valiant defender of the Community, was called to his eternal reward, just at a time when his help and advice was most needed for the Sisters.

Our Divine Lord, as if to console His " Messenger of Infinite Love " in this accumulation of trials, gave her a vision of the triumph of the Work :

" I found myself," she writes, " as if placed on the shore of an immense ocean, of a sort of profound abyss. It was Infinite Love ! My soul felt itself drawn towards it and I would have wished to plunge into it and become lost in it. Just then, it seemed to me, that a marvellously sweet interior voice said to me that I would soon become immersed in this abyss of love, and that I would not fall in alone, that Father (Charrier) would plunge into this abyss also, and after us a multitude of souls would come there too. When a soul falls into this divine ocean there is, as it were, a commotion in these waves of love, and this commotion extends in ever-growing circles, and the Blessed Trinity and the heavenly spirits and all creation receive the effects of it."

And another time Jesus spoke to her and said : " I have placed My love in the earth of your heart like a seed. It has germinated in the soil of the misery and corruption of your humanity, bathed in the dew of My grace, and warmed by the rays of My Heart, its young growth has appeared on the earth. A day will come when this young growth will yield an abundant harvest ; priests will be the first to come and be nourished with its fruits, and after them, the souls of the faithful will be nourished by it."

These were truly prophetic words which began to be realised before that generation had passed away. But in the meantime, the sensitive heart of Mother Louise Margaret bled for the sufferings of the Religious of France, but much more at the thought of the far greater sufferings that were soon to come on the whole Church of France, especially on the bishops and priests :

" Ever since the sudden rush of events burst upon us, my soul has remained immovable in a sentiment of adoration in the midst of the press of business and the general bustle. By a very simple act it adores the divine will and adheres to it from moment to moment without stopping to think whether it suffers or whether it acts.

" It fears nothing, desires nothing, wishes nothing ; it goes where the divine will brings it. One great thought is dominant in my soul : the Church of France. On that again I adore ; but in the sensitive part of my soul, a great sadness and a piercing sorrow make themselves felt. I suffer in my priests, all that threatens them and all that is going to happen to them strikes me in the heart, and my soul weeps with infinite sorrow thinking that perhaps there will be unfaithful ones.

" The persecution will indeed sanctify the good, and raise them higher ; but the weak will be shaken and many of them will fall. It is for the weak and the unfaithful that I suffer.

" Infinite Love urges me to suffer for them and to unite my sorrows and sacrifices to the sorrows of Jesus in order to obtain for them the grace to be strong and to remain faithful."

The final decision of the Council of State was given on November 21st. On that day when the Sisters were renewing their vows, a telegram announced the unjust decision.

Sister Louise Margaret sent the news to Father Charrier : " On the evening of the Feast of the Presentation, a telegram brought us us the news of the loss of the final appeal. Rev. Mother welcomed the announcement by smiling at the cross and renewing the act of confidence and abandonment to make which, now more than ever was the opportune time. The judgment leaves us completely in the hands of the liquidator. As soon as he has notified us, in a fort-night or so, we may expect the worst."

And on December 3rd she wrote to him again : " The liquidator has now complete control over us ; two days ago he said that in a month there will not be left a Visitation Sister in the Monastery. People objected to him that it would look very bad to put out so many old and infirm Sisters on the street in the dead of winter. He replied that they could go to the public hospital. As for me, I was so persuaded that we would be expelled that I have not been astonished. I suffer on account of the sufferings of others and especially of Rev. Mother, on whose shoulders falls the whole weight of the responsibility, and I suffer too at the thought of the sad state of poor France, and of the Church in France which is soon to be shaken by a terrible storm." (The Separation Law of 1905).

THE EXPULSION

The confiscation of the Monastery was then decided on. The local authorities, who were hostile and who coveted the property, wanted the Sisters to leave without protest ; they would take the old and infirm Sisters into the public hospital as paupers, the rest could go penniless and look for work—as many of the expelled Sisters of other convents had to do. The Rev. Mother gave no reply to the insulting offer. Her opinion was that they should remain until put out by force. She consulted Father Charrier ; he was emphatically of the same opinion ; he said that it was the duty of the Community to give the good example to the laity. The good example which they gave bore fruit later on under the Law of Separation ; when the vast property of the French Church was being confiscated, it was the vigorous, physical protest of the valiant minority that saved the churches from being sold.

We shall allow Sister Louise Margaret to describe the scene of the actual expulsion ; a scene which was enacted in every corner of France, but perhaps never so touchingly and so eloquently depicted :

On March 8th, 1906, she wrote to Father Charrier :

"You know already about our expulsion by our telegram of March 6th ; we wished to make you share immediately in the supernatural joy which we felt on suffering this violence for the name of Jesus. I commenced a few lines for you at Chambery ; I could not finish it. When we reach Revigliasco to-morrow, I shall write to you at greater length. Our good Mother has been visibly supported by Our Lord. Father, join your thanksgiving to ours.

" Pray for us, for your child who experiences ineffable delight in her suffering and who blesses Jesus for everything."

And on March 8th, when she had reached Italy, she gave him all the details :

" I have kept silence, O Lord, because it is Thou Who hast done this. Not, O Jesus, divine Friend, merciful Goodness, that it is Thou Who hast done the injustice from which we suffer, but it is Thou who hast permitted that we be the victims of it. And Thou hast permitted this in execution of eternal designs, designs of love and of mercy, for the greater good of our souls and for Thy greater glory. I would wish that my soul might be the alabaster vase of Mary, and that being broken, it might pour out a perfume on Thee, divine Jesus, and on all those who surround me ; a perfume of love and praise, a perfume of adoration and peace.

" After a month of agony, the decisive moment came. At one o'clock, I heard the sound of the drums for the mobilization at the barracks. I told our Bursar about it but she did not believe it ; however, at my entreaty, she went to the parlour to enquire. Our Portress told her that there was nothing the matter and she believed it. I had the inward conviction that the soldiers were mobilizing for us. At two o'clock, Sister X came to me very pale. Someone had just telephoned from V. that the expulsion was fixed for half-past two o'clock. Well ! I replied, ' have you told Rev. Mother ?' ' Oh ! no,' she said, ' will you go and tell her ?' Our dear Mother was writing in her room without suspecting anything. What impression was this news going to make on her ? Was I going to see her stagger and fall under the blow ? I approached her gently, and in a calm voice, as if communicating to her a simple supposition, I said to her : ' Mother, I really believe that we are going to have something strange to-day, they have been beating the drums at the barracks for the past hour, and a telephone message has just come from V. saying that it would be for to-day.'

" ' If that is so,' said she to me, ' we must prepare, we must tell the Bursar.'

" ' She knows it, my good Mother. If you wish I shall close your valise, for they say it will be soon. I was told it would be at half-past two.'

" Rev. Mother remained strong. ' Let us hasten,' she said to me. I helped her to gather her papers, I buckled her valise, all the time speaking gently and gaily to her :

" ' You need not be uneasy about anything ; everything is ready ; if you will kindly go down to your office, you can wait there reading over your protest.'

" Soon a crowd of our friends entered the cloister. Rev. Mother was moved but firm. Would she be able for the ordeal, I asked myself anxiously. O Jesus, Thou knowest all the anguish of my soul during these moments, and how my heart, unable to say any word, went up to Thee in mute supplications. We were all in the choir, in this choir where Jesus had lavished so many graces upon me, where I had been united to Him by the indestructible bonds of my profession ; where I had so often poured out my heart and my tears at His divine feet ; where our Holy Founder had blessed me, imposing his anointed hands on my head.

" How many memories crowded into my soul during that hour, while my lips recited the Rosary ! Around me, our friends were praying and singing, and outside, the workers of evil were hewing down the doors with axes, and were exasperated at our resistance.

" The last one had finally fallen. Some moments afterwards the liquidator, the agents and the soldiers invaded the choir. There was a moment of indescribable tumult, the soldiers were trying to push out the people who surrounded us ; they resisted and violent altercations took place.

" I looked over at Rev. Mother, who was standing up and calm ; I went over to her and asked her if she would be able to read. ' Yes,' she said to me, ' I can.'

" When a little order was restored, she read her protest in a perfectly confident, firm voice, pronouncing her words slowly, without appearing to be in the least impeded by her bad sight.

" Jesus was visibly helping her out. Oh ! divine Friend, how powerful and good Thou art !

" And then we were compelled to go out of our dear dwelling, to pass over the heaps of debris from our doors that had been hewn down, and like Thee, divine Master, without shelter or home, to seek a refuge provided by charity. When going down the streets amidst the cries of the crowd, leaning on the arm of a Sister, I felt my soul inundated with floods of peace. In this great despoiling of all things, God, this divine riches, gave Himself to me more liberally."

The Sisters were brought to the house of a friend, who felt honoured with their presence. On the following morning, their friends turned out again to escort them to the railway station ; the train which bore them to the land of exile moved out amidst the cries of a large, imposing crowd :

"Long live the Sisters ! Long live the Pope !"

BEGINNINGS IN A STRANGE LAND

"Poor dear France !" wrote Sister Louise Margaret, "the gigantic barrier of the Alps separates us from her now ; the familiar horizon, the beloved well-wishers have disappeared ; the sweet French tongue is no longer heard around us, and the voices that come up to us from the village bring us only strange accents.

"No more silent cloisters with white colonnades ; no more long corridors where, on meeting our Sisters, we bowed to them to honour their title of spouses of Christ. No more grilles to recall to us that we were separated from the world and that we were no longer to follow its maxims. No longer any exterior sign of our monastic life. But in the interior, in the intimacy of our souls, Christ, always ours, always ours, because we are always His !"

Their temporary residence, the castle of Count Berice, was situated on a plateau twelve hundred feet high. The castle was spacious ; it was surrounded by a well laid-out park and commanded a splendid view. Sister Louise Margaret, in a letter to Father Charrier, gives her first impressions of exile :

"We arrived in our new dwelling yesterday evening at four-thirty. You can understand our joy at meeting the other Sisters again and also the inward sorrow of our hearts when our thoughts went back from beyond the Alps to dear France, to our dear house now profaned ; to all those whom we had left and whom, perhaps, we would never see again. May the most sweet will of Jesus be done."

Besides the pain of exile, the many privations due to utter poverty, and above all, the disorganisation of Religious life, Our Lord gave her a glimpse of greater sufferings to come. These, Father Charrier encouraged her to bear cheerfully, for the love of her divine Master :

"Since Our Lord has given you a glimpse of many sacrifices in store for you, may this sight fill you with joy since you will be thus able to prove your love for Him better. Do you not wish to be His real victim of love ? And since the victim has delivered herself up, must not the Sacrificer immolate her ? I hope that the victim will let herself be offered without crying too much. Instead of weeping, let her utter cries of love to Jesus ; let her accept each wound for her heart, each suffering for her body, each torture for her soul, as so many arrows of love which the Beloved Sacrificer of the little victim discharges."

And not long afterwards, she was given a foretaste of the greater sufferings to come :

" Since I have come to Piedmont," she wrote in April, 1907, " I have been constantly ill, but thank God, not confined to bed.

" I assure you, I have great need of your prayers. I have a great desire to sanctify myself, but I do everything badly and cowardly. The only thing that I do well is the Lenten fast ; for the last three weeks I have abstained from all meat, and my nourishment for the day consists of two eggs and a little vegetables. The divine Master treats me admirably. If, when I came here, I had asked Rev. Mother for permission to fast and practise complete abstinence, she would most probably have refused me, but Jesus knows how to have His way."

After Easter, she was obliged to resume her Lenten diet, as she calls it, and she adds gaily : " Thus, while remaining in my dear Visitation, the reliquary of the love of the divine Heart, I can follow in a small way the Rule of the Carmelites and of so many other Orders vowed to perpetual abstinence."

But her sufferings, from whatever source they might originate, became for her sources of joy, for in the midst of them she got a prophetic glimpse of the dawn of Infinite Love :

" It has pleased Thee, my divine Jesus," she writes, " to light up my soul with a ray of joy. It seemed to me that I was witnessing the sun-rise. An immense horizon spread out before me and slowly became empurpled with the fires of Love, and this purple began to shine like molten metal. The Sun of Infinite Love had not yet begun to shine in the heavens, but some rays revealed Its presence, and if the valleys still remained in the shade, the mountain tops were being lit up. The mountain-tops—pure souls, holy priests—were already announcing the rise of the more ardent Sun. Oh ! to see Infinite Love casting Its rays on all souls, to see this divine Sun illuminate the world ! My God, how glorious !"

And as, by some mysterious law of Providence, participation in the sorrows of Calvary by some privileged souls is a necessary preparation for the realisation of some new merciful design, she glories in the generous contribution which her dear Visitation is making at that hour :

" When there is question of the glory of His divine Heart, Our Lord, as you know, is accustomed to address Himself to the Visitation. Well ! since He sends so much suffering to our dear Monasteries and since He levies a new toll on them, not only on one province or one nation, but almost everywhere, it is doubtless because He is preparing some glorious triumph for His Heart ! My God ! how that thought gives one a desire to suffer, to suffer much, to suffer patiently, in order that this glorification of the divine Heart may be hastened !"

And in his letter of December 27th, 1906, Father Charrier, while consoling her and encouraging her to suffer patiently, sums up beautifully this doctrine of participating in the sufferings of Christ :

" What sorrowful trials in your heart ! How Our Lord cherishes you ! I seem to see you crushed and exhausted. But you will accept all this from the Infinite Love of your Jesus, for all this comes from His Heart, as you know well. And it is so salutary to suffer for Him through Whom we suffer ! It is truly the mutual communication of goods, which is the best proof of love. Jesus gives us a share in His sufferings, and His sufferings are a blessing since they have saved souls. In our turn, we offer Him ours, and when united to His, they become a great blessing, since they permit us also to save souls, like Jesus, and in union with Him."

At the same time, Our Lord, as is His custom with all holy souls, inundates her soul with holy joy—the joy of seeing at a distance the dawn of the triumph of Infinite Love :

" My sweet Master," she exclaims, " Why dost Thou console me so ? Perhaps it would be better that I should suffer without seeing anything ; my Director prefers that I should suffer. Allow me then, if it be Thy holy will and if it serves the designs of Thy Love better, to suffer in darkness and desolation."

And with the incomparable tenderness of His Heart, Jesus replies : " I wish to give you joy in order to cure you."

When giving this news to her Spiritual Father, Sister Louise Margaret added : " It is true that since then, although constantly suffering, I have felt myself better and stronger.

" See how good Jesus is ! How like a mother !"

Her divine Spouse is careful too, to purify her from the smallest stain.

" There is on the part of Jesus," she writes, " a continuous merciful onslaught on my soul.   Like a husband who goes even to folly in order to adorn a spouse whom he loves passionately, thus Jesus goes to extremes of mercy in order to see me always adorned in white apparel, always as His love wishes me to be.

" Our Lord communicated Himself to my soul after Holy Communion.   He reproached me for my want of confidence in Him and for not abandoning myself to His love.   Showing me His Heart with ineffable tenderness, He said to me : ' If you are faithful, this will be your dwelling place !   Believe in My love.!   Has My Heart grown cold ?   Has my power been diminished ?   Have I not instructed you Myself ?   What is there that I have not done for you ?'   I shed tears abundantly seeing that my anxiety and my fears had saddened the Heart of my Saviour, but in my grief I experienced an ineffable joy at finding my Beloved again, Who had been so long hidden from my eyes."

And speaking of the Work of Infinite Love, Our Lord said to her in July, 1906 : " It will not be accomplished, like other works, with the aid of money ; it will be accomplished only by many sufferings, sacrifices and humiliations."

And in the following August she wrote : " For more than a fortnight, I have been getting a glimpse of a great cross, it is some suffering that I am to meet with in three or four months."   And at the date indicated, she had a profound, interior suffering which lasted several weeks.

In a retreat preached by Father Charrier in October of the same year, she received many heavenly favours in the midst of much suffering.   Jesus said to her : " Will you allow Me to pour into your heart a drop of Infinite Love ?"

" I felt my heart burning and my breast inflamed with mysterious fire," she writes ; " it seemed to me that my heart and my whole being would melt like wax exposed to the action of a great fire, by the contact with Infinite Love, radiating from the Heart of Jesus. In the midst of the delights and sufferings which Love caused me, I said to my divine Master :

" ' Why lavish so many blessings on me ?   Why give me so much love ?'

" He replied to me :

' **Because I have chosen you to reveal My Love to priests.**' "

So far from being elated by these divine favours, Sister Louise Margaret humbly acknowledged her unworthiness, thus giving proof that these favours really came from God ; for Our Lord's own criterion given to St. Margaret Mary was, that divine favours would make her humble in her own eyes and would draw down contempt from worldings.

BELIEF IN THE LOVE OF GOD

In the first Epistle of St. John (IV, 16) we read : " And we have known and believed the charity which God hath for us." And Mother Louise Margaret adds : " Indeed, we cannot see Jesus Christ, meditate on His words and actions, and study Him in His mysteries, particularly in that of His voluntary immolation on the cross, without believing in the love which God has for His creatures."

Belief in the love of the Sacred Heart of Jesus for each one of us is one of the essential elements of the devotion to the Sacred Heart as revealed to St. Margaret Mary. Mother Louise Margaret attributes God's special graces to her to the fact that she believed in His love for her : " It is not because I am good," she writes, " it is not because I am humble ; it is not because I am mortified, or faithful, or patient, or fervent, that Our Lord has granted me so many graces. Oh ! certainly not, for I am none of these things, but I am miserable and weak and poor in virtue, even to being completely devoid of it.

" If God has favoured me so much, it is solely because I have believed in His love : Yes, in the simplicity of my soul, I have believed that God, Who has need of nothing and Who alone was sufficient for Himself, had undertaken creation solely in order to be able to have something to love outside Himself. I have believed that in this magnificent creation, man was the one most special object of His love, and I have believed that nothing could come forth from God for this loved creature that was not also from love. I have believed that in His dealings with me, God has acted solely through love, and I have recognised this Infinite Love, less perhaps in the sweetness and the lights received, than in the manifold sufferings that have crushed my soul, my heart, and my body ; I have believed in love which consoles, which sustains, which inebriates ; I have believed also in Love which breaks, which crushes and which takes away.

" My God, I have believed in Thy love, and I believe in it with all the clearness of my intellect ; I believe it with all the precision of my reason, I believe in it with all the strength of my will, I believe in it especially with all the ardour of my heart. My God, I believe in Thy love, and I wish always to believe in it, whatever sorrows Thou mayst send me, whatever cross Thou mayst lay upon me, whatever help Thou mayst deprive me of, whatever good Thou mayst withdraw from me, I will believe in Thy love."

Intimate Notes : 24-9-1906.

OUR LORD CONTINUES HIS COMMUNICATIONS AMIDST THE SUFFERINGS OF EXILE

The troubles of the Community were by no means over when they arrived in Italy. The Sisters had no fixity of tenure in the rented castle, and after a short stay in it, had to find other accommodation at short notice. The castle itself lacked all the conveniences necessary for a community of fifty Sisters ; there was no water supply and the pump was out of order ; no cooking installation, no money to install these, no friends to help the Sisters in their difficulties. And then the Rev. Mother was old and infirm. In spite of her seventy-five years and weak health, she had risen to the occasion gloriously during the days of the expulsion ; on the one hand, she found a home for the Sisters after two journeys to Italy undertaken in the dead of winter, and on the other, she did her duty to God and to the Church of France by the splendid protest she made against injustice and tyranny. Then she collapsed completely. She was confined to bed for three months and was not even able to speak to the Sisters. Sister Louise Margaret was her Secretary and was also Mistress of Novices. She had been the companion and adviser of Rev. Mother during the first visit to Italy and in the dark days of the expulsion and now the care of the Community fell mostly on her. The Lord provided wonderfully for the Community ; if He had taken the Rev. Mother from the Sisters by sickness, He accepted her resignation and her ardent prayers and took charge of the Community Himself. He had brought the Community to Italy for His Own work, the Work of Infinite Love, and in the midst of the turmoil of preparation for exile and removing to a foreign land, He never ceased to speak to His chosen instrument and to prepare her to do His Work.

VISIT FROM ST. FRANCIS DE SALES

On January 29th, 1907, St. Francis de Sales, the founder of the Order of Visitation, appeared to her to assure her that she was not departing from the spirit of the Visitation by being the Messenger of Infinite Love, quite the contrary, for she writes : " **Our blessed Father (St. Francis de Sales), said to me that we had been established specially for the service of Infinite Love,** but that no soul could arrive at the love of God unless it had also a great and true charity for its neighbour. He gave me to understand that only rarely are souls raised to a high degree of love for God, because they do not carry their love for others far enough ; that it is not sufficient to serve them and merely to fulfil the commandment, but that it is necessary to have a very exquisite delicacy towards them in one's interior sentiments.

" In many souls there are vindictive sentiments and evil intentions which are not voluntarily cultivated, but which are not sufficiently combated, and which, being only venial sins, do not kill charity in the soul but prevent the work of Infinite Love in it. He taught me that delicacy and meekness of interior sentiments which render the soul so pleasing to God that the gift of Infinite Love is then given in very great abundance. He told me that we must always pardon every offence and always render good for evil ; then he told me that if I did so, Infinite Love would make Its sojourn of repose and delights in my soul."

CHAPTER VI.

SISTER LOUISE MARGARET ELECTED REV. MOTHER.

The second term in office came to an end for Mother Mary Emmanual on May 11th, 1907. Five days later, the choice of the Sisters for new Rev. Mother fell on Sister Louise Margaret. It was the work of the Lord ; she had, it is true, great capabilities, but very few of the Sisters were aware of them until she became Rev. Mother, and then there were three other Sisters in the Community who had had experience in that office. Besides the fact that the Lord had His Own special work to be done through her, He wished, no doubt, to reward the Sisters for their fidelity to Him in the days of trial by giving them as Rev. Mother one who would provide so ably both for their corporal and spiritual necessities. The Sisters welcomed the choice of God, and all, especially those who had experience in office, gave her their whole-hearted co-operation. Nor was their confidence in her misplaced ; before the end of her second term of office, she had restored the Community to the fervour of the days of St. Francis de Sales and St. Jane Frances de Chantal and had solved their great temporal problem by providing a permanent home for the Sisters.

In a letter to Father Charrier, written a few days after the election, she gives him the news :

" I received your card and good letter. I was waiting until the election was over to reply. I thought I could by the same letter announce to you the name of the Sister elected, and I had no idea whatever that it was to be myself.

" When the election was finished, the good Father said to us that he was going to announce to us with joy the choice of Our Lord ; then he mentioned my name. Ah ! Father, how can I describe for you what passed within my soul ; my breast heaved and I gave three sobs ; I thought that I was going to die. Soon the tears burst forth without my being able to stop them. Scarcely had I begun to read the profession of Faith when I felt myself completely taken possession of by God ; my soul was filled with strength ; I continued the holy words of the profession of Faith in a firm voice, without seeing anything around me. Our Lord was present : but at the end, when I came to the last words : ' So help me God and these holy Gospels,' this divine presence veiled Itself, and my tears began to flow again. My inner feeling was this : It is Jesus who has done it ; then it is good. I wish it also. I have confidence in Him and I abandon myself. At a quarter past nine, all was finished ; Jesus had made me the Mother of this dear family ; my heart was, and is since this hour, filled with the maternal tenderness which I feel descending from the adorable Heart of Jesus into mine. It is by the Heart of the Master that I love each of these souls ; and I understand that He has placed me in this position in order to make these souls ascend to His Heart by bearing them in mine. Help me, Father, to do in all this the Work of Love for which alone I exist."

Father Charrier's reply, while giving us an example of his vigorous, enlightened direction of this privileged soul, merits the attention of all who, like Sister Louise Margaret, are called to rule over God's elect :

" I know that you will be a good Mother for all your children and that you will make the Sacred Heart of Jesus loved. But you will need to have perpetual devotedness, to forget yourself constantly and to sacrifice your whole being to the needs of your children. This demands exalted virtue and physical strength, which perhaps you lack. I conjure you then, and if need be, I command you to take the same care of yourself as you would wish that anyone else in your place would take.

" Do it out of love for souls and in the spirit of simplicity. So much for the question of physical strength. As for the exalted virtue which you need, I recommend to you especially interior humility. When surrounded with homage, veneration and delicate attention, say to yourself that all this is for your office, but that the miserable person to whom Our Lord has entrusted it merits only the contempt of all, since she is the most miserable of all. You will have no difficulty, I imagine, in believing this. What would you be now, or where would you be, were it not for the merciful attentions of the infinite love of Jesus?

"It is my duty to speak thus to a soul which grace has sanctified, but which would be abandoned by grace if she did not remember that Jesus has raised her from the dunghill to make her a princess of His people. This sight of your misery, of your nothingness, of your past shortcomings, must not be a reason for distrust in yourself. On the contrary : being more loved than others, since Jesus has raised you up from a lower place, you should devote yourself more to His interests and love Him more. Jesus will give you His powerful assistance. If you remain in this state of humility, your virtue will increase rapidly. Place yourself sometimes in thought at the feet of others, at the feet of all. Meditate sometimes on Jesus, at the feet of Jesus, and ask yourself what ought to be your place.

"Have confidence then, confidence in Him Who has placed the burden on your shoulders and Who will carry it with you. Let nothing impede His action in your heart. The least sentiment of self-love would be so painful to Him that, I am confident, you will never yield to it."

And in a subsequent letter, he added the following beautiful counsels :

"Remember, however, that the dear Master has established you more as a Mother than as a Superioress. Have, therefore, a mother's heart for the dear aged and infirm Sisters, and never merit the reproach which a General of a great Order made to his Superiors : ' I have Superiors in abundance, but I find very few Fathers among them. Be above all a true mother by your delicate attention, tact and charity. Where is the love of God if it is not shown by love of your neighbour?"

In her reply to Father Charrier, she says :

"Your letter has done me a world of good. Yes, my whole desire is to be a mother, and I think the Sisters realise that I will be so."

And in a letter to him soon after, she tells him of the receipt of a little monetary help and gives us an insight into her great difficulties :

"You will, I am sure, join with us in thanking the good Master, for although it is only a temporal favour, nevertheless, it is a favour. When one is a Mother and has fifty children to feed, care for, and clothe, and see to it that the house does not get into debt, one has indeed some cares. It is true, Father, that I place all these cares in the Heart of Jesus. This divine and most amiable Heart is like a chest to which I come every day to deposit my cares, my fears, my troubles. And then from time to time this chest is opened, and all that I have placed in it is found changed into help, either spiritual or temporal, into graces of all kinds."

HER PROGRAMME FOR THE SISTERS

It was the duty of the Visitation Rev. Mother to give conferences to the Sisters at Chapter meetings. Fortunately for us, she wrote all her conferences with great care and submitted them to the Chaplain. She had taken a remark of Father Charrier " that she was incapable of writing anything but heresy " very much to heart ; but apparently she had not seen his qualifying remark, " of your own unaided efforts." At all events, he assured her in his next letter that he had never found the smallest error in any of her writings— a testimony which he repeated several times, as we shall see—and that she was under no obligation to submit her conferences to the Chaplain. However, she continued the custom, and these beautiful conferences which give the doctrine of Infinite Love as applied to the details of ordinary life and which happily have been preserved for us, are all the more valuable for the great care taken in their composition in order to ensure that they would contain no error or inaccuracy.

Our readers will find in Vol. II of this series a long selection of these conferences which she wrote down during her six years in office. They reveal at the same time Sister Louise Margaret as Rev. Mother, and how to live the doctrine of Infinite Love.

The following is the first of these Conferences, which was delivered two days after her election :

" My dear Sisters, when two days ago, it pleased Our Lord to impose on me this burden of office, always heavy to bear, after the first moment of emotion, and I will say even of intense dread, this thought occurred to my mind : If the divine Master chooses such a feeble instrument for His work, it is, doubtless, because He intends to do everything by Himself. We have resolved from this hour to leave to our adorable Master the direction of everything and to listen attentively to the inspirations of His grace and the dispositions of His will in order to accomplish it.

" The divine Will, which is the rule and form of our sanctification, on the part of God, is nothing else but love for His creature, and in exchange, the will of the creature should be nothing else but love for God. It is towards the increase of this heavenly love in ourselves that we, my beloved Sisters, shall work together continually endeavouring to give more strength and activity to this double current of sacred love which descends from the Heart of God to souls, and which goes up from our souls to God.

" Love is the great need of our hearts ; in these sad times which are troubled by so much dissension, frozen by so much selfishness, love is the constant, ardent desire of souls, who knowing God, are aware of what He deserves and what is due to Him, but which, alas, is almost everywhere refused to Him. Let us love this God, Who is so good and so worthy of being loved. Let us go to Jesus Christ, God made man ; let us seek His Heart, the source of love ; let us study It ; let us give all our affection to It ; and we shall come to the knowledge of the Divinity by entering into contact with His adorable Humanity.

" But, my beloved Sisters, a single way leads to Infinite Love, a single door gives access to this divine temple ; it is charity. Aided by grace and always attentive to the desires of the adorable Heart, we shall endeavour to remove the obstacles which might come to impede the exercise of this divine virtue. We shall strive to the best of our ability to unite our hearts, to bind them together so that they will form but one.

" Community of suffering brings hearts together more perhaps than community of life. It has been God's will, doubtless in order to cement still better the love and union of the members of our dear family, to make them pass through more painful trials. Each of your souls, my beloved Sisters, has had its own particular sufferings and anguish of heart. Several have had to leave dear works which had for them all the attraction of an apostolate ; many have seen mothers, sisters, loved families weeping, and have had to impose on them a sacrifice as painful as that of their own profession ; all have had to leave their native land, this unfortunate and so much loved France, and take the road for exile towards the uncertainty of the morrow and the unknown of the future. The Divine Master has seen the fidelity of your hearts and the generosity of your courage, and He will recompense you.

" But your souls fatigued by the struggle, and exhausted by the sacrifices have need of peace, repose and joy. Together, we shall seek all that in love, in Infinite Love, the source of light and of generous ardour ; in fraternal charity, the source of serene peace and trusting joy.

" For myself, my beloved Sisters, my sole ambition will be to aid the Master in doing His Work of love in this dear family. You will find in me neither the experience which age or long term in office gives, nor the talents of a superior mind, nor the virtues of the Saints ; but you will find—and I confidently promise you—a true mother's heart. Incapable of any good by myself, but sustained by grace, aided by the honourable Sisters who have preceded me in office with so much merit, and by the esteemed elders of the Community, whom long years of virtue have rendered so dear to me ; aided by the help and prayers of all, I undertake with confidence, with that entire confidence which trusts in God alone, the care of this dear family and the service of your souls."

And the resolutions which she made in the August retreat of the same year, resolutions which she observed with absolute fidelity, may be said to sum up the history of her six years in office. They were :

" To give myself, to sacrifice myself completely for the Community, in order to serve it to the best of my ability in all things spiritual and temporal ; and to do this in the spirit of immolation for the Church, for the souls of priests, for the reign of Infinite Love ; to be good like Jesus as far as that is possible for me ; to be a victim for souls, like Jesus immolated ; to love like Jesus and with Jesus."

And in a conference given to the Sisters the same year, she appeals to them to bring back the fervour of the Visitation in the days of St. Jane Frances de Chantal and St. Francis de Sales :

" On June 6th, 1910, our Holy Order will celebrate the third centenary of its foundation. Only three years separate us from this solemnity, which no Sister can hope to see twice in her lifetime.

" It is dear to our hearts because of the great memories which it re-calls, and it is capable of producing great fruits of sanctity in our souls.

" It has occurred to us to propose to you, dear Sisters, to make of these three years a sort of triduum of preparation during which, by applying ourselves with greater attention to the study of our holy Rules and by steeping ourselves in the primitive spirit of our holy Institute, we may dispose ourselves to receive the very special graces which our holy Founders will not fail to obtain for us from the divine bounty. Let us then enter into this period of renovation with holy fervour ; let us read again the holy books of our Order, let us study them ; let us nourish our souls with the holy food con-tained beneath the outward cover of our holy observances, and by our constant and loving fidelity, let us draw down the favour of the Blessed Trinity, Which has deigned to preside at the establishment of our holy Institute, and under Whose special protection we place these three years of preparation."

This was a very definite programme of work : to increase the love of God in the Community by an increase of charity towards one's neighbour ; to realise that unity for which Christ prayed for His Apostles :

" That they may be one as We also are one " (John XVII, 22) ; to restore the original observance of the Rule ; and towards that end to study carefully the books written by their holy Founders.

FIRST REMOVAL OF THE COMMUNITY

In spite of the difficult circumstances which she inherited, Mother Louise Margaret succeeded finally in making provision for the spiritual and temporal welfare of the Sisters. She acted gently and prudently and always took advice, but when her duty to God and the Community was clear, she never shirked her responsibility. Since the arrival in Italy, there had been no *clausura*; she restored the *clausura* and excluded unwelcome visitors. Some of the material difficulties, such as the want of a proper chapel (the fifty Sisters were cramped into a medium-sized room), and the primitive cooking arrangements, could be endured with patience; but the water-supply, inadequate as it was, had been found on analysis to be tainted and was responsible for an epidemic of sickness among the Sisters. It was therefore imperative to find a new home as soon as possible. But where? Just then a storm was raging outside; the masonic-controlled Press was clamouring for a law against Religious Congregations similar to that of France. The convent Chaplain, who went to Germany, brought back word that refugee-Communities would not be admitted there, and efforts made to divide up the Community among the German Visitation Monasteries ended in failure. Mother Louise Margaret went to France to consult the new Bishop of Valence, in whose diocese the Monastery of Romans was situated. His advice to her was to remain in Italy, but he gave her permission to get a house anywhere she could. Every effort to find another house had so far failed. In this sea of difficulties, Mother Louise Margaret's only hope was in prayer, prayer for a little nest for her family, no matter how poor it might be; just a place where they could continue their Religious life as Visitation nuns. The lease was expiring; two different parties were negotiating to rent the place. The Sisters had to pack up their little belongings to be ready to move.

"Such was the situation," writes Mother Louise Margaret; "half our furniture was packed up, it was bitterly cold, several of our Sisters were confined to bed with illness. I confess that I experienced a moment of profound sadness; it seemed to me that it was I and my acts of infidelity, that had drawn down these trials on the community; I besought Our Lord not to make my children bear the weight of my sins. And then it seemed to me that Our Lord's intention was to make me suffer for the good of His priests and, as the Community was what was dearest to me after them, that the good Master made the Community suffer in order that I might suffer the more."

Just when all hope seemed to have vanished, Our Lord came to their assistance. The Countess of San Marzano heard of their difficulties and rented to them at Mazze, a large house called 'La Torretta,' which belonged to her.

Mazze is situated in the diocese of Ivrea, about half way between Turin and Ivrea, and about four miles from the Monastery of the Sisters of Bethany of the Sacred Heart at Vische. The house was surrounded by a fine park planted with trees, was large enough to accommodate the fifty Sisters, was in good repair, and had an abundant water supply.

It was Divine Providence that brought the Community to the diocese of Ivrea, for the Bishop of the diocese was Monsignor Filipello who, as we shall see, was the man selected by Our Lord to initiate the Work of Infinite Love.

Mother Louise Margaret signed the lease on November 14th, 1908, willingly and joyfully, it is true, but she had been haunted by the fear of another legal expulsion, and contemplated leaving Italy. Later on, she wondered if this might not have been a manoeuvre of the devil to make her leave the country that was destined to become the cradle of the Work of Infinite Love.

THE TIME FOR ACTION COME

While these events were taking place, Mother Louise Margaret was getting intimations from her divine Spouse that the time for action was near. Only six and a half years of life remained for her. This fact was hidden from her until her work was completed, and then she announced that she was to die so as not to be an obstacle to making known the Work of Infinite Love. During these short years, she seemed urged on by a mysterious force. She did everything short of compulsion to persuade Father Charrier to act. She wanted him to do two things : to give a decision on the origin of her communications, and to undertake the composition of a book that would give them to the world, while she herself would remain hidden and unknown. Providence seems to have intervened on both these issues. On the first, Father Charrier would not go further than stating that he could find no error in anything she wrote and that, while it was his personal opinion that her communications were from God, he left it to the Holy See to decide ; on the second, after years of hesitation, he consented to compose a book for priests from her notes, but the amount of work given him to do by his Superiors left him no time to compose it and he was compelled to relinquish the idea. Our Divine Lord left Mother Louise Margaret in that painful state of uncertainty during most of her Religious life, and when the Holy See sanctioned the establishment of the Priests' Universal Union of the Friends of the Sacred Heart and the foundation of the new Monastery, which constituted the substance of her communications, her death was not far off.

We give here in detail an account of how she felt urged on to action by Our Lord and of the obstinate refusal of Father Charrier to yield to her entreaties.

" It seems to me," she writes in August, 1907, " that the profound calm which my soul enjoys is given to me by Our Lord as a preparation for a multitude of cares, business worries and complications of every kind which are to follow ; but even this thought does not trouble me in the least. I have a great interior certainty that it is God Himself Who has placed me in the position of authority which I occupy, all the more so, because, according to all human probabilities, this could not have been. God knows well my pitiable plight, my ignorance, my physical and moral incapacity, my powerlessness of every kind. If then He has given me this office, it is because He Himself is to see to the accomplishment of what I am incapable of doing, and that the end which He has in view cannot be other than His Own glory.

" I think I have been given a glimpse of what this end is this morning. **Jesus showed me the Infinite Love with which His Heart is filled and Which overflows from It, and He indicated it, if I am not mistaken, as the divine remedy which alone will save the world.** It seemed to me that perhaps the adorable Master has given me a little influence over souls and liberty of action solely for the purpose of revealing this saving love and diffusing it everywhere."

And soon afterwards she wrote : " I feel in myself a passionate desire to make God loved. I seem to have in my breast surging waves which want to find an outlet and escape ; waves at the same time burning like fire and refreshing like limpid water ; waves of love, active and enlivening, which are poured into me, not for myself but for others. God has made of my soul a profound reservoir of love into which He is always pouring anew. This love is not mine, it is not from me, it is the very Love of God. It comes from the Heart of Jesus, it descends into mine, but it is not in order to remain there. My heart is only a place of passage for this divine love. Where does this Infinite Love which passes go ? Towards what abyss does It rush? If goes from the abyss of divine Mercy, from which It issues, to the abyss of human misery."

On August 14th, 1907, she puts her case very strongly to Father Charrier and appeals for some decision :

" For the past eleven years you have been examining my way of life and my writings, or you have been getting them examined ; and you are still in a state of uncertainty.

" You have told me that I am incapable of saying or writing anything but what is full of heresy ; you often tell me that it is quite the contrary of what Our Lord seems to say to me interiorly.

" In reason, I should believe you rather than my own interior inspirations. Then, either you are deceiving me,—and if that be so, whom in the world can I trust when I can no longer trust my Father Director—or I am completely under a delusion. If I am under a delusion and if you think so, why do you not tell me?

" If I am not under a delusion, and if what I have believed to be the desire of Our Lord is really so, why do you not carry it out? Or if you have not sufficient courage to do so, why do you not get it done by others?

" Since my election, I suffer still more from all this, for if I am under a delusion, if I am incapable of producing anything but heresy, how will I be able to guide the Community?

" Every time that I have to give spiritual advice or to write a conference for a Chapter, I am afraid of doing more harm than good.

" To obviate this danger, at least partially, I submit my weekly conferences for the Chapter to the Chaplain, in order that he may point out any errors."

FATHER CHARRIER REASSURES HER

A few days afterwards Father Charrier sent her the following reply in which he assured her that he found no error in her writings and held out hopes of an early decision :

" I recognise that your grievances are well founded and I acknowledge that it is largely through my fault. Yes, I should not have left you so long in uncertainty. And I have not been able to rid myself of it. My numerous sins are, no doubt, the cause of this want of light. Nevertheless, I must correct an error in your letter. You quote me as saying that you are incapable of producing anything but heresy. Yes, I said that ' **of yourself** you are incapable of producing anything,' but I added : ' **However, in all your writings I have not found a word which is not in most exact conformity with Catholic doctrine, even in the most sublime subjects ; and this inclines me greatly to believe in the reality of the lights which you have received.'** Would you have forgotten this, or have I not expressed myself with sufficient clearness ?

" I wish to assure you that you are not bound to submit your conferences to the Chaplain, and that you can at any time dispense yourself from doing so.

" As for giving approbation to your writings, I do not feel myself competent to pronounce definitely on them, and I have not yet made up my mind to entrust them to someone else, although I believe I have met a person who is capable of clearing up my doubts."

And in a subsequent letter written in the following month, he told her that he had made a prudent beginning and had found a competent person to examine her writings :

" Here is just what I think about the whole matter : If I myself had not been designated as the person who is to assist in establishing the work and in diffusing the lights which I believe have come to you from Our Lord, I would be tempted to say ' yes ' to almost all your ideas. I have made a prudent beginning to do something. By having the prayer, ' O Jesus Eternal High Priest,' printed and indulgenced, I had the intention of entering into your projects. I had commenced a book of meditation for priests, giving prominence to the idea of the reign of Love, for which I got help from your writings. Then time was lacking. Can I say that I have not yielded to laziness ? I dare not. And then, even in the things that come from God, it is so easy to put in something of one's own, or to receive something from the enemy, that I have always abstained from giving a definite judgment ; this state of hesitation and suspense explains also why I have done nothing.

" In conclusion, I have found a person who, I believe, is certainly competent to give a definite judgment about your writings."

The prayer, O Jesus Eternal High Priest, referred to in Father Charrier's letter, was composed by Mother Louise Margaret in December, 1903. Father Charrier had it printed. It was soon translated into nine of the European languages ; and in February, 1905, Monsignor Henri, Bishop of Grenoble, presented the original and the nine translations to Pope Pius X, with a petition to His Holiness to grant an indulgence for its recitation.

The prayer, which was written before the Encyclical of Pius X on the Priesthood had appeared, contains ideas identical with those of the Encyclical. His Holiness was pleased to see that it expressed ideas so dear to his heart and granted an indulgence of 300 days once a day, and a plenary indulgence once a month for reciting it daily.[1]

It was gradually intimated to Mother Louise Margaret that what Our Lord had already told her was to be put into effect : Father Charrier was to be put aside for another, who would take charge of the active work. She continued to pray that her divine Master would enlighten him :

" I pray for you still more now than formerly and I await, with absolute confidence in Jesus, the full light which you are seeking. This interior suffering of my soul unites me more closely to priests. I cannot explain to you all that there is in my heart about this subject."

And in her letter to Father Charrier of November 6th, 1907, she explains what God wants from us and what virtues we must have in order to understand something of the mystery of Infinite Love :

" Our Lord is content to see us act faithfully under his inspiration, taking the proper means to promote His work, but He certainly does not want either natural eagerness or inconsiderate haste ; it suffices for Him that we go forward gently, without wishing to anticipate His hour. The hour chosen by God is always the best. However, our good Master is not pleased if we remain entirely inactive ; or if, either through cowardice, or lack of confidence in God, or from some other natural motive, we oblige Him in some way to delay His hour. For my part, Father, I shall die content whenever Jesus calls me, even though I should see nothing accomplished of what it seems to me He wishes done, provided that on my side I have employed myself faithfully in doing the little that I am able. Indeed, it matters nothing when we die, whether we have accomplished a work, whether we have succeeded or failed. It suffices that we have carried out courageously the part of the work that has been marked out for us. **Would that I could make even one soul understand clearly that God is Love** ! In order to understand it, a person must be very pure, that is to say, very humble, very charitable, very faithful to the inspirations from the Heart of Jesus, very mortified, and very supernatural"

[1] See 'The Sacred Heart and the Priesthood ', page 6 for this prayer.

FATHER HAMON, S.J., TO EXAMINE THE INTIMATE NOTES

On November 6th, 1907, Father Charrier announced to her his decision to hand over all her writings to Father Hamon, S.J., who had made a life long study of the devotion to the Sacred Heart, and who is still one of the great authorities on that subject :

" I shall see Father Hamon between the 24th and 29th of November. I shall give him all your writings. Pray fervently that God may give him light and prudence ! How happy I shall be, if he feels the same as I do ! If his judgment is that you are under no delusion, what acts of thanks I shall make to Our Lord !"

In his letter of January 4th, 1908, he tells her of Father Hamon's favourable impression and of his own sadness :

" I have seen Father Hamon on my way through Paris. What he has seen of your writings appears to him to be truly supernatural. His first impression was good. He admired the prayer for priests (" O Jesus, eternal High Priest ") very much and promised to keep the secret.

" I need hardly tell you that I am very sad. I feel that I am no longer of any use ; my strength is diminishing ; my activity is giving way to weakness, and it was never more necessary to work for the glory of God. Oh ! help me with your prayers, in order that I may not spoil the work of God too badly."

Mother Louise Margaret hastened to console him in the following beautiful letter written on January 8th :

" You say that it is needless to tell me that you are very sad. But on the contrary you should tell me. What is the cause of this sadness ? Sadness is never good ; it diminishes energy and paralyses all efforts to do good. We must not be sad, but always joyful in the service of our adorable Master. Are you sad because you are suffering ? Alas ! that you should be ! But suffering or complete exhaustion of our strength should not be a cause of sadness. It is a great source of joy to give our lives drop by drop for Jesus and in the end to feel that we have become worn out in His service and that we shall die for Him. Is the reason for your sadness because I told you that you have resisted Our Lord a little ? But, my dear good Father, in matters so delicate, and in things in which it is so difficult to find out the best course of action, this is only a very small fault in the eyes of the divine Master, and besides, it is a fault which was committed with such good intentions of humility and distrust in yourself, that Jesus cannot have been very much displeased with you. Is it, in fine, because living in the world, you see so much evil around you? God is able to draw good even from the excess of evil and, although He is much offended on earth, that does not prevent Him from being happy in heaven, because He is much loved."

CHAPTER VII.

THE SACRED HEART AND THE PRIESTHOOD

As we have already seen, Father Charrier ordered Mother Louise Margaret under obedience to write down the communications which she had received from Our Lord. He had in his possession for about thirteen years all these writings. They formed the material from which *The Sacred Heart and the Priesthood, The Book of Infinite Love,* and these new Volumes, now being published, were composed. The thoughts contained in these notes were most sublime, they were in perfect accord with Catholic teaching, and they appeared to be just what was suitable for the needs of the time. There was no reason then why some use should not be made of them, without pronouncing on the question whether they were inspired or not.

In May, 1903, Father Charrier wrote to Sister Louise Margaret :

" My dear child in Christ, I have read with edification and interest the thoughts which Our Lord has given you on the virtues of the priest. If it be the will of the Master, some use could be made of them."

Sister Louise Margaret replied :

" It seems to me to be the desire of Our Lord that the little extract which is to be made from them should be in very simple language without any attempt at style : that everything in it should be simple and humble like Jesus."

However, Father Charrier made no move for two years. In 1905 he wrote to her saying that he was thinking of preparing a little work on the Priesthood. He said that he was almost conquered by the " accent of truth " which he heard and the " seal of divine action " which he saw in all that she had written, and he asked her to pray that Our Lord would help him to overcome his doubts about His merciful intentions with regard to his own profound misery.

Nothing was done then : three years were to elapse before a serious attempt was made to give effect to Our Lord's wishes.

PROVIDENTIAL HAPPENINGS

Three events that happened in the January of 1908, which can hardly be called mere coincidences, co-operated in a marvellous manner in getting a beginning made to publish these communications.

During the month of January, 1908, Our Lord expressed His desire that a book be written as the first step towards establishing an organisation for priests ; in the same month, Father Charrier expressed his willingness to compose this book from the writings of Mother Louise Margaret which he had in his possession ; and in the same month, Father Hamon gave as his opinion to Father Charrier that a little book should be composed that would spread the ideas expressed in these writings.

The following is the letter of Mother Louise Margaret to Father Charrier, written January 18th, 1908 :

" My dear good Father, I have still something else which I must tell you. A few days ago while I was at prayer, **Our Lord showed me the immense desire which He has to be loved by His priests, whom He Himself loves as His dearest members. He wishes that they should all know that He has given them His Heart, and it seems to me that He demands that you write, or that you get someone else to write, a little book in which would be expressed all the desires that He has for His priests and all the effusions of His tenderness for them with the idea of founding this organisation** (which I have perhaps, understood so badly but which you understand better) **the object of which is to group them all around His Heart and in His Infinite Love ; that this little book should be presented to the Holy Father who, if he judges proper, would get the organisation founded according to his desires. It seems to me that the Master wishes this to be done this year and without further delay.**"

On January 23rd, 1908, Father Charrier proposed to write the book :

" My sadness has vanished. Your prayers have obtained for me this grace.

" I desire eagerly to compose the little book which you demand on the part of Our Lord. This had been my first thought in 1904, when during Lent I was contemplating doing something. I willingly return to this idea, but can I find the time ? The ideas for this work will be drawn completely from your notes. Thus I will be surer of not departing from what you consider to be demanded by Our Lord, and if the Holy See accepts it, Deo Gratias ! I shall be happy."

This letter was followed by another on February 10th, 1908 :

" Your writings are still in the hands of Father Hamon. I saw him on January 31st. He said to me : ' A little book must be composed that will spread the ideas expressed in these writings.' I have been so struck with this judgment so much in conformity with what you demand in your letter, that I have resolved to begin the work immediately after Easter. . . . . If you have a plan for the work, I ask you earnestly to communicate it to me, especially if it seems to come from the Master."

These letters expressed Father Charrier's good will, but his reluctance was not completely overcome. He had not yet begun the following April when he had the following extraordinary experience which he himself relates :

" I stopped at a convent in Turin to say Mass on April 20th, 1908. The Superioress gave me a note on which was written the following words : ' Our Lord wishes me to tell you that you should not delay any longer to do what He expects of you.' I asked to see the Sister who had sent this note to me and I questioned her as to what it meant. ' I do not know,' she replied, ' but at prayer this morning, Our Lord commanded me to tell you that.' I confess that I had the intention of refusing to do what Mother Louise Margaret had asked. From that moment, I resolved to work at the book."

In his letter of February 10th, Father Charrier had asked Mother Louise Margaret for a plan for the book, especially if it seemed to come from Our Lord. On February 17th, she sent him the following reply. The reply is interesting and important, firstly, because it gives the plan according to which she herself afterwards composed the book, and secondly, because it emphasises the fact that the book was a step towards the foundation of the Priests' Universal Union of the Friends of the Sacred Heart.

PLAN OF THE BOOK

" You ask me what I think about the plan for this little book. I think first of all that what you will do will be under the inspiration of the Master and that it will be good.   I must tell you, since you wish it, that when speaking of this with Our Lord yesterday at prayer, this thought has come to me :—

" It seems to me that it is Our Lord's desire that we should commence by saying that He has given His Heart to His priests, and that we should then point out how much He loves them, with what love of preference, and with what tenderness.   After that, we should say how priests can respond to this love of Jesus : namely, by loving Him, by imitating Him, by making His love known in the world, by continuing His very Person in themselves, by doing His work.   Then we should speak of the divine Work of Infinite Love, of this love which is, as it were, accumulated in the Heart of God, Who wishes that it be spread abroad in order to save the world, and Who wishes to make of the Priesthood a pure and sacred channel, through which It will pass, to bathe, purify and warm all souls.

" We should then deduce from this explanation the proof of what has been said at the commencement about the special gift of the Sacred Heart to priests, **and conclude by giving an idea of the organisation which will group the priests of the world around their bishops and around the Pope in order to form a chain of love with which to surround the world."**

Father Charrier, full of courage and good will, promised to begin work on the composition of the little book immediately.   He had already made out the plan for the first chapters.   Nevertheless, Mother Louise Margaret was under no delusion about the matter ; she knew his numerous and varied apostolic works of zeal, and in addition the difficulties of the task.   But Father was confident and full of promises.   The year, however, was to finish without anything being done.

The " Little Book " was constantly in her thoughts and in all her letters of this year she mentioned it.   On May 27th, 1908, she wrote to Father Charrier :

" Are you thinking always of the little book, my true and dear Father ?   You are thinking of priests ; of that I have no doubt ; I also am thinking of them and, in spite of pressure and multipliicity of business affairs which occupy me from morning to night, my soul all the same lives for them. I cannot think of the Heart of Jesus, and I think of It often, without thinking also of the heart of His mystical body, of the Priesthood, the true heart of the Church through which the blood of the Master should pass and in which His divine life should palpitate.

Father, you can do nothing more pleasing to the Sacred Heart of Jesus than work for His priests. Nothing is so pleasing also to the most Blessed Virgin, for she loves the Priesthood as the very Heart of her Jesus."

And on the following August 7th, she told him of the gracious promise made to her by Our Lord to help her, sustain her and direct her :

" Here I am on retreat near the good Master. Yesterday, He attracted me to Himself so strongly that I almost lost consciousness of things around me and I became completely absorbed in Infinite love.

" Since this, Our Saviour has, in a manner, effaced from my thoughts the memory of the business worries, cares, and inward pains which I suffered from latterly ; I am taken possession of by a repose of absolute confidence, and this morning, Jesus, drawing me to His Heart during holy Mass, said to me interiorly : ' Repose on me for all things, I am with you to help you, to sustain you and to direct you according to My will.' "

THE ENCYCLICAL OF POPE PIUS X ON THE PRIESTHOOD

By a Providential coincidence, it happened that while Mother Louise Margaret was receiving communications from Our Lord urging her to hasten the publication of *The Sacred Heart and the Priesthood*, His Holiness, Pope Pius X, composed and published his Encyclical to the priests of the world which contains so many ideas in common with *The Sacred Heart and the Priesthood* that it may be said to be a summary of it. The references to the end of the reign of Pius X and favourable judgment at Rome on her projects in the following letter are prophetic. Pius X lived just long enough to give his sanction to the establishment of the Priests' Universal Union of the Friends of the Sacred Heart and the foundation of the new monastery of the Visitation.

On August 12th, 1908, she wrote to Father Charrier :

" To-day I felt Our Lord to be very near me, attracting me strongly to Himself ; I felt that He wished either to communicate something to me or to get me to do something. I was well and I suffered at the same time for want of clear light. It was a state of suspense.

" In the afternoon I knew that Our Lord wished that, while giving myself to the Community as much as is necessary and as I am doing, it seems to me, I should also be entirely given to His priests."

PROPHETIC WORDS

" It seemed to me that the great anxiety which Community affairs have caused me for the past few months has drawn me away somewhat from my way of intercession for priests. After that, I became aware that it was high time for you to act, Father, that Jesus considered that we had delayed too long, **that the life of the present Pope (Pius X who died in 1914) would not be very long, that he himself was to arrange everything for the restoration of the Priesthood in Christ by love ; that the Pope should know about the effusions of Infinite Love and the special tenderness of the Heart of Jesus for priests.** While these lights were being given to me, which happened several times a day, I suffered and enjoyed pleasure at the same time as the result of an immense desire to labour and sacrifice myself for priests.

" I should also tell you, dear Father, that several times when conversing with very fervent priests or religious, I felt inclined to speak to them of Infinite Love and of the desires of Jesus for His priests ; but I have never done so. On such occasions I said to myself : no, it is Father who must speak, my part is to suffer and pray.

" This evening, when speaking of this to Our Lord, it seems to me that He said to me : ' he (Father Charrier) must speak first and commence the work, **but when the Pope has given judgment about everything and taken the matter in hand, then you can and must speak and communicate all that I shall give you."**

Father Charrier had not yet begun the composition of the book on September 18th, when Mother Louise Margaret wrote the following letter :

" In the midst of all these cares, I am happy, happy to give all the blood of my heart for my dear priests for whom I would wish so much to give my life. But I find it hard to see that you have no time to write.

The Encyclical of Pius X to priests has filled me with joy. One of our Sisters was astonished yesterday at the weight and number of the crosses which Jesus sends me, but she does not know that I must be a victim for priests. The good Master has placed me in charge only that I might suffer more and have the advantage of humiliation. I bless Him for it."

In the midst of all the turmoil caused by the installation of the Community at Mazze, Mother Louise Margaret found great consolation in the thought that Father Charrier was working at the little book. Indeed, his letters gave excellent promise ; we read in them :

" I am working most whole-heartedly at the little book that you know of."

In January, 1909, nearly a year after he had undertaken to compose the book, he wrote to her :

" You may rest assured that all my free time in this place is employed at the dear little book—

" The Master-piece of Infinite Love
—THE PRIESTHOOD—
" Appeal from the Heart of Jesus to His Priests."

" Does this title please you ? It is definite, and it seems to correspond with the thoughts in the book. Pray to Our Lord that He may help me to accomplish my purpose.

" The little remark in your letter touched me profoundly. Yes, you are right in thinking that Our Lord has chosen you, not to be a religious or a Superioress, but to be immolated for His priests. But first, be immolated for *your* priest, the poor man who is writing to you, in order that Our Lord may deign to have pity on his unfathomable misery and make him produce for Himself and others fruits of salvation and perfection."

Although the hopes expressed in the reply which Mother Louise Margaret wrote to him on January 19th were bound to be disappointed, it is interesting, because it shows that she wished to make sure that no change would be made in what she was persuaded was Our Lord's own message :

" I am very ignorant and it is quite possible that in what I have written or said to you, I may have made use of inaccurate terms. You will express these things very accurately and, with the help of your confreres, you will compose a very fine book theologically accurate. But if I have expressed my thoughts badly, will you be able to understand them? It seems to me, therefore, that it **would be advisable,** not from the theological view-point, but **from the viewpoint of the true desires of Our Lord that I should see your manuscript before it is printed.** It can easily happen that in correcting a wrong term or an ungrammatical phrase, that you may alter the meaning of the thought a little. When I have read it, I shall not tell you what to write. I am incapable of doing that, **but I shall tell you, perhaps, that here and there it is not altogether as Our Lord has said it.** It seems to me that Our Lord wished me to tell you this, but for the rest you will do as you judge best."

DIFFICULTIES AND DELAYS

Father Charrier, hindered by his numerous works of zeal, was always putting back the composition of the little book. Mother Louise Margaret, urged on to action by her interior lights, suffered from these delays. She expressed herself sadly to Father Charrier about it in a letter of April 14th, 1909 :

" . . . . . I suffer, Father (pardon me for telling you so), and it is because of you ! Your slowness causes me martyrdom ; I have to expiate your delays in meeting the wishes of Our Lord, in entering into His views, in realising His plan."

Father Charrier's reply, written on April 17th, shows that the final conclusion to which he came was justified ; that Providence did not intend him to compose the book, because the work which his Superiors gave him, left him no spare time.

In her letter of April 19th, Mother Louise Margaret tells him again of Our Lord's command to her to convey His message to His priests and of her own grief at having delayed so long in doing so :

" Perhaps I have caused you pain by my last letter ; pardon me, I pray you ; I would not wish to make you suffer ; but if you knew how much I suffer myself ! It seems to me, Father, that Our Lord is not pleased with me. It is seven years (it was in 1902) since He said to me : ' Show My Heart to My Priests,' seven years since, during the Octave of the Sacred Heart, He communicated His divine will and told me what He desires His priests to do, and what treasures of love which He has stored up for them in His divine Heart. Seven years ! and what have I done since then to accomplish His designs? What have I done to respond to His demand? You tell me that since Our Lord does not leave you the time to do what I ask of you, it shows that it is not His will that you do it. That is true ; but it puts me into another difficulty. Have I not been deceived? Is it not really you who were to help me in this work? I believe so ; but was it the confidence which I had in you that made me believe that you were the helper marked out by Jesus Himself? For seven years, perhaps through my own fault, I have been delaying the work of the Sacred Heart. Yes, it is true, it is not your fault ; but is it not mine? Two years ago, Our Lord gave me the heavy cross of superiorship ; was it not in order to give me more means to act, more liberty to do His work, more relations with the outside world in order to accomplish His desires? And I have done nothing. I feel an inward reproach in the depths of my heart, profound and sweet (for everything in Jesus is sweet, even His reproaches) saying to me : ' What have you done to manifest My Infinite Love to My priests ? ' And I have to answer, ' Nothing.' This night, Father, I wept for a long time in the dark at the feet of Jesus. I have not shed so many tears since the day when, two years ago at Revigliasco, I thought you were dead. I wept under the inward reproach of Jesus, thinking that perhaps all was due to my own infidelity. I thought, Father, that I should open my soul to none other than to you, to none other than to him who was to aid me in carrying out the desires of Jesus. Was I wrong? And now, Father, in the anguish which is choking me, what am I to do? Am I to reveal my soul and my trouble to Monsignor at the time of his visitation? Am I, Father, to seek light and counsel from another? I am alone on our hill of Mazze, far from all help, a prey to intense suffering ; I have need to seek counsel from someone. It seems to me that Jesus is saying to me interiorly : ' I have entrusted to you a treasure, the treasure of My Infinite Love, and you have buried it in the ground.' And this divine treasure of Love has been sleeping for the past seven years, and has remained unproductive.

" Oh ! Father, think, I pray you, of all this before Jesus ; think of the terrible responsibility I have in keeping this treasure of Love for myself alone. Tell me what I should do; whether I should open my heart to someone; tell me what I can do in my nothingness and weakness to please Jesus.

" I suffer much more from the reproaches of Jesus for not delivering His message to His priests than from all the other works and worries which I have. For the temporal and spiritual welfare of this dear family, it seems to me that I am doing practically everything in my power; for priests, to satisfy the desires of Jesus, I am doing nothing.

" I am suffering, it is true; but is it not suffering that Jesus wants from me? Yes, certainly, I would be very satisfied to suffer, if you would deliver Our Lord's message **You are doing a little in your preaching, but this great current of love which must pass through the priestly body, this new illumination of priests in Infinite Love,—where is it after seven years? and how can the Heart of the good Master be pleased with me? "**

FATHER CHARRIER'S DECISION

Father Charrier was profoundly moved by this letter. He delayed his reply until May 25th in the hope of being able to assure her that the book would soon be finished. Having written the letter announcing to her that he would have to relinquish the work, he waited until July 1st before posting it, in the hopes of being able to alter his decision :

" May 25th, 1909.

" I have waited, waited to reply to you, always hoping to be able to give you a satisfactory reply, favourable to your desires, and to my own—more than you can believe. I have been compelled to admit to myself that for want of time it would be impossible for me to compose the little book expected.

" If I were relieved of my very heavy missionary works, I could give my time to the book, as I most eagerly desire. It is a great heart-break for me not to be able to do this work. Thus I have sorrowfully resigned myself to tell you that you are free to seek someone else, and that I have at your disposal all your writings, which I have kept carefully, to hand them over to whomsoever you wish to indicate to me."

" July 1st, 1909

" I had hoped to be able to work at what you know ; and I would still hope, if I had not the sad experience of the past.

" I therefore go back to my decision of May 25th, namely, that I will give over your writings to whomsoever you tell me. I have only to excuse myself very humbly to you for giving you a hope which I have not been able to realise.

" Please write and tell me that you pardon me and believe that, in spite of this pitiful failure, of which, however, I can scarcely think myself to be guilty, I remain very united to you in the Sacred Heart.

" It will be a great heart-break to me to separate myself from my dear writings, but can I keep back a work, the importance of which I recognize ?"

On July 10th, 1909, Mother Louise Margaret sent him the following reply :

" You ask me to pardon you, I certainly do with all my heart, and I pray you, Father, to pardon me also if I have too long abused your patience and your goodness. A little later, if it pleases Our Lord, I shall write to you again ; in the meantime, be good enough to pray to the good Master for one who has so much need of prayers. Jesus wishes me to drink the chalice of all His sorrows, may He be blessed for it ; ask Him only to give me more courage and to increase my love for Him more and more."

Father Charrier arranged to send back all her papers, and gave further reasons to show that it had not been possible for him to compose the book :

" July 14th, 1909.

" I shall not be able to send you the packet of papers on the date indicated as you desire. I shall hold it at your disposal as soon as I return. Needless to say, it contains all your letters, all your writings, I do not think that there is a single one missing. Besides, I shall make it a matter of conscience to search for the smallest of your papers.

" I beg the good Master to give you the consolations of which you have need in the midst of the difficulties of all kinds which beset you. I beg Him to sustain you and enlighten you. I repent bitterly for not being able to make a better use of my time in view of the work to be done. I still continue to believe that it is not my fault, except in so far as I might have got some other person to help me besides the person whom I had first chosen, who was prevented by sickness. The desire of keeping the most absolute secrecy about this work prevented me from seeking some person of good will who might have been found. I shall not tell you of the inward pain which the reading of your letter caused me ; you understand it well."

FATHER POLLETTI'S PROVIDENTIAL VISIT

While Mother Louise Margaret was waiting for the reply from Father Charrier, which we have given above, Father Poletti, Superior of the Priest-Adorers of the Blessed Sacrament and Canonical Visitator to the Monastery, arrived. He was the proper person to give advice. His advice to do whatever Father Charrier would tell her was given while Father Charrier's letter was on the way.

The following is her account of that providential visit, written to Father Charrier on July 22nd, 1909 :

" Two years ago, Cardinal Richelmy delegated Father Poletti to make our canonical visitation. Since then I had seen him two or three times about temporal affairs ; however, while appreciating his exalted virtue, I had never spoken to him of the affairs of my soul. In the month of April, I wrote to you as your spiritual child, telling you about the sufferings of soul caused by the reproaches of Our Lord. You did not reply. The months which followed were for me months of painful agony and of trials of every kind ; not a word came from you to keep up my courage and light up my road; being unable to believe that you were indifferent, I thought that perhaps you had resolved not to write until you could announce to me that the little work was finished, for according to your previous letters, Father, I could justly conclude that it was much more advanced than it really was. On the eve of the Feast of the Sacred Heart, a card from Father Poletti announced that he was going to pass the whole of the following day here with us at Torretta. Was it not Our Lord Who sent him to me ? In the afternoon, on the Feast of the Sacred Heart itself, I saw Father in the parlour, and was interiorly inspired to open to him my soul, which was crushed and weary. From this confession I got a repose of mind and a peace which I had not tasted for a long time. Some days later, Father wrote to me saying that I should write to you very simply what I had told him and do what you would tell me. I was about to reply to Father Poletti that you knew everything already, that in March and April I had written to you absolutely everything that I had told him, when your letter of July 1st reached me. It broke my heart. I sent it to Father Poletti who replied to me : ' If I can help you in any way to carry out your dear trust, I am at your disposal. Allow Father Charrier to send you back your writings, read them again, put them in order ; and then if it be the will of the good Master, send them to your servant.' For my part, I did not wish to come to a decision on anything by myself ; is it not by the voice of others that we best find the will of God ?"

FATHER CHARRIER'S OPINION ON MOTHER LOUISE MARGARET AND HER WRITINGS

On July 25th, 1909, Father Charrier wrote to Father Poletti giving him his opinion of Mother Louise Margaret and her writings :

" I am sending back to Mother Louise Margaret, writings which I had thought I could utilise, but which for want of time, and probably because I was not worthy to do this work, I have not utilised as I desired.

" The following is my judgment on this whole matter, which, alas ! carries little authority :

" (1) I have never found anything in Sister Louise Margaret which was not in keeping with a good Religious, sincerely devoted to God.

" (2) I have found nothing in any of her writings which did not appear to me to be in conformity with sound theology ; and I have often been astonished at the fact that in her writings on most profound and sometimes very difficult matters she has always remained orthodox. Although she does not employ the terms used in the Schools, she seems to me never to employ an expression which cannot be fully justified.

" (3) I have long doubted about the certainty of the desires of Our Lord with reference to the work demanded. The principal reason for my doubt arose from the role that was attributed to me in this work and of which I felt myself to be more than unworthy.

" (4) I have got Father Hamon, the author of the recent life of St. Margaret Mary, to read all the writings and all the letters ;

he was of the opinion that a little book drawn from these writings should be composed, an anonymous work which God would make redound to His glory, if He was really the Author of the communications received by Mother Louise Margaret.

" (5) Now, without pronouncing a judgment which I have no right to pronounce, **I think that since our Lord does not leave me the time to compose the little work, the reason is that I was not to do it.**

" (6) I restricted myself to getting the Prayer for Priests, *Jesus Eternal High Priest,* published and having it indulgenced at Rome through the intermediary of the Bishop of Grenoble.

" These are, Rev. Father, ideas with which, it appears to me, I ought to furnish you on the writings which will be sent on to you.

" I shall be entirely at your disposal to give you all other information which may be useful to you."

On July 26th, Father Charrier wrote a second letter to Father Poletti.

" JULY 26th, 1909

" It is indeed true that I do not pass judgment on the divine origin of the communications received by Mother Louise Margaret. But the sole reason is because I have not the right to do so ; **only the authority of the Church can pronounce judgment on so delicate a matter. It none the less remains true that as a private individual I believe in this origin, because I have always found in the manner in which these communications have taken place and in their very nature, such marks as, after long hesitation, have enabled me to reassure the Sister and sustain her, perhaps not as much as I ought to have.**

" I cannot tell you the joy it gives me to hear that you are going to commence the work. With all my heart I pray Our Lord to bless it, and with my whole soul I ask Him to grant you abundant light to enter fully into the designs of His Infinite Love."

Mother Louise Margaret accepted Father Charrier's decision with resignation and wrote to him on July 27th, 1909, telling him of the great sorrow which it caused her :

" You cannot imagine, Father, the immense sorrow that your letter of July 3rd caused me. I so little expected the decision which you took to send me back my papers.

" Doubtless, the good Master has permitted all that. I plunge it into His infinitely bountiful Heart, and I beg Him to pardon us if we have been wanting in fidelity to Him. If He judges us unworthy of His graces, He will transfer them to others."
But still another cross was waiting for her, for on September 5th, Father Poletti announced to her his decision that she herself would have to compose the book :
" I take this occasion to send you back your dear writings safely. I have not been able to read them all, nevertheless, I have got from them sufficient knowledge to conclude that they will do good to priests. **To complete them and put them in form for the printer cannot, however, be the work of any other hand, or come from any other heart** but that of the person who has received these communications from her divine Spouse. Then, with the help of Jesus in the Blessed Sacrament, commence work and compose a perfect little book worthy of the Sacred Heart of Jesus, Who is the Author of these communications, and worthy of the priests for whom it is destined. Let your little book be simple and clear, well-ordered, full of life, presenting a general view of your subject and well connected. I pray for this myself and am having prayers offered for the same intention."

" THE LITTLE BOOK OF WHICH JESUS IS THE SOLE AUTHOR "

Mother Louise Margaret accepted Father Poletti's decision and commenced work on the book. In a letter written to Father Charrier on the following December 14th, she gives her reasons : " You know that in giving you all my papers for the past thirteen years I had but one desire : to allow you to do everything . . . . taking for myself the privilege of praying and suffering in obscurity. The good Master decided otherwise when He inspired you to send me back everything, and when Father Poletti and Father Choupin assured me that no one else but myself should undertake and finish the work of the book." In a few months, she had classified her notes, drawn up the general plan and finished the composition of *The Sacred Heart and the Priesthood*.
The little volume is composed of four parts.
I The Priest, the creation of Infinite Love. (Jesus teaching, Jesus pardoning, Jesus consoling, Jesus offering sacrifice.)

II   The Sacerdotal Virtues of the Heart of Jesus.

III The Love of the Incarnate Word for Priests.

IV   Sublime Reflections on Infinite Love and the Priesthood.

Mother Louise herself recognised that she had put nothing in the book which she had not received from Jesus in prayer. However, it was agreed that nothing should be said in the work which would indicate a supernatural origin. There should not even be mention of the organisation for priests contemplated and desired. It was a simple appeal to priests that would prepare the way for the organisation which was to group them around the Pope and bishops in a common bond of fraternal charity.

On October 8th she was able to announce to Father Charrier that progress was being made :

> " The book is making slow progress ; however, it is going ahead. Father Poletti wished that I should correct and finish certain parts that are incomplete and I am working at them, while one of our Sisters is copying what is ready. The little work will be very simple, with no straining after effect ; **It will be such as Jesus has prepared it.**"

She never for a moment attributed a single idea in the book to herself. In her next letter she speaks of it as **"the little book of which Jesus is the Sole Author."** It never even occurred to her to consult any of the books on the devotion to the Sacred Heart to guide her in the composition of *The Sacred Heart and the Priesthood.*

When later on, in May, 1911, Monsignor Filipello asked her what books she had read on the devotion to the Sacred Heart, she replied :

> " Father Charrier preferred that I should not read any, and my Superiors gave me none. Since I have become Superioress, I have had very little time to read anything for myself. During the past few years I got the life of St. Margaret Mary by Father Hamon read in the refectory ; I found it very interesting. I got a work of Father Tesnière on the Blessed Eucharist and the Sacred Heart read also."

Father Charrier was at Mazze on October 25th and 26th. He agreed then to revise the work, to verify the references from Scripture and to take charge of the publication of the French edition. He undertook also to write the preface.

On October 31st, 1909, she wrote to him giving him instructions about the preface and stating that Jesus was the sole author of the book :

" As I have told you, I saw Father Poletti on Thursday. He thinks that it is right and proper that there should be a French edition and that this edition should precede the Italian and all other editions. His opinion, that of Father Choupin and my own humble opinion is, that nothing extraordinary, nothing which would even vaguely indicate a revelation should appear in the first editions of this work. If then, Father, you are composing the preface, do not put anything in it suggesting a supernatural origin. **If this little book, of which Jesus is the sole author, makes its way in souls, we shall see about saying more on that question in the subsequent editions.**

I believe, dear Father, that Our Lord wishes that the revelation of His Infinite Love and the gift of His divine Heart to priests, be universal. I believe that Our Lord, Who has tender sentiments for France, as the eldest daughter of His Church, has been pleased to choose from France the first two instruments of His work of Love, you and my own unworthy self. I believe also that this good Master has marked out in other countries other instruments who, entering in their turn into the work of love, will labour for its extension throughout the world."

When he had finished the preface, Father Charrier submitted it to Mother Louise Margaret on December 4th and promised to undertake the composition of another book. In his letter he writes :

" What do you think of the phrase in the preface, which presents the little book as a gift from the Heart of Jesus, to His priests and which reveals to them the doctrine of Infinite Love ? What do you think of this other phrase which gives a vague promise of another more extensive work ? I shall begin to prepare this work after the publication of the little book : guided by the order adopted in the book and aided by your writings, all of which you will send back to me, I shall prepare a manuscript which perhaps will not see the light until after my death and yours, and which will give an exact idea of the desires of Our Lord on the subject of **Infinite Love, a doctrine which completes, enlarges and elevates the devotion to the Sacred Heart, forming but one with it, however, and being distinguished from it as the perfume from the flower which produces it.**"

In her letter to Father Charrier of November 16th, 1909, Mother Louise Margaret expressed the wish that he should present the book to His Holiness, Pius X, and should take advantage of the occasion to speak of the Work of Infinite Love to the Pope.

" I confess to you that the inmost desire of my soul is that it is you who should take it to Rome ; you who should present it to the Pope ; and that when presenting it you should speak of the idea of the Work and have it approved and blessed. Pius X already knows something of the desires of Infinite Love with regard to priests ; he knows that a little book is being prepared giving a first idea of this."

Father Charrier was unable to go to Rome. Mother Louise Margaret then wished him to compose a letter of explanation to be presented with the book. In her letter of December 14th to him she tells how she would have wished to remain hidden and unknown.

" If then you do not go to Rome, either you or I shall compose a letter of explanation, which we shall have presented to the Holy Father with the book. **The Pope already knows, though not in great detail, the demands of Our Lord and His desires with regard to priests ; he knows that it is the unworthy Rev. Mother of the Visitation, now in exile at Mazze, who has received these communications ;** he knows that this Rev. Mother has a Director who, after seven years waiting, is putting her writings in order for presentation to His Holiness. The Pope is awaiting fuller explanation of all this and the book that has been announced.
" You know, Father, that in giving you all my papers for the **past thirteen years** I had but one desire ; it was to allow you to do everything that was to be done, without any interference from me, taking for my part the privilege of praying and suffering in obscurity. The good Master decided otherwise when He inspired you in May and July to send me back everything, and

when Father Poletti and Father Choupin assured me that no one else but myself should undertake and finish the work of the book. By taking these papers out of your hands and placing them in mine, and by getting these two Fathers to tell me the same thing, Jesus has shown me, that His will is that I should continue to work, and that, if He does not wish to deprive you of the grace of labouring at His Work of love, nevertheless, He does not wish you to work alone. Now, not only must I assist you in the small measure of my capacity, but you will have other co-operators, not chosen by you but by the Master Himself.

"I cannot express to you how much I suffer to be obliged to speak myself of all this, to take charge of it and to see so many people acquainted with our affairs. All this might have been avoided, and I might have died without anyone but my Director knowing the secret of my soul, if you had willed it."

MONSIGNOR FILIPELLO PRESENTS THE BOOK TO POPE PIUS X

On June 10th, 1910, His Excellency Monsignor Filipello presented *The Sacred Heart and the Priesthood* to the Sovereign Pontiff in the following terms :

"Bishop's House,

Ivrea,

"June 17th, 1910

"Most Holy Father,

"Divine Providence, which always draws good from evil, has brought about that the persecution let loose these latter years in France against Religious Congregations resulted in transplanting into my dear diocese a choice family of the Order of the Visitation which Your Holiness praised in the Brief of December 13th last.

"Each Sister of the Community of which I speak diffuses the perfume of virtue. This is not to be wondered at, for this Community has as Superioress, a Rev. Mother who is a worthy daughter of the glorious Bishop of Geneva, a true emulator of the piety of St. Margaret Mary Alacoque.

" You will find, Most Holy Father, the confirmation of what
I say in the book : *The Sacred Heart and the Priesthood* which
I come to present to you. It has been composed from manu-
scripts written some years ago.

" In your sweet and gentle goodness, Most Holy Father, deign
to accept the filial homage which this pious Religious offers to
you, as well as this book which is the fruit of her love for Our
Lord and of her zeal for souls. And may your blessing obtain
that this book bear precious fruits of sanctity in priests to whom
it is addressed, and particularly in this Bishop and the dear priests
of his diocese where is now situated the Garden which the
author of this book cultivates, and which diffuses among us the
good odour of Jesus Christ.

" For myself and for all my dear children, kissing your sacred
feet, I implore the Apostolic Blessing and I profess myself

the most humble, most devoted and
most respectful servant and son of
Your Holiness,

✠ Matthew, Bishop."

His Holiness, Pius X, sent the following gracious reply through
his Cardinal Secretary of State, Cardinal Merry del Val :

" The Holy Father has received with particular favour the
presentation copy of the book entitled *The Sacred Heart and
the Priesthood*, furnished with the approval and encouragement
of ecclesiastical authority.

" The subject matter of the book is worthy of the deepest
interest. It contains an exposition of the sublime relations of
intimacy and love between the Heart of Jesus and the heart of
the priest, and of the touching harmonies between the Heart
of Jesus and the Priesthood ; it recounts all that the Divine Master
has done for those whom He calls ' His friends ' ; it lays before
the priest the necessity of forming his heart and inspiring his
life by this ineffable model of the Heart of Jesus.

" Sacerdotal souls, as well as souls exercised in the interior
life and formed in solid piety, will find in these pages edifying
and salutary considerations.

" The Holy Father, while praying Our Lord to bless this little book and crown it with precious fruit, sends the author a special blessing as a pledge of abundant heavenly favours.

" I unite my sincere thanks for the copy of the book which has been graciously presented to me, and I pray you to accept the expression of my devoted sentiments in Our Lord.

" R. CARDINAL MERRY DEL VAL."

The book has been translated into Italian, German, Polish, Dutch, Spanish, Croatian, Roumanian, English and Chinese. The Apostolic Benediction of the reigning Popes has followed the book into all the countries into whose language it has been translated. His present Holiness, Pius XII, has given a special blessing to the translator into English, for introducing the book and the Priests' Universal Union of the Friends of the Sacred Heart into Ireland England and America.

In her Intimate Notes of February 19th, 1910, Mother Louise Margaret wrote :

" Jesus communicated Himself to me this evening with divine abundance : He said to me : ' I am content.' How sweet these words were to me ! This adorable Master deigns to be content with the poor work of the little book. To see Jesus content and to hear Him say so is more than sufficient recompense for forty years of suffering and twenty years of martyrdom. I do not know whether this inward joy may not be the prelude of some great sorrow. Provided He is content and that He obtains His glory, that is sufficient for me."

CHAPTER VIII

THE ACT OF CONSECRATION AND DONATION TO INFINITE LOVE

JESUS DEMANDS THE ACT OF DONATION

This act of complete donation of themselves to Infinite Love was first demanded by Our Lord from Mother Louise Margaret and Father Charrier, as a condition for becoming His instruments in diffusing His message of love and mercy throughout the world. It has since become the official act by which priests are admitted to The Priests' Universal Union of the Friends of the Sacred Heart. Our Lord promised Mother Louise Margaret very special favours for making this act of donation.

In her Intimate Notes of 1904, she writes :

" After Holy Communion, Jesus appeared to me and said : ' When My servant and you will be completely given to Love by the consecration which I have demanded of you, it will be no longer on My Heart that I shall make you repose ; I shall make you penetrate into It. I shall introduce you into a mysterious dwelling of which you do not yet know. You will be enlightened by a living light on the nothingness of your being and of your own actions. Then, elevated above what is sensible, you will understand the mysteries of Love of which you are now ignorant. You will see that I am everything in all things and everything in you. Suffering may be able to reach you, but you will experience a plenitude of peace which you have not yet tasted.' "

Mother Louise Margaret, being firmly persuaded that it was Our Lord's wish that Father Charrier should make this act of donation of himself to Infinite Love, urged him repeatedly to make it ; but he hesitated for years giving as reasons his own unworthiness and his fear of not being faithful to it.

On November 13th and December 19th, 1909, respectively,

she wrote him the following very urgent letters, but it took two years more to persuade him to take the step. The correspondence is important because it brings out clearly the nature of the act and the great graces attached to it.

" November 19th, 1909

" As for the Work which our Lord demands, I think you would do well to think over it seriously. It is you who are to be the soul of this Work, and it would cost me much to see another take your place in the plan of Our Lord. However, that could happen for the Work, as it very nearly happened for the little book, if you are wanting in responding to the desires of Jesus. Our Lord is sovereignly good and patient, but when the instrument which He has first chosen remains inactive or escapes from His hand, He takes another, quite simply, and continues His work. Pardon me, Father, if I speak to you thus. I believed I saw, and that very clearly, that you were the instrument chosen by Jesus to commence His work of love, and how my heart bleeds at the thought that you might, by hesitating too long, lose this privilege. I thought I understood this, it is true, and **I found it again lately in a writing dating back some years, that this work should be first spread abroad in a foreign country before it should come to France ; however, it has always seemed to me that it was to commence in France and that you were to be the soul of it.**"

" December 19th, 1909

" Our Lord can do His Work without either you or me ; He has chosen us without our having merited this choice ; if we are unfaithful, He may withdraw the privileges and gifts which He has conferred on us first and give them to others."

FATHER CHARRIER'S REASONS FOR HESITATING AND MOTHER LOUISE MARGARET'S REPLY

In two letters written during the same month, Father Charrier gives his reasons for postponing the making of the act. The first was written on December 4th, 1909 :

" As for this act of donation of which I speak, I have never refused to make it. If I shrink from it, or rather if I have shrunk from it, it is because I felt myself to be too unworthy. Latterly, Our Lord seems to be granting me such graces that I am less reluctant, and while sinking down into the abyss of my profound misery, thanks to His grace, I feel myself a little less unworthy. Doubtless, I owe it to the prayers which you are saying for me. Thus I think that the year 1910 will not pass without this act being accomplished which will consecrate me entirely to Infinite Love. I feel myself very much attracted towards it ; and if I still hesitate, it is through fear of giving Our Lord only a tepid Heart and a languid soul, things which are repugnant to Him ; but perhaps it may be either cowardice or fear of the sacrifices which this act involves that is keeping me back. I cannot very well distinguish."

The second letter was written on December 21st, 1909.

" The act which you have been so long asking me to make to Infinite Love has not been made because I felt myself too unworthy. I have a horror that I might deceive Our Lord if I made the act demanded ; and I still hesitate because if I make it, I am firmly resolved, to bind myself absolutely ; and I do not yet see clearly enough what obligations will result from this act."

Mother Louise Margaret wrote the following reply on December 23rd, 1909 :

" Father, when Our Lord said to St. Peter : ' Lovest thou Me more than these ? " (John xxi, 15) there were many unknown mysteries of suffering for the Apostle in that question. He did not make much preparation, he did not make long reflections on the import of his reply ; he did not insist on seeing just to what he was going to bind himself, he did not put forward his own unworthiness. He replied straight out in a generous outburst from his heart, without calculation and without fear. Jesus had said to you : ' I have chosen you to propagate My Infinite Love, I entrust to you Its treasures. Are you willing to love Me more than others ? Are you willing to do more than others for My Love ? ' He expected you to reply by a total and absolute consecration to this Love."

On April 10th, she insists again on the necessity of the act of donation and on the marvellous effects it will produce :

" Infinite Love must be the supreme Master of our souls, It must rule them according to Its desires, It must make them carry out Its designs without any consideration, however good in appearance, being able to induce us to resist. Yes, I can understand your dread. Our poor human nature shrinks from being delivered up to Infinite Love, because we must lose our own being to such an extent in this divine fire, we must to such a degree do what we should never have wished to do, and so go beyond the possible and the feasible.

" Our Lord has no need of our action to accomplish His work ; He wishes merely to make use of our sufferings . . . . He takes them and unites them to His own and He operates prodigies by means of this divine mixture ; just as He did when He cured the blind man by mixing a little clay with His saliva and applying this mixture to the sightless eyes."

When in two of his letters to Mother Louise Margaret, Father Charrier in his humility alleged his own misery and unworthiness as a reason why he hesitated about making a total consecration and donation of himself to Infinite Love, she sent him the following beautiful replies :

" May 24th, 1910

" I cannot tell you what pain the latter part of your letter has given me. It is impossible for me to understand how your misery can be beyond the reach of the power of God. But, Father, your misery, my own, and that of the whole world are but atoms in comparison with Infinite Love and Divine Power. If I thought for a moment that my misery was greater than the mercy of God or beyond the reach of His power, I believe that I should be committing the greatest sin of my life.

" As for me, my confidence in God grows greater every day and my faith in sweet Providence increases from all the evidences of protection which we receive."

" June 10th, 1910

"Do you see, Father, that if you consent to make the act which Jesus demands (which is nothing else but an act of love and absolute confidence in Our Lord), you will have all possible facilities to make a success of the little book, and the Master will be pleased. On the other hand, I am persuaded that if you do not decide to make this act, you will not even succeed in making a success of your preface. Just say ' yes ' to Jesus once for all and you will not be sorry for it. He is so good ! It is an insult to Him to be afraid lest the obligation which you undertake with Him may prove too heavy. And as for these ideas of unworthiness which are paralysing you and preventing you from making acts of the love of God, they can be nothing else but temptations of the devil."

FATHER CHARRIER FINALLY CONSENTS

More than a year later, on January 5th, 1912, Father Charrier announced to her the good news that " he had given all to the Master without any reservation " :

" **I made my retreat which ended a little before Christmas, then on Christmas night I made the act of donation to Infinite Love with great consolation.** I am happy to have given all to the Master without any reservation whatsoever. Why have I made Him wait so long? Oh, would that my blood might not be too unworthy to flow for His glory."

And on January 11th Mother Louise Margaret replied :

" I cannot tell you how happy your last excellent letter has made me, announcing to me that you have finally done what Our Lord has so long desired you to do. I am confident that this complete and absolute donation of yourself to Infinite Love is going to be for you a source of new graces of incomparable value. It seems that the obstacle that came between us during the past few years has disappeared, and that in a complete blending of thoughts, sentiments and action, we shall be able to work together and with all our strength spread throughout the world the knowledge of Infinite Love, which is its life and its salvation because it is its principle and its end.

" Henceforward, we must forget ourselves completely, setting aside our own interests, our own judgment, our own desires and become the docile instruments of Infinite Love, Which wishes to do everything Itself and employs us only the better to show Its divine power and skill.

" When God acts on nothing, His divine power encounters no obstacles, it is free, but when it acts on a creature, or when it employs a creature in some work, it often encounters resistance in the will or in the passions of this creature.

" God has deigned that in this work of Infinite Love creatures should serve as instruments, and He has consented to see His creatures resist and cause long delays on His adorable designs . . . .

" Should not this thought make our hearts melt with love for this great God, good like a father who allows his work to be delayed and spoiled by his little child incapable of helping him."

Finally, during her retreat of July, 1912, she sees this act of donation as the bond which is to unite the priests of the world.

" To be *one* is to have one same thought, one same aspiration, one same impulse.   In order that all the priests of the world form but *one,* they must be united in one same will, one same act ; they must have a spiritual place of meeting where they can find each other.   This place of meeting will be the Sacred Heart of Jesus ; the act which will unite them to each other and all together to God, Infinite Love, will be an act of complete and entire consecration and donation to the Sacred Heart of Jesus Christ, tabernacle of Infinite Love."

The following is the formula for this act of donation to Infinite Love composed by Mother Louise Margaret.

1—ACT OF CONSECRATION AND DONATION OF ONESELF TO INFINITE LOVE

O Infinite Love, Eternal God, Principle of life, Source of being, I adore Thee in Thy sovereign Unity and in the Trinity of Thy Persons.

I adore Thee in the Father, omnipotent Creator Who has made all things.   I adore Thee in the Son, eternal Wisdom by Whom all things have been made, the Word of the Father, incarnate in time in the womb of the Virgin Mary, Jesus Christ, Redeemer and King.   I adore Thee in the Holy Ghost, substantial Love of the Father and the Son, in Whom are light, strength and fruitfulness.

I adore Thee, Infinite Love, hidden in all the mysteries of our Faith, shedding Thy beneficent rays in the Blessed Eucharist, overflowing on

Calvary and giving life to the Church by the channels of the Sacraments, I adore Thee throbbing in the Heart of Jesus, Thine ineffable Tabernacle, and I consecrate myself to Thee.

I give myself to Thee without fear with the fullness of my will ; take possession of my being, penetrate it entirely. I am but a nothing, powerless to serve Thee, it is true, but it is Thou, Infinite Love, Who hast given to this nothing and Who dost draw it to Thee.

Behold me then, O Jesus, come to do Thy work of love : to labour to the utmost of my capacity in bringing to Thy priests, and through them to the entire world, the knowledge of Thy mercies and of the sublime and tender love of Thy Heart.

I wish to accomplish Thy will, whatever it may cost me ; even to the shedding of my blood, if my blood be not unworthy to flow for Thy glory.

O Mary, Immaculate Virgin whom Infinite Love has rendered fruitful, it is by thy virginal hands that I give and consecrate myself.

Obtain for me the grace to be humble and faithful, and to devote myself without reserve to the interests of Jesus Christ Thy adorable Son and to the glory of His Sacred Heart !

Pope Pius XI granted the following indulgences to members for the recitation of this prayer : 300 days toties quoties ; plenary once a month, if recited daily.

CHAPTER IX

MONSIGNOR FILIPELLO AND THE ESTABLISHMENT OF THE ORGANISATION DEMANDED BY OUR LORD

Monsignor Matthew Filipello was born at Castlenuove, the birthplace of the great educator and Saint, Don Bosco. Young Matthew had the privilege of speaking to him several times and received his last blessing on January 30th, 1888, the eve of the death of the Saint. He was ordained priest in 1881, and after many years of fruitful work in the parish of St. Francis de Sales, Turin, he was appointed Bishop of Ivrea in 1898. During his long reign of nearly forty years, he was beloved by his priests and acquired a well-merited reputation for sound judgment, prudence and sanctity. On one occasion in 1926, when Monsignor Calabrose, Bishop of

Aosto, was asked his opinion about Mother Louise Margaret and the communications that she received, he replied : " If Monsignor Filipello approves of them, you can trust his judgment, for, in matters of this kind, he takes nothing for granted "

When, in November, 1908, Mother Louise Margaret wrote to him for permission to transfer her Community to Mazze which was under his jurisdiction, he welcomed the exiles to his diocese and paid a personal visit to them on the following January. In April, 1909, when he made his canonical visitation, he asked Mother Louise Margaret to get the Community to pray much for priests, and told her that he had an ardent desire to do something for them in honour of the Sacred Heart Mother Louise Margaret was profoundly moved and, in this solicitude for priests which he shared with her, she saw the hand of Providence. She eagerly assured him of the prayers of the Community and told him that one of the Sisters was very specially interested in this subject. When the Bishop asked her for more precise information, she gave him some of her Intimate Notes dealing with the love of the Heart of Jesus for His priests. Monsignor Filipello took them home, examined them at leisure, meditated on them, and soon declared that he was completely satisfied with them. Not only were the views expressed in these notes in conformity with his own, but they went far beyond them. At his next visit to Mazze, he asked Mother Louise Margaret to send him the Sister who had written these notes, and she, blushing with confusion, could only reply : " My Lord, she is here before you." He recognised that there was something great and mysterious in all this, but he prudently abstained from speaking to her about the subject for a whole year.

MONSIGNOR FILIPELLO DESIGNATED BY OUR LORD TO DIRECT THE WORK

During this time, Mother Louise Margaret was favoured with a communication from Our Lord about the person who was to direct His work. This she wrote to Father Charrier on December 10th, 1909 :

" This morning, during Holy Mass, I prayed and it seems to me, if I am not mistaken, that Our Lord has already designated someone for this Work. This person whom I do not know, is, it seems to me, a priest of the secular clergy. This priest will get his inspiration and impulse from you and from my papers. It is he who will direct the Work ; you and I shall remain hidden. Perhaps the little book will discover this priest who, seeing your name at the end of the preface, will go to you and enter into your views. We must allow Jesus to make the decision."

And on December 19th of the same year, she wrote again to him :

" As for the Work, dear Father, Jesus will do what is necessary. When the priest of whom I think I got a glimpse appears, he will come and receive from you all that the good Master has given us for this. You will be, I hope from the goodness of the Heart of Jesus, the spiritual founder of this Work of Love ; but, Father, I conjure you with all the filial affection which Jesus has given me for your soul, to be faithful in responding to the desires of Infinite Love."

As the time for the foundation of the Work of Infinite Love was drawing near, Our Divine Lord gave further signs to Mother Louise Margaret by which she could recognise the person whom He had chosen. On November 1st, 1910, she wrote to Monsignor Filipello : " The will of the good Master with regard to this Work seems to be revealing itself, and to be indicating that it is to be founded by a Bishop and a priest of the secular clergy."

The further sign given to her by which she would recognise the choice of Our Lord was that the priest who would be the first to consecrate and donate himself to Infinite Love was to be the founder. Now among the papers submitted to Monsignor Filipello by Mother Louise Margaret was the formula drawn up by her for the act of consecration and donation to Infinite Love, without any request or thought that he should make it. Great was her joy when she received the following letter from Monsignor Filipello :

" October 10th, 1910

" I thank you, Rev. Mother, for sending me a copy of your act of consecration to Jesus, Infinite Love. I am pleased with it, and if you consent, I shall keep it for myself. Would that I might be able to give myself totally to Jesus, Our Lord and Master,

Father Alfred Charrier, S.J.

Mother Louise Margaret

less by words than by acts, by works of virtue and annihilation of my own will."

On the following November 26th she told him that she had reason to believe that he was the Bishop marked out by Our Lord :

" I must tell your Excellency in all filial confidence a thing which I am sure will give you much pleasure. For many years past I have had an interior consciousness that the first priest who would consecrate himself to Infinite Love would found the Work demanded by the divine Heart of Jesus. For six years, Father Charrier has not been able to make up his mind to do this ; a thousand fears held him back. It was in vain that I asked him ; he did not dare to throw himself into the arms of Love. And so, Venerable Father, how great has been my consolation on seeing you in your goodness so willingly welcome this thought which I left to the good Master to suggest to the person whom He would choose."

In the meantime, Monsignor Filipello had been studying the writings of Mother Louise Margaret and getting all necessary information from her. He had been prompted to make these enquiries by reading *The Sacred Heart and the Priesthood*, which, he understood, was intended as a step towards something else.

On October 3rd, he wrote to her :

. . . . " Who knows but the Work will commence at Ivrea ? In my unworthiness, I dare not hope for so much. However, Mother, would it not be possible to formulate a programme for the Work ; to state briefly the end of the organisation, the means it will make use of, etc. ?

" From your ' Intimate Notes ' which I am at present reading, I see some information on this question here and there. If you would be so good as to write out in a few pages all that there is on this subject, perhaps we should be able to commence something practical."

A week later, on October 10th, 1910, Mother Louise Margaret, in obedience to his wishes sent Monsignor Filipello the following letter :

MOTHER LOUISE MARGARET GIVES MONSIGNOR FILIPELLO
A SUMMARY OF THE COMMUNICATION SHE RECEIVED

" As to my poor writings which I sent to you, I pray Your Excellency to use full liberty in questioning me or having me questioned on everything which you believe necessary. I shall reply with the most entire, filial confidence. Doubtless, it will cost me much to speak or write on a subject which concerns the inmost thoughts of my soul ; but I desire above all the accomplishment of the Will of Our Lord and the consolation of His Divine Heart.

" As I think I have already told Your Excellency, for several years the interior lights which I have received at prayer had reference solely to the Infinite Love of God, or rather to Infinite Love, God Himself ; and I felt that these lights and teachings were not given for myself alone. I was, it seemed to me, like a channel by which this Love would pass on its way to souls.

" In June, 1902, on the Feast of the Sacred Heart and during the seven following days, Our Lord favoured me with communications in quite a particular manner. Your Excellency will find among my papers a little double sheet of paper on which is written down all that was given to me during these eight days. Afterwards, and in the following years, other lights were given to me to the same purport, and they are written on the papers entrusted to your Excellency and on some others which are here.

" It was at the end of this Octave in June, 1902, that the Idea of an organisation for priests was communicated to me. I had always handed over my papers faithfully to Father Alfred Charrier, S.J., and in 1904 he seemed decided on undertaking something in response to the desires of Jesus. But, seized with terror at the sight of his own unworthiness, and being reluctant to believe that it was he whom Our Lord had called to establish this work, he did not dare to go forward. He wished to compose the little book and promised to begin work immediately. As his spiritual child, I pressed him, for Our Lord urged me interiorly, but time and courage were always wanting to him.

" In March, 1909, it seemed to me that Our Lord complained that nothing had been done. Indeed, almost seven years had elapsed since Jesus made His demands. I transmitted these complaints to Father Alfred Charrier and feeling myself suffering,

I wrote a letter to the Sovereign Pontiff. It was doubtless great audacity, but I suffered so much from the complaints of Jesus and I had no other course open to me. I enclose the rough draft of the letter which I wrote to His Holiness. However, after more than two months of interior struggles, in July, 1909, Father Charrier, overcome by discouragement, sent me back my papers and told me to entrust them to someone else. I then gave them to Father Poletti, who, having given only a hurried glance over them, told me that I myself should finish and prepare for publication the writings suitable to form a book.

" As your Excellency sees, the work has not yet been commenced; some months ago I had a communication to the effect that it was not to be a Religious who should direct it, and I wrote to Father Charrier.

" I think, Most Reverend Father, that I have replied to all the questions asked in the letter of Your Excellency. As to the Work, I have such fear of mixing up my own mind and ideas with the mind and ideas of Our Lord, that I have never dared to formulate anything definite. I am so ignorant and wretched, and it is so easy to mix one's own ideas with supernatural communications. However, I shall tell Your Excellency in all simplicity that **it seems to me that Jesus wishes an organisation that will unite priests,—the good and faithful ones, those who are truly attached to sound doctrine,—and group them around their bishop in each diocese and that all the dioceses be linked together and grouped around the Pope,** the headquarters of the organisation being wherever the Pope resided. The priests of this organisation (which would not be merely a work of prayer like that of Father Eymard but an active work) would labour in the spirit of the little book to diffuse the knowledge of Infinite Love around them and preach love for Jesus Christ, God and man, and fidelity to the Church and the Pope.

" As to the exterior organisation of this work, it seems to me that the person whom Our Lord will call to found it will know better than I the most suitable way to establish it. Besides, I could, if Your Excellency would kindly send me back my papers, get copied out all the passages in them which have reference to the Work, as well as those passages in the papers which we have here."

On October 22nd, 1910, Monsignor Filipello wrote to her asking her to draw up a plan for the statutes in order to give the Work a concrete form, and enquiring whether she thought that it would be necessary to wait for some order from the Holy See to commence the Work (the Bishop knew that she had submitted a part of what concerned the Work to the Holy Father); His Excellency asked also if the person who would commence the work was to be a priest or a bishop.

THE FIRST DRAFT OF THE STATUTES OF THE PRIESTS' UNIVERSAL UNION

On November 1st, she replied :
" I shall begin to-day to draw up the Statutes of the Work according to the desire expressed by Your Excellency ; but how incapable of doing so I feel myself ! The will of the Good Master with regard to this Work seems to be revealing itself, and to be indicating that it is to be founded by a Bishop and a priest of the secular clergy. The more I see, the more I believe that Father Charrier was not called to establish it and direct it. He himself also seems to think so. I have written to him recently, telling him vaguely that the Work which he knows is demanded by Our Lord was perhaps going to be started and that I was about to try to write the Statutes for it. In his reply to me yesterday, he manifested his joy saying : ' The little book has already done so much good ; I feel quite sure that Our Lord will not leave you without special help, and that these Statutes will be the starting point of a work which will do immense good.' "

With Monsignor Filipello's consent she kept Father Charrier informed of the new development. On October 26th she wrote to him :
" Are you willing that your personality like my own should disappear entirely behind that of a bishop and a priest chosen by him ? If so, reply to me immediately and tell me if you could come and spend two days at Mazze before November 10th.
" I have received an order under obedience to write the Statutes for the organisation and would like to have your co-operation in writing them if it be the will of God."

Father Charrier replied that while willing to co-operate he was unable to come in person.

In her letter to him on November 2nd, besides giving him the important information that Monsignor Filipello was to take the statutes to Rome and consult the Pope, she emphasised the fact that the book was but a preliminary step and that the real work was to commence :

" At the canonical visitation this year, Monsignor questioned me about the origin of the book. **He had already understood that this book was but the commencement of something else** ; he read several of my papers that had reference to the Work ; then, he took them away to examine them at leisure. Finally, a few days ago, Monsignor came and spent some hours here ; he had brought a little list of questions to which I replied as well as I could ; then he told me to draw up these Statutes and to send them to him ; he intends to go to Rome in January and wishes to speak to the Holy Father about all this. Pray then, Father, that Jesus may have His Will put into effect. Monsignor is most discreet and wishes that absolute secrecy be observed about this matter. As for you, Father, as Monsignor did not tell me to keep it secret from you, I regarded myself at liberty to write to you."

MONSIGNOR FILIPELLO PROMISES WHOLE-HEARTED CO-OPERATION

On November 4th Monsignor Filipello announced to Mother Louise Margaret his willingness to give her whole-hearted co-operation in the founding of the organisation for priests, and gave her very practical directions for the drawing up of the Statutes :

" I congratulate myself with you that you are working at the Statutes of the Work which seems willed by Our Lord and Master In this matter, it is not a question of you, or of me, or of others, but solely of the glory of God and the good of souls redeemed by the Blood of Our Lord Who has loved them so much. Certainly if I considered my numerous and real defects, I should refuse to take part in this work, so noble and so delicate. But since God has been pleased to send me to this diocese and entrust it to my poor care, **most willingly, according to the little means at my disposal, shall I undertake the foundation and the propagation of this Work in the hope of obtaining from the Sacred Heart the grace to know how to conquer and renounce myself.**

" **Furthermore, I have here with me a holy priest who has experience and who, on account of the great esteem in which he is held, will be able to help greatly in the propagation of the Work.**

" Besides, it is Jesus Himself Who will bring this Work into being ; we shall be His instruments if He deigns to use us.

" May God enlighten and sanctify us ! When drawing up the Statutes, be sure to state very clearly the end of the Association, the means to attain its ends, the persons who may be members of it, the obligations which they will assume, who are to be the directors, etc."

On November 9th, 1910, she submitted the first draft of the Statutes. In this draft she made no reference to any supernatural help received in composing them, but stated her willingness to append on a separate sheet for the inspection of the Holy See the sources from which she composed them. In her accompanying letter she says :

" As Your Excellency will see, I have drawn up these Statutes in such a way that nothing supernatural appears tn them. If. however, Your Excellency thinks it opportune that I should write in a few pages the different communications which I received on this subject, in order to submit them to the Holy Father, or for any other reason, I could write them concisely and join them to the Statutes.

" I did not dare to insist on Infinite Love in these Statutes, I have rather dwelt on the Sacred Heart, Which is Its most touching manifestation."

In his letter of November 24th, Monsignor Filipello directed her to append the sources from which the Statutes were composed.

" In my humble judgment, you might write out in a few pages the different communications which you have received on this subject. Then in a personal interview, the Holy Father could be informed about these things, or what you will write on this subject could be presented to His Holiness separate from the Statutes, and perhaps this could be presented beforehand to some pious, influential personage.

" I believe that we shall find some Cardinal to take charge of this.

" I regret to cause you this fatigue, but there is question of the glory and of the love of Jesus, your only and beloved Spouse.

" I find indirect references to the object of this work mentioned in the book entitled : *History of a Soul : Life of Sister Teresa of the Infant Jesus,* which I am reading at present."

In her letter of November 26th to Monsignor Filipello, Mother Louise Margaret tells him the reasons which she has for believing that he is the Bishop chosen by Our Lord to commence the work. She suggests that the Statutes should have the character of universality, that details should be left to each individual diocese, and that an appeal to priests should accompany the Statutes. In the end of her letter, she predicts her early death, though she was still only forty-five and in normal health :

. . . . . . " In your goodness, Venerable Father, you will ask the Heart of our Sweet Jesus to give me the help necessary to be able to retouch and complete these Statutes. I feel myself so devoid of all that is needed for this : and now in the very active life which my position as Superioress imposes on me, I have so little time for recollection and prayer.

" If I be not mistaken, Jesus wishes the organisation to be universal. If Your Excellency, as I believe more and more, is destined by the good Master to give the first impulse to this Work, to bring it into being, if I may so express myself, from the very Heart of Jesus I say that it would perhaps be best that the Statutes which you, Venerable Father, will present to Rome, have from the beginning this form of universality. It will be time enough to add the little particulars when it commences for the first time in this diocese.

" It would be necessary also, it seems to me, to write a kind of ' Appeal to Priests ' which would precede the Statutes. If the worthy priest whom Your Excellency has in mind could do this, would it not be best ? I am incapable of anything good, Monsignor ; I could pass on the ideas of the good Master, but a holy priest would draw up this appeal much better. **I desire only to die, Venerable Father, to go and be united to the good Jesus. When I have said all that He wishes, when His Work of Love is commenced, He will perhaps grant me this favour.''**

In his letter of December 17th to her, Monsignor Filipello instructed her to make the changes she suggested in the draft, and to compose the appeal to priests herself.

" You, yourself compose the Statutes according to this conception of universality. I will then examine them and discuss them with this priest who seems to me very well qualified ; he is certainly a true friend of the Divine Heart.

" In addition, prepare the ' Appeal to the Priests '[1] who are to be members of this Association ; we shall then make any changes or additions that we think necessary.

" It would be best that we should have, very complete and very clear, all your ideas on this subject ; these will then be expressed in different form, if necessary. But Jesus wishes that you should be the first to speak ; and since you are in haste to go to Paradise, it is proper that you should tell us quickly all that Jesus desires from His priests."

PREPARATION OF THE PIONEERS

The first draft of the Statutes was ready in December, 1910. Six months were to elapse before they were presented in Rome. In the letters and Intimate Notes of Mother Louise about this time we find lights on many aspects of the work, particularly on the preparation needed for priests who were to take part in it, the way in which the work was to be propagated, and what was the part that the Religious Orders were called upon to play in it.

In the *Book of Infinite Love* Mother Louise Margaret writes : " There is question of choosing those priests marked out by God to be the first to receive the revelation of Love ; to penetrate them

---

[1] This " Appeal to Priests " has been included in *The Book of Infinite Love* without a heading. It is found on page 102, No. IX beginning with the words "On the vigil of His dolorous Passion," and continues to the end of the chapter, page 106.

with this love, and they will communicate the divine fire to their brethren. And thus, Infinite Love will do Its work and make progress like a fire lighted in the corner of a wood and gradually spreading to all the trees, causing a general conflagration."

And in the same book she writes : " The end of the Work ; souls saved by Love and Mercy. The means of action of the Work : the priest ; the holy, zealous priest, filled with love so that he will pour it, as if naturally, into souls."

THE WORK TO BE COMMENCED BY A SMALL NUMBER

She has no dreams of a spectacular beginning for the organisation. In her letter of June 18th, 1911, to Monsignor Filipello she writes :

" It seems to me that there are priests, at least some, who are quite disposed to receive the abundance of graces prepared by divine Charity for the souls of priests.

" *Five or six priests* of the diocese who would give and consecrate themselves to Infinite Love would become a precious acquisition for the Work at the time of its foundation."

And in her letter to Monsignor Filipello of November 24th of the same year, she indicates that the Work must be first begun in secret, in a humble and unpretentious manner :

" It was a great joy to me to read in your last letter, that Your Excellency is not losing sight of the Statutes and the Work of Love.

" I will tell you in all filial simplicity, Venerable Father, that on the 15th of this month when I was at evening prayer, Our Lord favoured me with an interior communication from Himself according to His usual manner. He said to me : ' I wish to fill souls with my Infinite Love.' Then He added in an account of prayer : ' Open the hearts of priests to Me, in order that I may pour into them and through them into the world, the love which presses me.' . . . . . . Then the good Master gave me to understand, if I am not mistaken, that we must make love the dominant note in the Statutes and that the Work must be commenced in secret first. **It seemed to me that a dozen priests of the diocese, the best ones, should be taken first, the mysteries of**

Infinite Love and the desires of the Sacred Heart should be revealed to them. They would consecrate themselves together to Infinite Love, become permeated with it, and then gradually they would communicate to their brethren the gift which they had received ; and when they would be sufficiently numerous, they would commence the Work in the open. Your Excellency will find in the diary for June, 1902, a statement of Our Lord[1] which I did not then understand and of which the explanation was given to me this time. It seems that He wishes that the Work of His Love should begin in humility and secrecy, as the Holy Church has commenced.

" It is with the most humble respect that I submit my poor thoughts to Your Excellency, leaving to you the care of judging and deciding everything. It seems to me that the good Master will be very pleased the day when He will see His first priests consecrate themselves to His Infinite Love and commence to enkindle this Divine Fire and make it burn in the hearts of men."

And in her letter of December 2nd of the same year she writes to Father Charrier :

" The desire of the good Master is indeed that the Work be truly the Work of His Infinite Love. If this work were launched without preparation, several people might join it, attracted only by the exterior good, without being called by Infinite Love. It is necessary then to prepare some souls first, to imbue them with Infinite Love, and then only when they are prepared and sufficently numerous, the exterior Work will assume a body and will be manifested to the world.

" On the 15th of the last month, I had a very clear communica-cation on this work. I ask you therefore, Father, to labour at this preparation."

Finally, in her letter of December 18th, 1911, to Monsignor Filipello and her Intimate Note of 1913, Mother Louise Margaret insists that it is Our Lord's wish that Love be the dominant note

---

[1] Most probably this statement is : " Nineteen centuries ago, twelve men have changed the world ; they were not mere men, they were priests ; now a second time, twelve men can change the world."

in this work, and that the Statutes would have to be revised to give prominence to that idea :

" I pray Our Lord to give Your Excellency the abundance of His graces and His lights so that the Work may commence well and make good progress. Jesus is in haste to open His Divine Heart to priests, for He sees that because they do not know of His love, many are lost by turning from the true doctrine. Faith declines and becomes extinguished when it is not warmed by love."

Intimate Notes : 1913

" Just now, at prayer, Our Lord manifested Himself to me interiorly : He said to me : ' I wish to fill souls with my Infinite Love.' Then He added in an accent of prayer : ' Open to Me the souls and hearts of priests in order that I may pour into them, and through them upon the world, the Love which presses Me ' Then great sadness came over me ; my eyes became filled with tears and I said : ' O Lord, what can I do to accomplish this ? I have told everything to Father Charrier and he has done nothing ; I have entrusted everything to Monsignor. I can do nothing more except suffer.'

" Our Lord then said that the Work was destined to reveal His Infinite Love to His priests ; that the Statutes drafted did not reveal love sufficiently well. It seems to me that His wish is not to create an ordinary work, but that a small number of priests should first be selected out of each diocese, chosen souls who will be nourished on the doctrine of Infinite Love."

THE PART RESERVED FOR PRIESTS OF RELIGIOUS ORDERS IN THE WORK OF INFINITE LOVE

They are to remember that besides being Religious, they are priests, and that Christ's special message of love for priests and the special donation which He makes of His Sacred Heart to priests is meant for them as well as for the secular clergy.

In July, 1918, Mother Louise Margaret writes :

" While I was before the Blessed Sacrament, Our Lord made known to me several things about His priests, He wishes that we should work to uplift them not only in the esteem of the world, but also in their own esteem, in order that they may become more and more attached to their sublime vocation. **Jesus makes no difference in His Heart between Secular priests and priests of Religious Orders.**"

While the Priests of Religious Orders are to leave the control of the work to the bishops and priests of the Secular clergy, they are free to join branches as ordinary members ; but Religious, whether they join or not, are expected to do   pioneer work.

In a letter of June, 1911, to Monsignor Filipello, Mother Louise Margaret writes :

" Our Lord addresses His Work of Love to His priests, and His object is to bring the priests of the secular clergy together and unite them more closely to their bishops.

" Religious are sufficiently united by their rules, their constitutions and their vows. They can nourish themselves on the doctrine of Infinite Love, become penetrated with it and preach it everywhere.

" It would be very desirable that Directors and Presidents of Conferences of the Priests' Universal Union should invite Religious to preach at their meetings."

RELATIONS BETWEEN THE PRIESTS' UNIVERSAL UNION OF THE FRIENDS OF THE SACRED HEART AND OTHER CLERICAL UNIONS

The Priests' Universal Union has a special work of its own, different from that of other clerical associations ; this work is (1) to provide a universal bond uniting all the clerical associations of the world ; (2) to promote a deeper study and more zealous preaching of the devotion to the Sacred Heart of Jesus, and (3) to associate all others besides priests, both religious and people living in the world, with the Work of Infinite Love, the aim of which is to reconquer the world for Christ.

It is therefore in no sense a rival of, and in no way interferes with the work of other clerical unions. On the contrary, it aims at assisting them, and so far from taking members away from other clerical societies, its work will result in increasing their numbers. Members of other clerical societies who join will still remain members of their societies and will become more zealous members ; clerical associations which become affiliated will retain their identity and will receive valuable help.[1]

THE STATUTES PRESENTED TO POPE PIUS X

As he had announced, Monsignor Filipello brought the first draft of the Statutes with him to Rome on the occasion of his visit *ad limina* in May, 1911. Cardinal Gennari, Prefect of the Congregation of the Council to whom they were first presented, fully approved of the Priests' Universal Union and the Statutes, and urged Monsignor Filipello to commence it in his diocese in order that it might be propagated from there. His Holiness Pius X was already in full sympathy with the work ; for him it was only a question of the most opportune time to begin. Just then Cardinal Dubillard of Chambery was getting approval for his work called *Pro Pontifice et Ecclesia,* and if this other work were launched at the same time there was danger that they might be confounded, and so His Holiness advised Monsignor Filipello to wait. Besides, Providence was soon to arrange to have Mother Louise Margaret herself brought to Rome in order that this work with its principal component part, the new Monastery that was to be a spiritual foundation for it, should receive approbation together.[2]

---

[1] For further information on this question see appendix page 222.

[2] See Appendix, page 222, for the Statutes of the Priests' Universal Union.

CHAPTER X

MOTHER LOUISE MARGARET'S SECOND TERM IN OFFICE

The duties of Superioress to provide for the spiritual and temporal welfare of the Community had been carried out so perfectly by Mother Louise Margaret, that no one could suspect that another great burden had lain on her all the time. The beautiful conferences which she gave at the Chapter meetings (a number of which will be found in Vol. II) are evidences of her rare talents as spiritual director, while on the material side, she solved all the pressing material problems which she had inherited. All this she made to serve the Work of Infinite Love. What she had written at the time of her first election was carried out to the letter : " To give myself, to sacrifice myself for the Community to the limit of my capacity, in all things both spiritual and temporal, and this, in the spirit of immolation for the Church, for the souls of priests, for the reign of Infinite Love ; to be good like Jesus if that were possible for me ; like Jesus, to be a victim for souls, immolated to love like Jesus and with Jesus." When the time for re-election came, May, 1910, she wanted to be relieved of the burden of office, but the Sisters could not entertain the idea ; she had been most successful in extricating them from what appeared to be unsurmountable difficulties, and there still remained a pressing problem to be solved ; to find a permanent home for the Community. Besides, Our Divine Lord had His own designs. Monsignor Filipello, who presided at the election addressed the Sisters after it, and terminated his address with these words : " Does not the heavenly Father seem to say to you to-day : This is My beloved daughter, be guided by her ! "

On the following day she wrote in her Intimate Notes :

" On the day after my re-election, at evening prayer Jesus took my soul to Himself and gave me to understand that He wished to give me again many sufferings and many graces. During part of this prayer I tasted the sweetest consolations by a very close union with Jesus.

" On the day which followed, I suffered much corporally, while at the same time keeping that intimate union so sweet to my soul.

" During the Octave of Corpus Christi, my soul entered into a period of great sadness, a kind of most painful interior solitude which continued a little beyond the day of the Feast of the Sacred Heart.

" On my knees before the altar, for some moments I lost consciousness of exterior things around me. It seemed to me that from the Heart of Jesus in the tabernacle, Infinite Love poured forth on me like a torrent . . . . But this love which rushed on me was not given for me. I was a channel that served to make these waves of love pass on. Infinite Love, life, true life in its strength and intensity passed on and went from God to souls ; to the souls of priests, for it is to them that Infinite Love goes first.

" I asked Jesus what I am to do. He replied : ' Nothing, just allow My will to be accomplished in you.'

" I have the feeling that I am going to pass through great suffering and that from it the Work of Love will issue forth. These abundant graces which have been given to me these days are a preparation for sorrow. O Jesus ! Infinite Love, I wish only what Thou wishest and I love all that Thou dost ! "

SECOND REMOVAL OF THE COMMUNITY

The problem of finding another home for the Sisters remained to be solved for nearly two years, and in the meantime continued to weigh heavily upon her. In any event, another house had to be found, and there was the further question of the possibility of being expelled from Italy. In February, 1911, she wrote to Father Charrier :

" You know that we are threatened on all sides. A decree against Religious Congregations is expected in the course of this year, or at latest, next year. Where are we to go ? I have not the slightest idea. The Austrian bishops have been ordered by the Government not to receive any foreign Religious Communities into their dioceses. This prohibition has been made last September, no doubt in view of the events here in Italy that may drive all the Italian Communities to the Austrian frontier. France is closed to us. Switzerland will receive us no more.

Belgium is full up. Bavaria not only forbids the admission of Communities, but will not even allow the convents there to receive individual Sisters. Pray for us, Father, for me in particular, for I have the heavy responsibility of this large family. I count on the adorable Heart of our good Master, Jesus."

The good Master was pleased with her confidence in Him, for on February 19th of the same month, she wrote :

" I was in great trouble for several days past about the future of the Community. Yesterday at evening prayer, the good Master made His presence felt and said to me : ' Fear nothing, I will hide you under the shadow of My wings ! ' Then I said to Him : ' Not only myself, protect also the family that Thou hast given to me.' He replied : ' My protection will extend to all ! ' Then my soul was filled with peace and consolation, and Jesus, keeping me united intimately to Him, showed me that I had yet much to suffer, but that He would be always with me."

In the following March, the Count of San Marzano, the owner of the house in which the Sisters were living, arrived with a purchaser for the house, who wanted immediate possession.

Mother Louise Margaret appealed for advice and help to Monsignor Filipello to make provision for her family of fifty Sisters, most of whom were old and infirm.

On her part, she succeeded in gaining a few months' respite, and in the meantime Monsignor secured for the Community a large house at Parella, a few miles from Ivrea, which was in every way suitable. The house was situated at the foot of the Alps in a healthy situation ; with its spacious rooms, large enough to provide chapel, refectory and Community room, long corridors and interior courtyard that reminded them of their Monastery of Romans, it looked as if it had been built for a monastery. Mother Louise Margaret took charge of the transfer, organised the new house, and before the end of her term in office, left everything in order for her successor.

In the midst of all this bustle and turmoil, Our Lord continued to favour her with His communications, but as in the case of all His servants, He gave her just sufficient for each day, and allowed her to be troubled with doubts about her mission and uncertainty about the future. All these, the lights and favours, the doubts and difficulties, she humbly submitted to Monsignor Filipello and sought his advice and guidance.

HER ATTITUDE TOWARDS THE COMMUNICATIONS SHE RECEIVED

During this period and especially in 1912 when she was coming near the end of her second term in office, Our Lord allowed her to be tormented even more than usual by doubts about the communications which she received; He did this for His own wise ends, for by humbly submitting these doubts to proper authority, she at the same time found light and guidance and left us another proof that her communications were from God. On August 26th, 1912, she wrote down from the beginning a brief account of her attitude towards the communications which she had received:

" My education and my positive character have naturally put me on my guard against the supernatural and the mystical. When, after my profession, I commenced to receive interior communications from Our Lord, I resisted for a long time and I suffered great interior combats. The clearness of the supernatural action in me and the direction of Father Charrier got me out of this state of internal struggle. Abandonment to divine Providence, obedience, and above all, simplicity conquered my resistance.

" Since I have become Superioress I have been in a position to see many illusions in certain souls and much false mysticism; and above all, states of religious hysteria and unhealthy elation. This had already put me on my guard against so-called interior graces and supernatural states. Then, what I saw in Father Charrier (his slowness in giving credence to the communications which she received), while causing me much pain, in the end made me doubt about certain interior communications, and gradually, I began again to resist the interior impulses, lights, and words which I received.

" This made my soul dry and arid like a land without water. And then I no longer dared to say or write anything.

" I feared to be myself the victim of the same unhealthy illusions as I had seen in others; I was afraid I might deceive my bishop and all those whom I had told about the communications which I received. Then I relapsed into silence again and wrote nothing for more than ten months.

" At the retreat a month ago, I felt my resistance abating for

ten days ; I received what God gave me ; with my former simplicity I noted down some of it, and in this simplicity and peace,
my soul brightened up. But soon after the retreat, my trouble
became more acute. When the Holy Office refused to grant
indulgences for the two prayers[1] I drew the conclusion from this
that I must have written heresy, and that consequently, all that
I thought, felt, and received, was only the effect of my imagination. Then I wished to reject everything, and my soul was as
if torn asunder, feeling itself on one side urged on by grace and
by Infinite Love, and on the other as if frozen by cold reason
which said : 'All that, is but the result of imagination or disease.'

" I have confidence in Monsignor Filipello, because he is very
prudent, very calm, and slow to act."

She might well say that Monsignor Filipello was slow to act,
for when she first showed him her Intimate Notes, had he not waited
a whole year before even making mention of them to her ? It was
not the fear of being kept waiting for a reply, however, that made
her hesitate before consulting him, it was rather her fear of abusing
his goodness towards her, and her difficulty of explaining her case
in Italian. On the advice of Father Poletti, she finally decided
to open her heart completely to her bishop and received the following
re-assuring reply with instructions to continue noting down the
graces and lights which she received :

MONSIGNOR FILIPELLO SOLVES HER DIFFICULTIES

" September 1st, 1912.

" I understand perfectly the cause of your moral sufferings
and I believe myself bound in conscience to declare to you that
it is your duty to be entirely free from anxiety. There is no
question of hallucinations ; for already great good has resulted
from all that you have done, and I am confident, that not only
will this good not cease, but that it will go on increasing.

---

[1] These prayers were subsequently indulgenced and are included in the Raccolta.

" Contrary to what you fear, I come to the conclusion that your trouble is a trial from God, Who permits the adversary of good to come and disturb you.

" Remain calm and tranquil; continue to abandon yourself to the will of your divine Spouse Whom you have chosen. Note down always, under obedience, according as you have time, the interior impulses, lights, and words which you receive.

" When I come, arrange things so as always to have a little free time for your soul, then unburden yourself freely of your troubles, without worrying either about taking up my time, or about the manner in which you are to express your sentiments. As for me, I am ready to aid you as a Father; I am even prepared to come this very week."

In her Intimate Notes of September 4th she wrote :

" Monsignor's letter has done me good; I have renewed my act of abandonment, but this afternoon, I have gone through great sufferings of soul.

" I felt myself at times as if taken possession of by the divine presence ; a supernatural force lifted me up and attracted me to itself, and in the inmost depths of my soul there was a kind of plenitude of love which would have been very sweet, if I had not resisted it vigorously."

During those very days, Divine Providence gave her a gracious confirmation of the decision of Monsignor Filipello.   The reading in the refectory happened to be from *The Doctrine of Love*, by Monsignor Gilbergue, Bishop of Valence, who afterwards in 1918 along with the Cardinal of Lyons, helped to establish the Priests' Universal Union in France.

On September 5th, 1912, she wrote in her Intimate Notes :

" This morning, in the refectory, a passage in the reading suddenly filled my soul with light and consolation.   It answered word for word the doubt which was torturing my soul for some time.   I was in mortal dread of being deceived, of having fallen into error in this doctrine of Infinite Love, which was communicated to me.   I transcribe here the passage which corresponds so well to what I have known and seen : ' God is Love.   Love is less an attribute and a perfection of God than the very Being and Substance of God. If God is Love we may invert the definition of the Apostle and say : ' Love is God.' "

Intimate Note, September 8th

" This reading of *The Doctrine of Love* **by Monsignor Gilbergue is doing me good and reassuring me. I see in it written by a person of authority, and duly approved, all that has been communicated to me in my inmost soul about Infinite Love."**

Mother Louise Margaret understood that the organisation for priests demanded by Our Lord should have the support of the prayers of Religious, and in her loyalty to her dear Visitation, she wished that it should have that honour.

She consulted Monsignor Filipello on making a beginning in her own Community :

" It seemed to me these days that Jesus wished our dear Visitation to be the praying helpmate of the Priesthood and several ideas were given to me on this subject. I feel an impulse urging me to form our Sisters in the Noviciate in this spirit of devotedness to the Church and the Priesthood, and to reveal a little about Infinite Love to them, but I never yet have dared to do so. I have never, up to the present, spoken either to the Community or to the Noviciate on these subjects. Thus many of our Sisters read *The Sacred Heart and the Priesthood* without suspecting by whom it has been written."

Monsignor Filipello encouraged her to do so :

" I assure you therefore that you are doing right in forming the young Sisters in this spirit and that you would do well, especially at this season, to speak to the whole Community of Infinite Love in connection with the Passion of Our Lord which the Church now commemorates. And if some of your Sisters come to know that you are the author of the book, what harm would that be ?

" Speak of the Love of Our Lord and pray that we may love Him with our whole hearts.

" You who have such great zeal for souls, should obtain the conversion of one very quickly.

" I earnestly recommend this soul to your charity. You have already obtained conversions of this kind and even greater ones ; obtain this one also.

✠ " Matthew Bishop."

THE BOOK OF INFINITE LOVE

" Infinite Love : It is the substance of Catholic doctrine ; it is its centre ; it is the explanation of all the mysteries of our Faith ; it is not only the love of God for His creature ; it is God Himself. God is Love ! He wishes to be thus known ; He wishes that this knowledge be diffused throughout the world that it may inflame it and renew it."

So wrote Mother Louise Margaret in her Intimate Notes. All her writings are full of references to Infinite Love. Her mission was to reveal God as Infinite Love. And so Monsignor Filipello, towards the end of her second term of office, ordered her to write a little book in which she would bring together all the lights which she received on this sublime subject. In the following letter to Monsignor Filipello, expressing her gratitude to him for the many favours he had conferred on the Community, she announced to him, that the good Master had given her the plan for the work.

" Powerless to give Your Excellency a fitting testimony of our gratitude, we ask the good Master to pay our filial debt, and to pour out the abundant graces of His Infinite Love on your person, on your dear family, on all the souls that God has entrusted to your pastoral care, and on all your works.

" It is with unspeakable joy that on Saturday next I am going to resume the lowest place and the interior life of prayer of which my soul has such great need. **During these last few days, the good Master, if I am not mistaken, has given me the whole plan of what I must write on the doctrine of Infinite Love,** but my ignorance and misery will ever prevent me from becoming capable of writing it alone."

MOTHER LOUISE MARGARET'S SECOND TERM IN OFFICE
COMES TO AN END

In a letter to Sister Margaret (who was afterwards her companion on her journey to Rome and first Superioress of Bethany of the Sacred Heart), she announced the news of the election of Mother Frances Pauline as Rev. Mother and adds :

" On Saturday last I have been at last relieved of the burden of office. It seemed to me that Our Lord took off my shoulders a weight of a hundred tons.

" Since that happy day, I have been lodged in the infirmary waiting until there will be an empty bed somewhere to receive me. It is from there that I write to you, from that sunny room still filled with the memory of the sweet and holy death of our dear little Sister Mary Anthony.

" How sweet it will be to die when one has laboured hard and suffered much ! "

One of the Sisters of the Community writes the following beautiful testimony to the humility of the retired Rev. Mother ; it is written also to Sister Margaret, who was absent on business at the time :

" May 25th, 1913.

" The health of this venerable Sister Louise Margaret is good and it is a pleasure for us, each one in her turn, to enjoy her conversation in the Community, where she occupies the lowest place and effaces herself with charming humility and simplicity. No stranger could suspect from the way that she acts that this Sister of such humble appearance, who disappears in the crowd so naturally, is the same as she who has just occupied the first place for six years, and showed such superior talents and such eminent virtues.

" I confess to you, dear Sister, that the sight of this touches me more than I can express, and often furnishes me with a subject for my meditation these days ; it also serves to engrave deeply in my soul her teachings and counsels, and I would wish, according to my limited capacity, to reproduce in my own conduct what I admire in her. Is not the secret to succeed in doing so, to give oneself without reserve like her to the love of Him Who ought to be all in all to us ? I beg you, my sister, to pray for me that I may follow faithfully and courageously the path which has been so well traced out for us by the words and example of our former Rev. Mother, and that I may give our dear new Rev. Mother, the consolation of gathering some fruit in my poor garden."

CHAPTER XI

THE JOURNEY TO ROME

" The good Master came to me. He said to me, if I am not mistaken : ' Be faithful, cast yourself into My Heart and have confidence. You will leave this house and you will carry elsewhere the overflowing abundance of My Love ' "

Relieved from the burden of office and longing for rest and solitude after these six years of continual work and worry, we should think that Mother Louise Margaret had excellent reasons for looking forward to the future with calmness. In her humility, she did not realise that, after remaining for six years at the head of the Community and exercising profound personal influence over it, it would be difficult for her to efface herself completely.

The ways of the Lord are not our ways. He reserved for His faithful servant many painful trials before taking her to His eternal kingdom. Various things that happened led Mother Louise Margaret to think that for the peace of the Community it would be better for her to go away, at least for a time, from the convent in which she was professed. As we may well guess, it caused her a veritable heart-break to come to this decision.

The extraordinary confessor was consulted and he approved of her departure ; he told her that she must make people forget her by withdrawing for some time to another monastery of her Order.

Monsignor Filipello had at first some difficulty in agreeing to this proposal. It was a big sacrifice for him to allow the Sister whom he had directed for many years to leave his diocese.

Nevertheless, he soon sided with the Superioress, and recognised that this departure was the will of God.

At first, Monsignor Filipello contemplated sending her to some of the monasteries that had asked for her towards the end of her second term in office ; but when the idea of sending her to Rome was suggested to him by the Superioress of Parella, he eagerly seized upon it, for he desired to have further enlightenment on the work and writings of his spiritual daughter. He considered that he would find at Rome advice and support for the Priests' Universal Union, which he was already endeavouring to found according to the ideas of Mother Louise Margaret. He therefore sent her to Rome with the mission of getting the lights which she had received in prayer judged by competent authorities.

This decision was taken at the beginning of August, 1913. As the great heat and the humid climate of the Eternal City might prove fatal for the health of Mother Louise Margaret, who was always delicate, it was decided that she should go to Rome by slow stages, and as she went along, should ask for hospitality in some of the monasteries of the Order.

THE COMPOSITION OF THE " BOOK OF INFINITE LOVE "

It was during this journey that Mother Louise Margaret began the composition of *The Treatise on Infinite Love* which Monsignor Filipello had asked for some time previously.

The treatise was destined to remain unfinished, but it has been published as she left it, except that the chapters which she left incomplete have been completed according to the plan which she left from her own writings.

She had to stop at the beginning of the chapter of Love Creator. Her intentions had been to condense into one little volume all the lights which she had received from God on Infinite Love during the space of eleven years. Even such as it is, this little volume is precious, for it is the resumé and the synthesis of all the ideas of Mother Louise Margaret. As we turn over these pages which were written at the most painful period of her life, we feel ourselves unconsciously moved to holy emotions. This little volume contains sublime passages on the most profound doctrines of our religion ;

on the mystery of the Trinity, on Infinite Love and gives instructions about the Priesthood ; we read it and re-read it without ever becoming tired of it.

On July 5th, in a letter to Monsignor Filipello, she tells him that the good Master assured her that it was His desire that she should leave Parella.

" On Thursday morning the good Master came to me. He said to me, if I am not mistaken : ' Be faithful, cast yourself into My Heart and have confidence. You will leave this house and you will carry elsewhere the overflowing abundance of My Love.' "

SHE LEAVES THE MONASTERY OF PARELLA

On August 6th at 6 a.m. the Feast of the Transfiguration of Our Lord, she left the monastery of Parella and went to Ivrea, a few kilometres away, to get the train. However, she first went to the Cathedral with her travelling companion, to hear Holy Mass, receive Holy Communion and get her letter of instructions, as His Excellency had arranged. Then she left for the Visitation Monastery of Turin, the first stage of her journey.

On this journey, by the arrangement of her superiors, she visited all the Visitation Monasteries from Turin to Rome, and by their orders, had to retrace her steps from Pisa to visit the Monastery of Bologna. In all the monasteries, the Sisters regarded her as a person of altogether remarkable virtue and talents. On the journey she continued the composition of *The Book of Infinite Love* and kept both Monsignor Filipello and Father Charrier acquainted with the progress of the book.

On August 11th, 1913, she wrote to Father Charrier from the Monastery of Turin :

" How consoling our meeting on Friday has been to me ; I think that the good Master must be well pleased, now that those whom He Himself has united are again united. In my inmost soul a more profound peace reigns ; Infinite Love will now flow like a great wide river, and pass through our souls without obstacle. Your interview with Monsignor has very much consoled me. I see that you two have the same inspiration and impulse for the Work, both of which come from Our Lord.

" Ah ! I certainly do not grieve over my present sorrows if Infinite Love can make use of them for His glory. Ask Our Lord therefore to grant me the necessary help in order to write what you and Monsignor wish me to write ; I feel myself so incapable of reproducing what I see on Infinite Love. I am unable to find appropriate terms to express and explain what I understand. You could not believe how painful it is to feel one's ignorance in face of a command to be carried out and a good to be accomplished."

On August 14th, she added :

" Yes, the further I go on, the more I feel that it is Jesus Who is directing everything. What will be the result of it ? It is still a mystery in which I must hide myself without seeking to comprehend it.

" Nothing is so good as to abandon oneself to divine Providence. However, my heart suffers constantly and the remembrance of Parella often brings tears to my eyes. The dear souls whom I loved as my children often come before my mind ; then I recommend them immediately to the good Master and bury myself in my obscurity."

On August 16th, 1913, Father Charrier replied :

" I was very much struck by what I read in your notes (for the treatise on Infinite Love), which I sent back to you.

" This adorable name of God which was revealed in definite form for the first time by St. John when he said : ' God is Love ' (1 John, IV 8 and 16); the manner in which you express this remarkable truth, and all that I have read in your notes prove to me that Our Lord is guiding your pen with divine simplicity, which is the hallmark of divine assistance. Yes, without doubt, your plan pleases me very much. If you realise it, you will be realising a wish which I expressed at the time of the publication of *The Sacred Heart and the Priesthood*. By all means, speak of Infinite Love, reveal it to souls, since Our Lord reveals it to you. Do not keep this treasure for yourself. Have I told you that I wear my Act of Donation to Infinite Love on my person each day at the Altar ?

" Go on where God is guiding you ; with humble confidence seek in His divine Heart the lights of which you have need to write on Infinite Love.

" You will leave to me the verifying of the texts of Scripture, as in the case of the first work."

Mother Louise Margaret left Turin on August 12th and after a short stay at the Visitation Monastery of Genoa, she arrived at Pisa on the 14th, and on August 20th she wrote the following letter to Monsignor Filipello :

" It is from Pisa, where we arrived on Wednesday last, that we are addressing these lines to Your Excellency. We rested one night with the Sisters at Genoa, and here, the Rev. Mother insists on keeping us until the feast of St. Jane Frances de Chantal, on which day a novice will be professed.

" On Friday we shall take the mountain road for Massa where we intend to remain until Your Excellency tells me to set out for Rome.

" In the sweet peace of this dear Monastery of Pisa, I am meditating on Infinite Love and preparing to write what Your Excellency desires. I expect to commence at Massa, if the good Master inspires me, for without Him I can do nothing.

" My soul is in great peace and continually adores the Divine Will, which arranges all things for God's glory. My heart, doubtless, suffers ; it becomes more capable of understanding the inner sufferings of the Heart of Jesus and thus of uniting itself to Him and consoling Him."

The following letters from the Superioress of the Visitation Monastery of Massa to Monsignor Filipello and to Sister Margaret show the esteem which Mother Louise Margaret inspired :

Letter to Monsignor Filipello :

" Permit me to express to Your Excellency my profound gratitude and that of the Community for the honour which you have conferred on us and the consolation which you have procured for us in putting our little Monastery in the itinerary of the former Rev. Mother of Parella.

" I can assure Your Excellency that we all appreciate the favour which has been conferred on our humble religious family; we admire the virtues of this honoured Sister and her perfect religious spirit; we knew her already, it is true, and therefore our joy was great in having the privilege of opening our door to her, but now that we have her among us and see her virtues at closer quarters, we esteem her still more.

" We make bold to ask Your Excellency to put Massa on the itinerary when she is returning, in order that we may be able to be again edified by this estimable Sister."

Letter to Sister Margaret:

" We are at the eve of the departure of dear Sister Louise Margaret, former Rev. Mother of Parella. It is a great sacrifice for us all, for we were all profoundly attached to this venerable Sister, who has been a constant source of great edification to us during her stay here.

" Try to bring her back this way on your return from Rome and do not fail. The hope of seeing her again will alone sweeten the sacrifice which we must make.

" This dear Sister has kept in moderate health, just as you left her with us. We should have wished to give her a little colour and make her less thin, but we did not succeed."

On September 25th, 1913, Monsignor Filipello wrote to her:

" I have read through the manuscript which you have sent me by Sister Margaret and the plan of the work which you have made out, and I consider all very good. You must therefore continue. I am very glad that you are employed in the Noviciate at the Monastery; that will help the Work.

" I enclose an order for you instructing you to set out for Pisa where you are to remain until the time of your departure for Rome, which will be about the middle of October.

" I intend to leave for Rome during the second week of October."

THE FUTURE BENEDICT XV LEARNS OF HER WORK

In this providentially arranged journey to Rome, undoubtedly the most extraordinary thing was the way in which Mother Louise

Margaret was brought to Bologna, and how Cardinal della Chiesa, the future Benedict XV, learned of her work and received a copy of *The Sacred Heart and the Priesthood*. It was the Rev. Mother of Parella who requested Monsignor Filipello to order her to go there, and to write a second letter, ordering her to suspend her journey to Rome. It was Pope Benedict XV who, after the death of Mother Louise Margaret, intervened in favour of the new Monastery and finally had it formed into an independent Sisterhood. Truly the ways of Providence are wonderful!

On October 10th, she received an ' obedience ' from Monsignor Filipello to go to Bologna. She obeyed immediately. Soon afterwards, she received a second ' obedience ' from Monsignor Filipello to suspend her journey to Rome and to wait at Bologna until the will of God should be manifested. She communicated the news to Father Charrier in the following letter:

" I am not going, then, to Rome, at least for the present; this sacrifice is easy to make, and perhaps it would be even better to go there when the Work will be a little better known and the Act of Consecration a little better circulated and indulgenced by more Bishops. It is Jesus Who permits all this. We have only to kiss His Divine Hand that is always so good, so holy, and so adorable."

The Rev. Mother of Bologna, uneasy on account of the situation in which Mother Louise found herself due to a combination of circumstances, and desiring to find a definite solution, had taken counsel with His Eminence, Cardinal Della Chiesa, Archbishop of Bologna, the future Benedict XV. The reply which she received was that, as the first order which Mother Louise received, assigned Rome as the end of her journey, it was to Rome that she should go, and that she would find light there. This reply harmonised with the inner sentiments of the Rev. Mother and she wrote to Monsignor Filipello, Bishop of Ivrea, on October 27th:

" I wish to assure Your Excellency that I had nothing to do with the request which this worthy Rev. Mother makes to you with reference to my departure for Rome. I desire absolutely nothing but to carry out my obligations of obedience. During these days of retreat, I have felt more clearly that God, in making me suffer in a most unexpected manner by taking me out of the Monastery in which I was professed, had very special designs upon me. These designs He manifests to me only gradually.

"Are not the desire and the insistence shown by the Venerable Rev. Mother here, by her predecessor in office, and the dear Mother Treya, to send me to Rome a new indication that such is the will of the good God.

"Our Venerable Rev. Mother of Bologna presented Monsignor de Camerino who is on his way through here, and **Monsignor Della Chiesa, Archbishop of Bologna,** with copies of *The Sacred Heart and the Priesthood* which Your Excellency takes pleasure in circulating. She also gave them two copies of the ' Act of Consecration.' "

On October 29th Monsignor Filipello wrote to her :

"God is submitting you to a trial which, in human language, is called hard and difficult. You must now set out for Rome. Will it be the last stage of your long pilgrimage ? It does not seem so . . . .

"We must say now and always : ' Not what I will, but what Thou wilt, my God ! " (Mark XIV, 36).

"I think that you should give the Rev. Mother Superior notice of your departure for Rome.

"I ask you to recommend the members of my flock and myself to the divine Heart ; and I, on my part, shall not cease to pray for you, with the intention that matters may be cleared up so as to permit you to work in peace for the good of souls, and particularly for that of the souls of priests."

She wrote immediately to Father Charrier :

"Bologna. Oct. 31st, 1913.

"We came out of retreat yesterday after ten days passed in the company of the good Master. And behold ! a letter from Monsignor was handed to me : it was excessively kind and contained an ' obedience ' to continue my journey to Rome. During the retreat I had put myself in a state of complete indifference, wishing for nothing, and ready to return to Parella, if my superiors asked me to do so. Behold! Providence has arranged that I am to do quite the contrary, for on to-morrow evening, with the blessing of all the Saints, we are to take the road for Rome where we shall arrive at 6.30 a.m. on Sunday morning."

And Father Charrier replied :

" November 2nd, 1913

" There is no further doubt possible. Our Lord wishes you at Rome. Deo gratias! He knows how to reach His ends in spite of all obstacles. May the divine Heart be blessed !

" I am very happy at the turn events are taking. Providence has arranged everything well."

PAINFUL TRIALS

The necessity which obliged her to leave the Monastery of Parella which she had just acquired for the Sisters, the contradictory orders which she received on the way and the new kind of poverty which left her without a home, caused her intense suffering, as we shall see from the following two records which she has left !

" *Intimate Note.* Bologna, Oct. 23rd, 1913

" After passing through the most painful inward sorrows, I commenced my retreat. My heart became even more broken and sorrowful, but my soul was in a state of abandonment and peace. I am not surprised at the heavy crosses and crushing trials through which I have passed, especially for the past six months. It is Jesus Who wills or permits all that. I have offered myself as a victim, to Infinite Love ; it is His Love which performs in me His work of immolation. I ask but one thing of Jesus : to have the strength and patience necessary to support without flinching, without offending His Sacred Heart, the weight of so many sorrows. At the beginning of this painful crisis, my poor heart was so sorrow-stricken that I gave way to complaints : I said things that I should have had the strength to keep back. I humble myself for these things before Infinite Love, and I thank Him once more for having permitted these weaknesses which have humiliated me before creatures and discredited me in their eyes. Yes, I am happy not only to suffer, but still more to be humiliated.

" I suffer at feeling myself without family or permanent abode, a burden to all the Monasteries which receive me as I pass, as if for charity : and I am happy on account of this sorrow, of this humiliation. Jesus also had not a stone on which to lay His head."

Letter to Father Charrier.

" Monastery of Bologna,

" October 20th, 1913

" I see that you are troubled about the number and severity of my present trials and sorrows ; but believe me, they will go on increasing to the extremity and become more profound and more intense. I have offered myself as a victim to Jesus, and the Work of His Love will be established only on the complete immolation of my whole being ; even before I offered myself, Infinite Love had already exercised Its sacrificial action over me, and from the time of my infancy I have never ceased to suffer. May love be glorified ! that is all we must desire and wish for."

But the principal source of her suffering during this journey was the fear lest, in expressing in human language what was given to her to understand about the mysteries of Infinite Love, particularly with reference to the most adorable Trinity, she might have fallen into error. Our Lord was pleased to console her in her trouble :

" *Intimate Note.* October 9th, 1913

" When I awoke and during the whole morning, I was suffering slightly from my mouth ; a broken tooth had wounded and inflamed my tongue, which became swollen and painful on one side. It was of no consequence but pained me a little when I spoke or swallowed.

" Before Mass and during Mass, I suffered in my soul from feeling my powerlessness to write what I am commanded under obedience, and I was afraid that I might have written things which were erroneous on the Blessed Trinity and which, perhaps, were not according to the spirit of Our Lord. Still feeling this pain in my tongue after receiving the Sacred Host, without reflecting, I said to Jesus : ' Thou art always the same, always as powerful and as good : when placing Thyself on my tongue, Thou canst indeed cure it.' Immediately the pain disappeared. The movements of the tongue did not cause me the least trouble ; it was not even tender.

" Seeing this, I smiled at Jesus and said to Him : ' Thou perhaps art not displeased with me or with what I have written, since Thou hast done this for me.'

" Yes, Jesus is indeed always the same ; always as good towards His poor spouse, towards this sinful nothingness which, however, would wish to love Him and to make Him loved."

CHAPTER XII

THE HOLY SEE SANCTIONS THE WORK OF INFINITE LOVE

The reader will remember that in November, 1899, Mother Louise Margaret, when at prayer, had got a glimpse of a house which was shown to her as a future Monastery of the Visitation. In the course of her journey to Rome, two of the Superiors of monasteries through which she passed spontaneously advised her to found a new monastery or to co-operate in the foundation of one. At Rome, Mother Louise Margaret heard their Eminences Cardinal Gennari and Cagiano de Azevedo, as well as her confessor, not only advise her, but assure her that it was the will of God that she should do so, and she saw that they favoured the idea of a monastery of Sisters whose vocation would be to pray and immolate themselves for the Church and for priests.

While at Rome, she was ordered by Monsignor Filipello to speak to different Cardinals and Bishops about the Priests' Universal Union. All of them looked with favour upon the idea of this Union, presented under the aspect of a universal bond of charity, uniting priests and even existing associations without absorbing them or depriving them of their distinctive character. She was told that it would be easy to obtain indulgences for the Act of Consecration and Donation to Infinite Love as soon as the first branches of the Union were founded, and that she was to remain at Rome until the question was settled.

Thus it was providentially brought about that the projects so long contemplated by the Bishop of Ivrea and by Father Charrier were submitted to the judgment of the Holy See. Mother Louise Margaret had been told by Cardinal della Chiesa to go to Rome and that she would find light there. During her stay at Rome all her projects were realised; the Priests' Universal Union was approved, and arrangements were made for founding a new monastery of Sisters, who were to pray and immolate themselves for this work.

FIRST AUDIENCE WITH POPE PIUS X

On November 14th, 1913, she wrote to Monsignor Filipello:

" It will soon be a fortnight since we arrived in Rome, and by the grace of God we have already received several favours that we scarcely dared to hope for.

" On Friday last, the 7th, the dear Rev. Mother here, with the intention of showing her kindness to us by procuring for us a confessor who spoke French, introduced us to Monsignor Galardo, a very holy priest belonging to a very rich family from the Argentine. Having formerly been a lawyer, he entered the priesthood, and devotes himself with profound humility to all kinds of good works.

" This worthy priest, having learned of our desire to receive the blessing of the Holy Father, arranged all without telling us anything, and on Saturday evening sent word to the Rev. Mother that on the following day at 9.30 a.m. the Superioress of the Sisters of St. Joseph would conduct us to the Vatican. He took it on himself also to procure for us all the necessary permissions. On last Sunday, then, we had the very great consolation of seeing the Holy Father and receiving his blessing; there were only about twenty of us. We saw in our Holy Pontiff what seemed to be a shadow that came from the other world; his voice during the short discourse which He addressed to us, appeared to come from beyond the tomb.

" Afterwards we went to St. Peter's and, in order to take advantage of our outing, the good Superioress of the Sisters of St. Joseph, before bringing us back to the monastery, showed us the Mamertine Prison, the Coliseum, the Catacombs of St. Sebastian, and St. John Lateran's.

" I wonder if the time has not come to commence the foundation of the house, a vision of which I had formerly.   The Venerable Rev. Mothers of Bologna and Pisa encouraged me to do so, and they asked themselves, as I did, whether the present inexplicable situation was not a Providential manifestation on the question of this foundation.   Monsignor Galardo questioned me on this subject, and approved and encouraged this foundation, the object of which is to pray for priests.

" I tell this in all simplicity to Your Excellency ; we seek and wish only the will of God ; and certainly if you had the inspiration to come to Rome, we could speak of all this and of other matters besides, which would completely clear up the situation."

SHE HANDS IN ALL HER WRITINGS FOR EXAMINATION

At this date Mother Louise Margaret arranged her spiritual writings, both published and unpublished ; manuscripts, letters and prayers, and handed them over to competent authority to be examined and afterwards to be burned or employed for the glory of God according as it would be judged proper.

She declared : **" All that I have written, I have written in the simplicity of my heart and before God ; being profoundly ignorant, I have doubtless, made many mistakes.   I retract anything that may be contrary to the spirit of the Church or to sound doctrine, for I am above all a loving child of our Mother, the Holy, Catholic, Apostolic and Roman Church, in the most pure faith of which, I have always wished to live and die."**

On December 1st, Monsignor Filipello, while blessing her and encouraging her to accept all her suffering with ever-increasing love and abnegation for the benefit of the Work, gave her the following new order under obedience: " As far as it depends on me, I authorise you to remain in Rome until the complete conclusion of the matters which are at present being discussed by the Holy See."

On December 15th, after piously mounting the Scala Santa to obtain grace and courage, Mother Louise Margaret, in obedience to an order which she received, went to the Holy Office to see Cardinal Cagiano to whom she had been sent.

CARDINAL CAGIANO AND THE PRIESTS' UNIVERSAL UNION

On December 16th, 1913, she wrote to Mosignor Filipello :

" When speaking of the Work to Cardinal Cagiano, I explained my ideas not quite in the same way as they are expressed in the Statutes. **I showed the Priests' Universal Union as a universal bond of charity, destined to be, strictly speaking, not an additional Association for priests, added to others which are already numerous, but an all-embracing bond, uniting together all other Associations for priests and completely fusing all the priests of the world together,** It was precisely this **universality** which pleased the Cardinal ; he saw that this Union, far from creating an extra, particular organisation, would on the contrary, fill a gap and would make unity in multiplicity.

" Naturally, I did not say that these ideas were my own ; I simply said that a Bishop of Piedmont and a Religious from France were commencing to lay the foundations of this Work."

CARDINAL GENNARI AND THE FOUNDATION OF THE NEW MONASTERY

On December 26th, 1913, she wrote again to Monsignor Filipello :

" On Sunday last I received a card from His Eminence Cardinal Gennari telling me to go and speak with the Cardinal Prefect of the Sacred Congregation of Religious. I expected that he would give me a reply to my case of conscience ; he did not discuss that question. After making mention of it, he began immediately to speak on the subject of the foundation ; he asked me why I had not sent in a request to make the foundation at the same time that I submitted my case of conscience ; and after asking me many questions and interesting himself in this project he told me to prepare all the documents relating to this matter and to bring them to him at the earliest possible moment.

" It is proper that the indication of the diocese chosen for the new foundation should come in the first place. The filial attachment and profound gratitude I have always had for Your Excellency, makes me wish not to leave the dear diocese of Ivrea where Our Lord has been so liberal to me with His many graces and also with many crosses. If Your Excellency does not think that two houses of the Visitation Order would not be too much in your diocese, and if you deign to welcome this new family, personally, I shall be very happy.

" It seems that the will of Our Lord with regard to this humble foundation is making itself clear, for all those who are interesting themselves in our affairs are turning in this direction. For my part, I abandon myself to God, allowing Him to direct events according to His will, and I lovingly offer Him the sufferings and humiliations which continue to come to me."

On December 28th, 1913, Monsignor Filipello wrote to her :

" I am very much obliged to you for all the information which you are sending me in your letters.

" As to the new foundation, I wish very much to have it in my diocese, and I shall be very happy, if it can be so arranged. In my opinion, there is no difficulty about having two monasteries of the Visitation in this diocese. In the meantime, we must pray that the Will of God may be accomplished, and especially that it may be manifested by means of your Venerable Superiors.

" I have only praise for the communication which you have made to the Holy Office concerning the Work.

" Yes, certainly, I see it in that way, and I am willing to devote myself to laying the foundation of this Work and to propagating it, when the Holy See judges it opportune.

" Since you have explained the nature of the Work in a manner that gives it a wider scope than it had in the first Statutes, it is proper that you should rearrange them in conformity with the ideas which you have submitted. And in this connection, I think that in order even to group some priests together with their Bishop at their head for the purpose of obtaining the realisation of the Work, it would be necessary that the Statutes be first approved, so as not to expose these priests to disappointment.

" We shall certainly find here priests who will accept these Statutes and live in their spirit, especially when they see that the Work is intended to bind them together by a golden thread of charity and to unite them to other similar organisations.

" In the meantime, tell all the secrets of your heart completely and simply to those persons at Rome who are in a position to help you in the holy Work. It is truly providential that, in spite of so many contradictions, you have been able to get to Rome ; now speak."

On 30th December, 1913, Father Charrier wrote to her :

" I see more and more clearly that the designs of God over you are providentially mysterious. You have only to abandon yourself to His Wisdom. What you tell me impresses me very much, but does not surprise me. All I can do is to pray with my whole soul. Your affairs are in the hands of too high authorities for me to dare to pronounce a judgment. But I shall receive with submission all that may be decided.

" I should like very much to have the Statutes drawn up so as to make the Work universal. This work of love and generosity appears to me to be more and more necessary."

On December 31st, 1913, she wrote to Monsignor Filipello :

" The letter of Your Excellency, so paternally kind, has given us intense consolation. We have communicated its contents to Monsignor Galardo who has also been highly pleased with it.

" We are to see Monsignor Cherubini on Friday next ; he is to give me officially the reply to my case of conscience and directions for the foundation.

" How happy we shall be, if it pleases Jesus to put the finishing touch to His Work, to repose in the humble little nest which you will choose for us, and, as our Holy Founder says, like mystic bees distil the honey of Infinite Love and pray continually for your dear diocese.

" Monsignor Galardo appears to believe that this foundation is useful for the Work ; he says that it is necessary to nourish by a life of prayer the beginning and the development of the Priests' Universal Union."

THE DECISION OF THE HOLY SEE ON THE PROJECT OF THE NEW MONASTERY AND THE UNION FOR PRIESTS

In the beginning of January, 1914, Mother Louise Margaret, at the request of Cardinal Cagiano, Prefect of the Congregation for Religious, presented to that Congregation a petition for permission to found a new monastery of the Visitation, which was to serve as a spiritual foundation for the Priests' Universal Union. This petition was received and carefully studied by the Congregation, which granted the permission requested, and authorised Monsignor Filipello to proceed with the foundation.

On January 2nd, 1914, she wrote to Monsignor Filipello :

" As humble children of Your Excellency, we thank you once again with our whole heart for your paternal goodness in opening your dear diocese to our little foundation just coming into life.

" The Cardinal Prefect of the Congregation for Religious fully approves of our object, which is to pray very specially for the Church and for priests. At our last visit, the Cardinal asked us to put down in writing the idea underlying this foundation and its spirit. We have drawn up in all simplicity and truth the little memoir which I enclose, and which I ask Your Excellency kindly to read. His Eminence, the Cardinal, is waiting for it.

" Monsignor Galardo, who has the extracts from my writings relating to the Work and who is studying them, says that the foundation of the convent goes along with it ; **that the two things are connected, and that the convent founded must aid the development of the Work by prayer.** And so he is delighted, as Your Excellency will see by the card which I enclose, that you are receiving the foundation into your diocese and that the Priests' Universal Union is to commence there also."

On January 5th, 1914, Monsignor Filipello wrote to His Eminence Cardinal Cagiano de Azevedo, Prefect of the Sacred Congregation for Religious, as follows :

" I, the undersigned, not only consent, but deem myself happy that a new foundation of a Visitation Monastery with special objects, under the direction of the pious Sister Louise Margaret Claret de la Touche, be opened in my diocese.

" Knowing for many years the religious spirit of this good Sister and her spiritual outlook, and knowing also the good will of the Sisters who are united with her for this holy work, I hope that this foundation will redound to the glory of God, and that it will be of particular profit to one's neighbour especially to priests."

" ✠ MATTHEW FILIPELLO."

Father Charrier hastened to offer his services to " the little family " which he saw already in being :

" Need I tell you how heartily I love this little family ? You can count on complete devotedness on my part. I sympathise with you in all your crosses. How many has the Sacred Heart yet kept in reserve for you ? But He will give you strength to bear them, and they will be the most solid basis for the Work that is going to come into being ; I have much confidence that it will be so. I think that the foundation will follow closely on the approbation of the Holy See. You seem to wish me to speak to these dear souls. I shall be free from April 25th to May 22nd, and from June 22nd to July 12th. If you wish, I shall give a retreat. It should be at least ten days. Get Monsignor Filipello to write to me and I shall easily obtain permission to give it.

" May the Sacred Heart of Jesus continue to guide you to attain its ends ! You, my child, continue to abandon yourself completely to divine Providence."

On January 18th, she wrote to Monsignor Filipello :

" During these past days I have revised the Statutes so as to make them universal and have given them to Monsignor Galardo to be examined, asking him to correct, abridge, or lengthen them as he pleases. I think that he must have got them examined by Monsignor Zonghi also, who is President of the Academy of Noble Ecclesiastics, who is his intimate friend and with whom he lives at this Academy. Yesterday Monsignor Galardo brought me back these Statutes which I send herewith to your Excellency. He found nothing to be changed or corrected ; everything that is marked corresponds closely with his ideas. He told me that he thinks that this Priests' Union will be well received, that it is very simple and clear, and capable of being accommodated to all places and all dispositions, being above all a spiritual bond of charity."

On January 31st, 1914, she wrote to Monsignor Filipello :

" I hasten to give Your Excellency the good news. Yesterday at the meeting of the Sacred Congregation, **they finished the examination of our dear little foundation, and sanctioned it . . . . . .** They decided to give Your Excellency full powers to make the foundation. Monsignor Cherubini said also that you would be notified about this in four or five days at latest.

" On Thursday, I went to see His Eminence, Cardinal Gennari to recommend the foundation to his benevolence and to explain to him our desire to see the undertaking hastened. I spoke to him also about the organisation for Priests. He has the ' Statutes ' still and *The Sacred Heart and the Priesthood.* He told me that if Your Excellency would send him the new Statutes approved by you, with a letter petitioning the approbation by the Holy See, he would have them examined by the Council of which he is the Prefect.

" But I hope to see Your Excellency soon, and we can talk about the Work and the Statutes, to which Father Charrier proposes a little addition.

" Indeed, Most Venerable Father, if you approve of it, we could take the road back to Piedmont in eight days."

On January 31st, 1914, she wrote to Father Charrier :

" Sister Margaret went to the Chancery this morning and at the first free moment which I have, I write to you to communicate the good news. On Friday, at the meeting of the Council, our case was again examined and it was decided that everything was to be left in the hands of the Bishop to make the foundation. They stated that the Bishop would be officially notified in a week. You see, dear Father, that we have only to bless the Lord, now that His will is clearly manifested.

" It is probable that I shall set out for Piedmont immediately after the notification is given. I shall probably stay in a convent at Turin to make suitable arrangements with Monsignor, to visit the house and get it ready.

"You can well believe, dear Father, that I am making acts of faith and abandonment as I have never done in my life before. We should require at least three or four hundred thousand francs[1] for the first installation—the bare necessities for a humble chapel, linen for the house and a wooden grille, which is indispensable for the most primitive enclosure. Well! I have not got this three or four hundred thousand francs.

"You see then, that I must practice blind faith and abandonment to Providence. Yesterday, when writing to Monsignor to announce to him the good news, I asked him very humbly if he would kindly lend me three hundred francs for travelling expenses for myself and Sister Margaret and the expenses which we have incurred here. Naturally, that was painful to me, I assure you. It is the first time in my life that I have asked monetary assistance for myself. But this real poverty, which has nothing for the morrow except confidence in Providence, is very sweet to the soul. Later on, when we are installed, we shall have sufficient for our necessities. But for the beginning, with the expenses of these long journeys and the installation, it will be complete poverty.

"It is not to complain about these things, dear Father, that I tell you this ; it is because I wish as your child to tell you what I think.

"As to the Statutes, I have already looked over your corrections ; I shall speak to Monsignor about them as soon as I shall see him. But as to what you say about people in the cloister or in the world, it is our little foundation that will bring about that.

THE ASSOCIATES OF THE WORK

"Yes, Father, souls that are free, who are called to the religious life and who wish to live by offering their prayers and immolating themselves for the Church and priests, will come to us and will be able to make profession among us. Others, living in the world who,

---

[1] The franc was then twenty-five to the pound sterling or a little over six to the U.S. dollar.

on account of the necessity of their state, cannot join us, or those already bound by their vows in other Religious Orders, can unite themselves in this spirit, can become affiliated to our Community and joined to it by a spiritual bond.

" The three founders of the new Monastery have been the first to make the act of consecration of the Association, and our little Monastery of the Visitation, although it will be a real Visitation Monastery, will have the spirit of the Association as its particular spirit. How I would wish to be able to explain all this orally to you ! We must wait until June and then, if it please Jesus, we shall discuss it at our leisure, and you will see how similar your thoughts are to my unworthy ones.

" On Thursday, we had an audience with His Eminence Cardinal Gennari. You could not imagine how painful it was to me ; I wish so much that my person should disappear in this work. His Eminence was extremely kind to us. At the end of the interview he blessed us with such a kindly, heavenly air.''

On February 6th, 1914, she wrote to Monsignor Filipello :

" Yesterday, God in His divine goodness granted us the remarkable privilege of an audience with His Holiness. We had the intention of asking for an audience before our departure and on Wednesday I sent Sister Margaret to present our request. Scarcely had she arrived when Father Pifferi told her that he had just seen the Major-domo and that he had asked and obtained an audience for us.

" At mid-day yesterday, we had the great consolation of seeing the Sovereign Pontiff in the Throne-hall, of speaking to him, of kissing his venerable hand, of receiving his paternal blessing for Your Excellency, for our humble foundation, our families and all our intentions. At the end, His Holiness placed his holy hand on my head, pressed it firmly and for quite a long time and blessed us again. I cannot tell Your Excellency what sentiments of faith and of filial love my soul felt during this precious audience, the memory of which will never fade from Sister Margaret's mind nor from mine. We found His Holiness in much better health, more lively, more cheerful, and so holy ! May the good Master deign to preserve him still for the Holy Church.

" The Venerable Cardinal Gennari has entered into eternal happiness. This very sudden death has profoundly grieved me. Two days before, we had seen him so kind, so paternally disposed towards our affairs. He was entirely in favour of our little foundation, which he urged us to undertake at our first visit in the beginning of December. On January 29th, he had shown himself so happy about our foundation and had promised to expedite matters at the meeting of the Council on the following day. Indeed, he occupied himself with our affairs on Friday morning, and when giving us his final blessing on Thursday with an altogether heavenly fervour, at the same time he blessed Your Excellency and our humble newly-born family. He will certainly be a good protector to us in heaven.

" We do not think that the notification of the Sacred Congregation will contain many details about the foundation. The Sacred Congregation, which has taken the trouble of examining this matter so carefully, might have opposed its erection, and its approbation consists in entrusting Your Excellency with everything which regards this foundation in detail. We are very pleased with that, Most Rev. Father, for if the Sacred Congregation had itself assumed the responsibility for the details, the matter would have taken much longer to finish. We are truly the children of the Bishops, as our Holy Founder said, and we are much more so from the fact that we have only simple vows.

" Father Charrier wishes to come to us in June ! If Your Excellency approves of it, would you kindly write to the Rev. Father Provincial at Lyons, and ask him to allow Father Charrier to come to us.

" Monsignor Galardo advised us, (His Eminence, Cardinal Gennari being no longer in this world), to recommend the Work to another Cardinal of the Sacred Congregation of the Council before our departure from Rome. To-morrow we are to have an audience with His Eminence, Cardinal Merry del Vai, who has kindly consented to receive us. Monsignor Galardo wishes us to tell him everything and to give him a copy of the Statutes in order that he may become acquainted with the Work. It cost me a good deal to do so, for I am most reluctant to speak of this, but it is for Jesus and His glory that I do it. Yesterday, he again spoke to us saying : ' The profound study that has been made of your ideas and your writings is an assurance that you are acting perfectly according to the will of God in undertaking this foundation, which is truly willed by God. And now you are so completely with Our Lord that, in my humble opinion, you and all those who are to co-operate in this foundation would be guilty of an act of real infidelity to grace, if you do not put your hand to this work immediately.'

" Your Excellency sees that all possible assurances have been given to us. This will give us courage to surmount the difficulties which will not be wanting to us at the final stage.

" We thank Your Excellency for the trouble which you are taking for us to find a place to shelter us at Turin."

POPE PIUS X BLESSES THE WORK OF INFINITE LOVE

Mother Louise Margaret and Sister Margaret addressed a petition to the Pope in which, while setting forth the object of the foundation, they asked the Apostolic Blessing for themselves, their co-operators and for all those who would aid in the establishment of this Community.

Pius X, of venerable memory, deigned to write with his own hand at the bottom of this petition the following :—

" Praying that the Lord may be liberal with His choicest graces to our dear Daughters, in order that they may correspond with their holy vocation, we grant them with all our heart the Apostolic Blessing.

Pius PP.X."

February 8th, 1914.

CHAPTER XIII

THE FOUNDATION OF THE NEW MONASTERY AT VISCHE

Mother Louise Margaret and her companion arrived at Turin on February 18th, and received hospitality which had been prepared for them by the Sisters of Charity. Their first care was to seek out a house suitable for the new foundation. Efforts previously made to find one had brought no result.

However, in the beginning of March, 1914, a house at Vische was offered to Monsignor Filipello. The owners wished that it should be acquired by a Religious Community. The negotiations for the leasing of this house were quickly concluded. Mother Louise Margaret, at her first visit there, recognised in it the little house that had been formerly shown to her by the divine Master on October 29th, 1899.

After the death of Mother Louise Margaret, Miss Louise Rossi, the daughter of the proprietor of the Vische House, told of the providential circumstances in which the house was acquired :

" It was certainly Providence that brought me in contact with this good and gentle Sister who in such a short time has been able to inspire me with sentiments of such profound esteem and such pious and profound affection.

" My mother had frequently expressed her desire that one of our houses, which enshrined sacred memories of dear friends, should be inhabited by Religious. On a certain rainy day, (a Saturday, a day dedicated to the Blessed Virgin), my mother urged by a secret presentiment, went to see Monsignor Filipello and told him about her intentions. Now while she was at the Bishop's residence, Sister Margaret, the worthy companion of the Rev. Mother Superior Louise Margaret de la Touche, happened to be there at the very same time.

" The two Religious were in search of a house ; my mother was in search of Religious to live in one of her houses, and recognising this happy coincidence, Monsignor himself exclaimed : ' This is providential ! it is truly providential ! ' My mother was also of the same opinion. A moment's conversation sufficed to arrange the day for a visit to the house."

The property was leased and on March 19th, the Feast of St. Joseph ; the Bishop of Ivrea issued the decree of foundation. On March 25th, the Feast of the Annunciation, the first Mass was celebrated in the new Monastery. Religious life began, as the Foundress had desired, in poverty, simplicity, and humility.

However, in various circles outside, people found it hard to understand the necessity for this new monastery, and Mother Louise Margaret was judged severely. " It is so good to be humiliated," she writes, "to be regarded as an imposter, and yet to feel that the good Master is not angry."

Before leaving Rome, she wrote the following letter to Monsignor Filipello on February 15th, 1914:

"We expect to leave on Tuesday next, by the 6 p.m. train and arrive in Turin on Wednesday at 8 p.m.

"Yes, we can say that we are leaving Rome laden with rich blessings. Yesterday, we saw Monsignor Virili (Postulator at Rome for the cause of St. Margaret Mary) and with his heart so full of affection for our dear Visitation, he blessed our little foundation, promising to come and visit it; he conversed with us for nearly an hour with a simplicity and confidence which very much edified us.

"This morning, it was Monsignor Zonghi who came to bless ourselves and our little future family. Being a man of great piety, he appreciated *The Sacred Heart and the Priesthood* very much and has taken a very keen interest in the foundation.

"Your Excellency sees that Jesus is always Infinite Love and that, if sometimes He makes us suffer much, He gives us consolation also. One of the greatest consolations that we have had is the assurance given us here that this foundation is really in accordance with the Will of God. On the day before yesterday, Monsignor Galardo, when he came for our confession, said to me: 'Perhaps you will have to suffer much yet, but you can be certain that this foundation is according to the Will of God, and that you are carrying out this Divine Will in making it.'

"Our Venerable Rev. Mother wishes me to thank Your Excellency cordially for the letters which you have written to her. She is overwhelmed by your great kindness and purposes to reply to Your Excellency in a few days, but she does not wish to wait till then to express her gratitude and profound respect."

Monsignor Galardo, who had followed this whole question of the foundation with keen interest, gave Mother Louise Margaret and her companions great encouragement. But on the last but one occasion that he saw them he said to them:

"Go and do the work of God, sacrifice yourselves, immolate yourselves for His love. Unheard of sufferings, such as you cannot even suspect, await you. If you are faithful, Jesus also will be faithful. But you must not be astonished, above all, you must not be discouraged, if everything does not go as you have planned, and if at certain times your plans seem to be upset. That will be the time to be still more faithful, to abandon yourselves more, to immolate yourselves still more   Yes, **this work of yours is necessary to help the Priests' Universal Union ; they go together."**

THE LITTLE HOUSE

On February 21st she wrote to Father Charrier telling him about the little house :

" Thanks with all my filial heart for your paternal solicitude. When it is a question of goodness and charity, I am not astonished at anything you do.

" It is certain that from every point of view this little house will suit us perfectly. It is suitable for the life of the cloister. It has a garden, many fruit trees, good air, a view of the mountains, friendly neighbours, a doctor quite near, and a charming family that will be a real help to us. Nothing better could be desired.

" The house is very clean, healthy, pleasant and enshrines religious memories ; true, it is very small. But for the present it will be sufficient and as all the furniture in it is very simple, iron beds, tables, chairs, etc., we could go into it to-morrow if the lease had been signed.

" By raising it a storey higher later on, which the doctor says would cost from about six to eight thousand francs, we could easily accommodate twenty Sisters in it. As it is at the present time, we could have about eleven beds.

" A little chapel could easily be made in the great entrance hall, also an enclosure and the choir could be installed in a room close by which has a ceiling.

" But the difficulty is that the doctor insists on selling it and does not wish to lease it, or he will agree to let it and give us a long lease if we promise to buy it later on.

" For us, that suits our present necessity perfectly. They wish that the deal be concluded on Saturday at Turin, because they have prayed to the Blessed Virgin to get their house leased, and they consider that day suitable as it is consecrated to Our Lady.

" It seems, as you said, Rev. Father, that it is Providence that has prepared this little house for us, and even the proprietors are very well disposed."

On March 16th, the eve of the opening of the new monastery, she wrote to Monsignor Filipello :

" What is certain is that Providence, which has arranged every-thing up to the present, will finish its work, and that the souls marked out by Infinite Love will be brought to us when their time comes.

" In the hope of receiving Your Excellency's blessing to-morrow and of being soon shut up in our silent nest, I remain with the most profound and filial respect . . . . . "

On March 19th, when the house rented at Vische was sufficiently ready, Monsignor Filipello, when greeting the Sisters who were to be its first occupants, said to them :

" Peace and consolation in the Holy Spirit to you ! Having received from Rome the Rescript authorising your foundation in this diocese under our licence and good pleasure, we order you to proceed there as soon as possible in order to co-operate in a good work which tends towards the greater glory of God and the salvation of many souls. We exhort and command you to live there in the perfect observance of the rules and constitutions of your Order and according to the spirit of your holy founders.

" And praying God to guide you and keep you always under the protection of His Mercy we bless you."

LIFE IN THE LITTLE COMMUNITY

The foundation of the Visitation Monastery at Vische was an accomplished fact. Religious life was quickly organised, with, however, the usual preoccupations about material things incidental to every foundation. Then in August ,1914, war broke out ; the hearts of those exiled Sisters were grieved at seeing their native land, which they were forced to leave, now under the heel of the invader.

The letters of Mother Louise at this time tell us little about her interior life. She had to think of the needs of the foundation before everything else. However, the following few lines give us a glimpse of it.

" My soul is almost continually in a state of adoration and contemplative immobility before Infinite Love, Which guides all things with strength and sweetness."

As for the Priests' Universal Union, in view of the external difficulties, it was considered advisable to wait till peace was established in men's minds and hearts before proceeding with its establishment. Besides, it was in accordance with the designs of Providence that the establishment should be deferred until all questions regarding the new Community were finally settled by the Holy See and the Community became an independent religious congregation with full freedom to carry out the work that Providence entrusted to it, which was to be the spiritual foundation for the Priests' Universal Union.

The following letters to Monsignor Filipello and Father Charrier written by Mother Louise Margaret in the last year of her life give us interesting details about the life of the little Community ; a life of intimate union with God and holy joy amidst privations and contradictions :

On March 23rd, 1914, she wrote to Father Charrier :

" . . . . . We also were impatiently awaiting a letter from you. Finally it has come bringing sorrow and consolation, like all things in this life ; sorrow, because of this new storm which is raised against us and which, for a short time only, I hope, will prevent you from coming to us ; consolation at seeing your paternal goodness in remaining faithful to us all the same, and in procuring for us assistance which is very useful to us at this moment. We must entrust all to Our Lord, and without doubt His adorable Heart will arrange everything. It is certain that the devil is not pleased with our little foundation, and he is always thinking out some new kind of persecution : but Jesus is the stronger. In these days of His holy Passion, let us unite together more than ever, and afterwards will come the hour of the Resurrection."

On March 25th, 1914, she wrote to Monsignor Filipello :

" This morning at eight o'clock, we had the great consolation of hearing Holy Mass for the first time in the humble chapel of Alberetto. Madam Bolocco (the wife of the proprietor) and her daughter who assisted were very much touched, and about twenty people who knew the time of the Mass, we do not know how, asked permission to assist at it ; as the *clausura* did not yet exist, we permitted them to enter the garden and from there they assisted at the Mass with great recollection.

" We are putting our whole hearts into the preparation of this House of Infinite Love and we feel that He is aiding us and sustaining us in a very special manner."

And again on 30th March, 1914 :

" . . . . . The good people of Vische continue to come in considerable numbers to our Holy Mass. On Friday there were fifty-two, and to-day there were still more. The pastor is to come to hear confessions to-morrow and on Friday, the First Friday of the month, he will give a sermon at Mass. It is, then, in our little chapel that the devotion to the Sacred Heart will begin to be known here."

MISUNDERSTANDINGS

Like St. Margaret Mary Alcoque, Mother Louise Margaret was misunderstood by the Sisters of the monastery in which she had lived. In the case of St. Margaret Mary, the misunderstanding was cleared up before her death, but in that of Mother Louise Margaret, it was humanly speaking impossible. It was only when her writings were published after her death, that those Sisters understood that in all that Mother Louise Margaret had done, she acted under obedience to the proper authority, and, we may even say, had been compelled by a divine command. All these misunderstandings have happily disappeared, and all Visitation Monasteries have a warm welcome for the Sisters of Bethany of the Sacred Heart wherever they travel. During her life, Mother Louise Margaret suffered intensely from being misunderstood and misrepresented, but never showed the slightest trace of resentment.

In reply to a letter from Father Charrier of April 30th, 1914, she wrote :

" As for me, I allow many matters to drop, and I count on the adorable Heart of Jesus, Who will give light when the time comes and when it will be for His glory.

" You tell me that I must above all excuse people's intentions. I endeavour especially not to stop to think of the intentions of those who judge me wrongly. Whether their intention is good or bad, I wish to pardon them and love them in charity. The Heart of the good Master has still more to suffer than mine on the part of so many creatures who despise Him and forget His love, and yet He loves all creatures and would wish to save all. He knows well that people's intentions are not all good and yet He is merciful to all."

And in her letter of May 12th to Father Charrier, she shows the same beautiful spirit of charity and trust in God in the midst of the most complete poverty.

" I am not troubled about anything ; either about what people may say, or what they may think about us.

" Let us allow the storm to pass. Whatever comes from creatures, whatever is merely external, lasts only for a time and can do very little against the works of God.

" If this foundation is willed by Our Lord, He will be able to preserve it, if it is not, we do not want it either. I am completely tranquil about all that comes from the exterior ; but for the interior of our little foundation, I wish that the pure spirit of charity and humility should be established there.

" . . . . . We have to count our last farthing to live. We do a little exchange ; yesterday we sold three small heads of asparagus from our garden for nine pence, and with this bought some vegetables to help to nourish us for a part of the week. Our garden, which was sown very late, has still nothing except a few poor heads of asparagus."

And in a letter written to Monsignor Filipello in May, 1914, she shows the same forgiving spirit :

" Without troubling about anything that is being said or done against us, we are following our life of prayer, pleading each day for the Holy Church, for you, Most Rev. Father, and for priests in general, especially those of this dear diocese.

" It is good for us to feel that we are in the hands of Our Lord, and it is from Him and His divine Heart that we expect everything. Too happy shall we be, if our present humiliations can serve the glory of the good Master and His Work of Love."

In her letter of June 21st, 1914, to Monsignor Filipello, she tells him of the celebration of the Feast of the Sacred Heart :

" On Friday last we celebrated the first Feast of the Sacred Heart in our humble chapel. We asked the Pastor if he would consent to have Exposition of the Blessed Sacrament ; he willingly acceded to our wishes, and from Mass time up to Benediction in the evening, the good people of Vische surrounded the good Master in great numbers. We decorated the altar with flowers and lights, and our humble adorations went up to Our Lord the whole day. Our Sisters chanted the litanies at Benediction, the people gave the responses, and all were very pleased with this pious function. The pastor himself came to join in the adoration. Your Excellency promised us a visit in June : May we still hope for it ? "

In her letter of June 25th to Father Charrier, she suggests that people in the world, as well as Religious, should co-operate in the Work of Infinite Love :

" I have almost completely recovered. Just a little weakness still remains : I have not yet resumed the office in choir, but I assist at the six o'clock Mass almost every morning and we are working as hard as we can to prepare an alb, a chasuble, and altar linen for the Feast of the Visitation. You see that there is no further reason to be uneasy about my health. I have been very well taken care of, and our Sisters surround me with their filial attentions.

" Last Friday we had the first Exposition of the Blessed Sacrament ; natural flowers and lights furnished the decorations of our little chapel. It was a memorable day. There were people from the six o'clock Mass until Benediction in the evening in adoration at the feet of the good Master. And they prayed most fervently. Sister Margaret Agnes and her sister chanted beautifully both the Litany of the Sacred Heart and the hymns for Benediction, and everyone was very much pleased with our little ceremony. And what consolation for us! We all recited the Act of Consecration to Infinite Love together in choir.

"While I was ill, I had several ideas about uniting souls in the world with us in the same spirit. We must write something on that question and circulate it among those who are called."

BEGINNING OF HER LAST ILLNESS

In her next letter written in July, she tells Father Charrier of the beginning of the illness that was to prove fatal:

" I must tell you of the illness which the good Master sent me. At first it was only a severe cold caught on the eve of the Ascension when I was taking in the fifty-eight parcels from Madame Grange. At first I did not notice it and in spite of feeling somewhat uncomfortable, I kept on my feet. Besides, I did not wish to alarm my good mother who was going to leave. After her departure, thinking lightly of it, I continued work as usual, although coughing and feverish ; finally, on the following Thursday, I had to give in and go to bed with a severe attack of bronchitis. Then, during the night from Sunday to Monday, I became worse and my heart grew weak. I understood that I had an attack of Bright's disease. The doctor found that as a matter of fact I had, and so severe was the attack, that he was alarmed and wished to have a consultation, offering to go himself for a professor from Turin. We contented ourselves with our local doctor."

DEATH OF POPE PIUS X

In her letter of August 12th, 1908, to Father Charrier, she had foretold that the life of Pope Pius X would not be very long ; in her present letter of August 20th, 1914, to Monsignor Filipello, she tells him of her grief at his death :

" The sorrowful news of the death of our Holy Father, Pius X, which came t his morning, has profoundly grieved us, and we thought immediately that your heart, which was so devoted to His Holiness must have been sadly moved by this loss.

" As daughters of the Holy Church and of the Holy See, we are going to devote ourselves to prayer in a special manner during these days of mourning and expiation. To-day we shall make the Holy Hour, and to-morrow, at the feet of Jesus exposed on our humble altar, we shall beg Him to console and sustain His Church.

" The Pastor, who is full of delicate attention for our little foundation, was very pleased at the idea of having Exposition of the Blessed Sacrament to-morrow and encouraged us to have it ; also all the people around are pleased. We are having it in honour of our holy Foundress, St. Jane Frances de Chantal, in order that she may protect our little family.

" Divine Providence continues to send us help. In spite of the war we are getting many useful little presents. Our sacristy is being furnished gradually and we shall soon be able to return to the parish all that has been lent to us.

" We offer special prayers for Our Holy Mother the Church until the election of the successor of the late Holy Father. In order to add the merit of obedience, would Your Excellency tell us that you wish us to do so ? After Holy Mass the faithful can join in our prayer but we cannot keep them praying too long."

On August 28th she tells Father Charrier of the priests conscripted for the war and of the arrival of a postulant :

" We are also praying fervently for the poor fallen soldiers and in what numbers ! Nearly all our good Capuchin Fathers have gone to the front ; there are only five remaining—aged or sick—in the convent of Chivasso. The priest who hears our confessions and says Mass on Sundays for us has not left, being ailing, but the Father Guardian himself has gone to the war. Poor, dear France ! What is going to become of her ? It seems that, without a miracle, such as that of Joan of Arc, we are going to be completely defeated.

" A young girl who presented herself to-day seems to have all the conditions required for us : intelligence, true vocation, a disposition already inclined to prayer and immolation for priests."

THE FUTURE ASSOCIATES OF THE PRIESTS' UNIVERSAL UNION AND FAITHFUL FRIENDS OF BETHANY OF THE SACRED HEART[1]

Letter to Father Charrier, September 26th, 1914 :

"**The will of God seems to me always to be that we should unite souls in the world who have an attraction for Infinite Love and for praying for priests, to our little Community.** The people who have consecrated themselves to Infinite Love are all marked out for that. But we need to bring out an explanatory leaflet and those people should be united with our Monastery.

" Write to me clearly what you think ; tell me the names and the number of those who have been initiated by you, whether ladies or priests. Tell me whether, in the leaflet in question, we can speak of our new Community, of union with it, etc. This work would have to be commenced and approved before asking for indulgences for it at Rome. How have you spoken of this to those who have made the act of consecration ? Should not these people be put in touch with our little Monastery ? Should the matter be secret and hidden ?

" For myself, I think that the book to give inspiration for the exterior life should be *The Introduction to the Devout Life* by St. Frances de Sales, and that the impulse for the interior life should be got from the knowledge of Infinite Love and from the act of the consecration, and that the end should be to pray for the Church and for Priests.

" I beg of you to reply promptly about this question, for I have two people here who wish to know exactly what they must do and in what this union consists.

" No, I do not know the present Pope. He was Archbishop of Bologna when I was there ; we sent him a copy of the book (*The Sacred Heart and the Priesthood*)—I believe that it was he who decided my departure for Rome, but I have never seen him and perhaps he does not even know my name.

---

[1] For further information about the Associates and Faithful Friends see *The Little Book of the Work of Infinite Love*, price 1/6.

" I would like to have some young women representing all countries in order to imbue them with Infinite Love and make It circulate everywhere. If it be the will of Jesus, He will send them one day."

On September 8th Father Charrier wrote to her to console her on her many trials :

" May the sweet peace of the Lord be all the more profound in your soul as everything around you is naturally calculated to extinguish it. You are suffering alone ! Oh, no ! The Master, who is sending you these trials, does not leave you alone. If He seems to do so, it is in order to try your faith and love. But He is surely with you, because He is sending so many crosses. All these crosses and contradictions prove to me that you are doing the work of God ; and God laughs at the opposition of men to His will. At the moment when men believe that they are prevailing against His, it is He who triumphs gently but mightily, and men are obliged to recognise His victory. The last word always belongs to God ; in your case, you may rest assured that He will have the last word. And even if He were to make you pass through still more painful trials, His end will be attained by means of this poor little instrument, which you will never cease to be in His hands. Bury yourself then in deeper and deeper humility, and increase your confidence as difficulties around you grow greater.

" I have great pity for your extreme poverty, and my powerlessness to relieve it increases my pain. Just now in France, everything goes to help the innumerable cases of distress caused by the war. The shutting down of industries and closing of work-shops have occasioned such misery that all the resources of charity are needed to relieve it. Even the rich have no longer money at their disposal, for the law prevents them from withdrawing their money from the banks where it is deposited. What numbers of afflicted ! My heart bleeds for all your sufferings, but I enter with these sufferings into the Sacred Heart which imposed them, and I ask It to sustain those who bear them. You also enter into this tabernacle of Infinite Love and wait there patiently for the end of your present trials, knowing that they are fertile for the work undertaken for Infinite Love. If Divine

Providence puts any gift that can be of service to you in my way, you know how glad I shall be to send it on to you. That at least is permitted to me. I recommend myself to your prayers and sufferings."

In her letter to Monsignor Filipello, written in October, 1914, she expresses her one desire : **the establishment of the reign of Infinite Love :**

" We are going to make our annual retreat from the 9th to 21st, all together with Jesus, our good Master. We have but one desire : to establish the reign of Infinite Love in this little family, to prepare the diffusion of it among priests by our self-immolation and prayers."

Father Charrier again consoles her :

" Diano Marino, October 19th, 1914
" I feel that you are in the midst of such suffering, such uncertainty, such obstacles that I have great pity for your condition. I think of them continually, and if I did not know that divine works are founded in misfortunes and contradictions, I should not have such great confidence in the final success, and I should, be inclined to be alarmed at this uninterrupted series of trials through which God has made you pass.

" My child, remain humble and full of confidence at the feet of Our Lord. Let your love for Him be nourished on the thousand crosses laid on your shoulders and causing your heart to bleed. Courage and confidence ! When this terrible scourge which is devastating Europe ceases its work, I hope that with peace among the nations, your work will begin to prosper for the greater good of those souls who will consecrate themselves to Infinite Love."

POVERTY OF THE LITTLE COMMUNITY

In her letter to Father Charrier, begun on November 27th and finished on December 2nd, 1914, she tells him of the poverty of the Sisters, her illness, and gives us a glimpse of the Community life :

" On November 10th, all three of us entered retreat, which I made as well as I could.

" We abandon ourselves to Divine Providence and live as economically as possible without, however, depriving our Sisters of nourishment; we have not yet lighted any fire except that of our little stove in the kitchen. All three of us endure the cold valiantly, but my hands are covered with chilblains. One catches cold less easily when everywhere is cold than if one goes frequently into changing temperatures."

" December 2nd.

" I am beginning my letter again after receiving a double mail. And first, I received your card announcing the serious illness of your brother, which is causing your heart such grief. Yes, we are all praying for him, who was so good to us at Revigliasce. He is a faithful servant of God who will enter without difficulty into the repose of the Lord. And will your dear sister be able to take care of him?

" I recommend to your good prayers the soul of my brother-in-law who has just died. I have not had many details, but I know that for the past year and a half he has had two attacks. Our Lord makes us all perceive His divine action tangibly every day. We are all, thanks to His favour, enjoying extraordinary health."

On December 23rd, 1914, she wishes Monsignor Filipello a happy Christmas for the last time:

" The humble little Community of the Visitation of Vische is happy to present to Your Excellency its respectful and filial good wishes for the Feast of Christmas and for the New Year.

" Each day after Matins we pray very specially for Your Excellency, and again each morning after Holy Mass. It is a very pleasant duty which nothing can make us omit. We hope that this severe cold is not trying for Your Excellency's health and that your respected mother and your dear sister also are able to endure it well.

" Here we have not had a single cold yet and our whole little family is passing courageously through the winter without any other heating system than foot-warmers. As we are frequently obliged to go to the garden and to the parlour, 1 think that we should have got cold oftener if we had the house heated.

"Besides, we are all conscious of special graces, the graces attached to foundations, which enable us to do and to endure things which we could not have done at other times."

LAST ILLNESS AND DEATH OF MOTHER LOUISE MARGARET

During her last year, Mother Louise Margaret wrote a few more letters with her own hand or dictated them to her faithful secretary, letters which show confidence in divine Providence and in the future of the foundation. The number of postulants increased gradually, and visible blessings from God continued to descend upon the humble house. During the first months of the year 1915, the Holy See was petitioned to withdraw the authorisation which it had granted to the Bishop of Ivrea in his diocese, and the reply given was a confirmation of the authorisation granted in the preceding year.

Everything seemed to make for a stable situation when Mother Louise Margaret became seriously ill in February. Unable to stand on her feet or lie in bed, she had to remain in an armchair night and day for the last months of her life. Despite this, she continued to take charge of the spiritual and temporal direction of the Community and of the Novitiate until her last day, and took part in all the religious exercises. In spite of nights of painful agony during which the divine Master associated her mysteriously with His Cross, in the morning, she found the energy to smile and hide her martyrdom from the Sisters. Three hours before her death she still gave 'obediences' to the Sisters, appointing their duties and their work for the day. On Friday, May 14th, the day after the feast of the Ascension, at three o'clock in the afternoon, Mother Louise Margaret, after pronouncing the sacred name of Jesus for the last time, went to sleep peacefully in the Lord, at the age of forty-seven years.

Happily, her companions and those with whom she came in contact have preserved for us the impression which her exalted virtue and her heroism in suffering during her last illness made upon them. The testimony of Sister Margaret is particularly valuable ; she was her constant companion during these last years, and knew the secrets of her mystic life. But even those who saw only the exterior are unanimous in proclaiming their admiration for the heroic patience with which she bore the sufferings which caused her death.

They say : " Her heroic patience was never for a moment ruffled."
" A complaint never escaped from her lips."

Her doctors say : " A person can have no idea of how painful her disease was, or express in words what she had to endure."

HER LAST LETTERS

On January 12th and February 25th, she wrote to Monsignor Filipello to tell him of the arrival of postulants and of their training :

" Jesus is gradually sending labourers into His little vineyard of Vische. Two postulants entered last March and we are now five. A young girl from Turin is waiting to be free to come to us, also the daughter of M. Chivasso.

" A dozen girls from Vische come to the parlour once a week for lessons in embroidery ; they appear to be very pleased, as is also our Pastor."

" At our common meetings we read passages from good books to supply for preaching, and we are endeavouring to form our Sisters to this life of union with Infinite Love, which is the end of our foundation."

In her letter of March 15th, 1915, to Monsignor Filipello, she refers to the Monastery of Vische as " the root hidden in the ground of the Work of Infinite Love." :

" The remembrance which Your Excellency has kept of the anniversary of our little foundation has touched us deeply and we thank you heartily for the paternal sentiments which you have so kindly expressed to us.

" Indeed, Divine Providence has shown itself liberal towards **our humble foundation, whose function is to be the principle and the root hidden in the ground, of the Work of Infinite Love,** we can say that each day we receive marks of divine protection and of the sweet attentions of the Heart of Jesus.

" Some persons from France sent us the requisites to have

exposition of the Blessed Sacrament on First Fridays of the month and on our great feasts. These divine acts of benevolence encourage us to bear our present poverty and to go through these difficult times.

" How grateful we are to Your Excellency for the goodness which you show us on every occasion and for your proposal to help us by a subsidy. We are very happy in our poverty and personal privations do not trouble us, but it is very painful for me to contract debts, and I beg Our Lord to enable us to pay them as soon as possible.

" For some time past, the good Master has been keeping me on the cross of sickness, obliging me to remain night and day in an arm-chair.

" Nevertheless, I am able to look after the Community as before, and each day I give instruction in the Novitiate.

" The people of Vische still come in good numbers to our little chapel, but they complain that our bell is too small and that it cannot be heard at a distance. Does Your Excellency know if there is anywhere at Ivrea, or in the diocese, a bell sufficiently large which could be lent to us ? that would be very acceptable.

" We confide all this dear little · family to the Sacred Heart of Jesus and we shall comply with whatever Your Excellency desires for the settlement of our present affairs."

In her letters of April 1st and April 11th, 1915, she tells Monsignor Filipello of the trials of the Community, and of the appeal to the Holy See to have the Monastery closed :

" While respectfully offering our filial good wishes for a happy feast of Easter, we write to thank you for the paternal letter which you have so kindly written to us.

" Yes, the trials of our little foundation are great and numerous ; but those who know them say that they are a mark of the works of God, and that we must not let ourselves be discouraged by them.

" The present war is one of our greatest trials and it is God Himself directly Who sends it to us.

" How grateful we are to Your Excellency for the help which you have so kindly offered to us in spite of present difficulties. I think that Sister Margaret will be able to go to Ivrea at the beginning of Easter week.

Bishop Filipello

The Little House

The New Wing of the Monastery

The Grave of Mother Louise Margaret

" I had to write a note to Madame Balocco to-day asking her to wait a little for the payment of our rent. Jesus knows how painful to me that was."

" April 11th, 1915.
" I take the liberty of sending to Your Excellency a letter which I have just received. It informs us of the re-examination which is being made at Rome of the question of our foundation.
" As for us, Most Rev. Father, we wish only the will of God, and this news does not trouble us in the least.
" God is able to obtain His glory from everything and we have only to abandon ourselves into His Divine Hands and especially to His love."

On April 11th, Father Charrier wrote to her to express his joy at the news that the Holy See had confirmed the foundation :

" May God be blessed ! The little Monastery of Vische founded in poverty and amidst trials has been again approved.
" I bless Our Lord Who has thus re-affirmed His will by this new decision of Rome."

On May 12th, 1915, Sister Margaret wrote to Father Charrier to tell him that Mother Louise Margaret was dangerously ill :

" I am writing to you in the midst of the most sorrowful affliction. I am by the bed-side of our good, saintly Mother who has just had a severe attack of nephritis, with Bright's disease and other complications. The doctor warned me that her life was in danger, and I called in the Pastor, who heard her confession and administered the last Sacraments. Some days previous she had been improving ; her complete cure seemed to be only a matter of days. Even to-day she insisted on being brought down to the Community room, but all the time she felt a kind of drowsiness and was like wax. When the doctor came, he found her very ill. She kept saying all the time that she was better and not to be uneasy about her, as it was the result of the attack of Bright's disease.
" I said to her several times that I was going to write to Monsignor ; she replied to me : ' I forbid you ; you will needlessly alarm him.'

" I do not know how to write to you this evening, Father, as you can well understand, my heart is full of the most poignant grief. A miracle alone can save her. Ask for this miracle with us, Father ; pray and get prayers said. You know what a treasure we wish to keep. When you receive this letter, how will she be ? Jesus alone knows. It is the time to make a great act of faith and abandonment.

" Our Mother desired so much to write to you these last days. She was waiting, she said, to be better in order to give you more details and open her soul to you fully. Poor Mother, what a martyr in soul, body and heart !

" Just as I am writing, she is very ill. Bless her ; bless us and accept . . . . . "

TOUCHING DESCRIPTION BY SISTER MARGARET OF HER LAST ILLNESS AND DEATH

On May 14th, 1915, Sister Margaret sends Father Charrier the news of her death :

" The consummation of the great trial has come. Jesus has taken back from us the treasure which we possessed, in our most honoured and loved Mother. We were not worthy to possess her, and perhaps we did not know how to correspond with this favour, and Jesus has taken her away from us.

" Her beautiful soul went to sleep in the Lord in the greatest peace. She was in the state of the most complete abandonment to Providence either to live or to die. If it had been the will of God, she would have gladly lived for her little foundation which was increasing, and at the sight of all the daily marks of Providence, the spiritual and temporal works already commenced by our good Mother, a person would be inclined to think that her death was impossible. She herself often said : ' Oh ! I think I must resign myself to be cured and to suffer still for a long time.'

" This morning she reassured us and told us that she was feeling much better. Her clear intellect remained unimpaired, but she had difficulty in speaking. At midday she still gave us the orders for the day ; after that she spoke only a few words more.

" But when I see you, Father, I shall relate all that in greater detail ; to-night I am crushed by sorrow, fatigue, and the great responsibility which falls on my shoulders."

And on the following day, Sister Margaret told her mother, Madame de Chamberet, about her last illness and death :

" Our dear Mother was suffering from nephritis which brought on Bright's disease. She began to feel the first symptoms last November, but up to February she bore her illness standing, and displayed rare energy and angelic virtue.

" However, the swelling persisted and walking became painful to her. It was agreed that we should install her downstairs so that she could continue to look after everything and direct everything more easily. We changed the refectory into our little Community-room, and the refectory, which is beside the kitchen where we keep up the fire day and night, became the infirmary, and the Community-room at the time of the Sisters' recreations. There, during three months and a half, our beloved Mother continued to give us the most admirable examples of the Christian virtues, of the sweetest patience, and the most complete abandonment to Providence. There also, she passed days and especially nights of martyrdom. There, after suffering like a person in her death-agony, in the morning, she was found possessed of a supernatural strength which enabled her to carry out all her duties, of Foundress, Superioress and Mistress of Novices. Not a single time did she miss any of the Community exercises or fail to give her instruction to the novices, and God alone knows what such efforts cost.

" I never left her either day or night ; I had the honour and the great consolation to be the witness of her heroic sufferings as well as of her heroic virtues, and the confidante of her joys and sorrows.

" Even the heart and eyes of a child could understand the greatness of her sufferings, so that I often wondered if she was not enduring her purgatory on earth . . . . . but her strength of soul, her rare energy, her self-possession, were so great that the Sisters never suspected her sufferings.

" Sometimes in confidence she would say to me : ' Because people see me sitting in an arm-chair, looking after everything they do not imagine that I am ill and that all this costs a painful effort ; but you see, I have always the grace to carry out my duty, which proves that Jesus wishes it so.' Her pleasant countenance was in no way altered. She grew even younger looking and rosy, like a person in perfect health

" During the nights, however, and in the morning when I was alone with her, I remarked that a change was coming over her and that she had an expression like one crucified. Several times I told her of this. ' Yes,' she said to me, ' there is something supernatural about this illness.' Indeed, everything in this angelic existence was a miracle, and up to the end, I hoped for a miracle. It seemed that she was indispensable to us, and that Jesus could not take away our treasure from us.

" When she saw me saddened by her condition, she would say to me : ' Why are you grieving ? If I am useful to the foundation Jesus will keep me ; He has brought me through worse illnesses. If I am not useful, oh ! well, I will go with Jesus. How grand it will be up there to be lost in Infinite Love !

" Often she repeated : ' I give myself to the good God ; if I am to remain an invalid, be it as He will. I am not saying an Our Father either to be cured, or to die.' ' Oh ! Mother, since we are so eager that you be cured, do you not wish to be cured for our sake.? ' ' Oh ! yes, I say to Jesus : If what my children ask of Thee is according to Thy holy Will, with all the heart of a Mother, I beg of Thee to hear them.'

" How many prayers said, how many novenas made, how many acts performed to obtain her recovery ! How many candles burned ! If Jesus has taken her, it is indeed because she was not to remain any longer on this earth.

" At the very time when Jesus was coming to pluck His ' precious flower ' we were getting back hope of seeing our dear, edifying Mother cured. She herself said to us : ' Now it is only a question of days ! I feel well, even very well. If the swelling does not return, and if I do not get another attack of dropsy, it seems that I am on the road to recovery.' And indeed the whole month of April and the first days of May had been as good as possible. Our Mother worked at various kinds of embroidery either for the decoration of her dear little chapel, or to sell in order to increase our income.

" She said again : ' Now I think I must resign myself to be

cured. The many proofs of His Providence that Jesus gives us show us that our little house is pleasing to Him; then, if I am useful to this house, I must resign myself to continue to endure great suffering.'

" And then, being as generous as she was indifferent to living or dying, she accepted all the most painful remedies that were thought necessary to help cure her.

" At the chapter meetings, how often did she not heroically control herself so that not a muscle of her face or a sign of dejection in her countenance revealed to our Sisters the martyrdom which she was enduring. The doctor said to me after her death : ' You can have no idea how painful this disease was. One cannot express in words what she had to endure.' I who knew something of what she was suffering, said to her when our Sisters were leaving the meeting to make the Holy Hour : ' If you wish, Mother, we shall make the Holy Hour together.' She accepted and said to me : ' Yes, my child, let us both suffer along with Jesus.' Her suffering increased and became so violent that some tears gushed out from her eyes. Smiling all the same, she said to me : ' It is the Holy Hour, do not be alarmed.' Nevertheless, I endeavoured to give her some relief, but my efforts were in vain ; her suffering lasted the whole night, ' Jesus, Jesus, Jesus,' she repeated at each breath which she drew. I wished to send for the doctor but she objected, saying that Jesus wished her to suffer like that, and that the doctor would be no more successful than myself. ' My poor lamb, what a night I am making you pass again after so many others,' she said to me, ' go to bed and let me suffer alone.' But I did not do so. In the morning, everything calmed down, and when the Sisters came to see her after Mass, her gracious countenance was as serene and as fresh as if she had passed an excellent night. She said : ' I am not too bad,' and, as usual, did not wish me to tell what she suffered. She had received Holy Communion. As usual, I dressed her wounds. It was much more painful than on the previous occasions.

" But our saintly Mother forgot all her sufferings during Benediction of the Blessed Sacrament when she heard the French hymn being sung in the choir : ' Bless, O tender Mother, this cry of our Faith : we will serve God, for He is our Father ; we will serve God, for He is our King . . . .' and when she learned that our three zealous, fervent priests had been in the choir for the past hour she was intensely consoled. Some tears—this time of joy,—gushed out of her eyes, and she said : ' It is curious how profoundly this ceremony has touched me.'

" When the doctor came on Wednesday at five p.m. I saw by the expression on his countenance that he thought our Mother was very bad, and I learned that my misgiving was only too well founded.

" The night which she passed, however, was rather good. While we were talking with Sister Margaret Agnes about our grief, she said to us with a gracious smile and an interrogating look : ' I hear you talking and I do not understand what you are saying.' We told her and soon after she dozed off to sleep again ; at six o'clock she received Holy Communion. When the doctor came at five o'clock he could hardly believe his eyes to find her still alive. He found that she was much better. The crisis had passed. All that day was good ; our Mother attended to many things ; she received visits from Dr. Delgrossa and from our chaplain, Father Trovera, talked to them for quite a good while, dictated a letter to me for Monsignor in which she made me write : ' Our dear invalid wishes me to tell you that she abandons herself completely to the will of God.' Between times, I told her of the fright which she had given us and of the danger in which she had been. ' Won't you promise to warn me if it re-curs ? ' ' Yes, Mother,' and I began to weep. ' Come now, courage ! Don't be crying like that : if I am useful for the newly-founded house, God will keep me ; if I am not useful, well ! He will do what must be done.' Then we talked familiarly ; she was perfectly clear in her mind ; her great intellect was un-impaired. These fits of oppression which seized her from time to time took away nothing of her presence of mind. She passed a good night up to two o'clock in the morning. At that time, she began to suffer and had a little fever, but she was able to receive Holy Communion at the usual hour.

" However, our beloved Mother continued to sink gradually. At eleven a.m. I gave her the injection which the doctor ordered, but it produced no visible improvement. At midday Our Mother could still give us the orders for the day, but soon after she sank rapidly. Her breathing became laboured. The priest and doctor, who were sent for, came back immediately. She spoke kindly to both of them. At two p.m. I gave her another injection. These injections were very painful to her; this time she just looked at me as if to say : ' Yes, still another for Jesus,' but she did not speak.

" After kissing the cross lovingly she pronounced the holy name of ' Jesus '; it was her last word. At 3 p.m. our dear lamented Mother rendered her beautiful soul to her Creator. It was the sleep of a child going to sleep in its mother's arms, without agony, as simply as she had lived, with the same calmness, the same abandonment. She left this earth, her children, this foundation which she built up at the price of such sufferings and such love.

" To see the saints die, what a lesson ! My dear, venerable Madame ; what a grace for me to have closed the eyes of her who was a mother and a friend to me in every sense of the word, but alas what sorrow !

" It is Infinite Love Who came our way. He came to take into His Heart her who, for His love, was a martyr in soul and body. He came to seek her for His own glory and to recompense this beautiful soul who loved Him so much, who was so faithful, and who passed over this earth like a seraph."

One of the members of the Community writes :

" On the night preceding the death of our Mother, I had the consolation of assisting Sister Margaret in watching the dear invalid. That night was for me a night of edification and instruction. Up to midnight Rev. Mother's suffering was not extreme, but after 2 a.m. it became so intense that no words can describe it. Nevertheless, not a word of complaint escaped from those blessed lips which had so eloquently inculcated love of suffering. At times she pronounced the holy name of Jesus in such a suppliant tone as to bring tears to our eyes, but fearing that she had been wanting in patience, she immediately made reparation by a sweet smile. On our asking her if she suffered much, she replied calmly and serenely : ' It is Jesus Who wills it, and all that Jesus does is well done.'

" Even in the last moments of her precious existence, when any liquid was presented to her lips, dear Rev. Mother would collect all her feeble strength and make the sign of the cross with the vessel itself. In the morning a Sister came and asked her if she had passed a good night. Dear Rev. Mother replied vivaciously : ' Fine, splendid,' thus hiding from others the sufferings of the preceding night. Far from complaining, she bore every-thing with sweet patience and profit for eternity.

" On every occasion and in all circumstances our good Rev. Mother was the first to put in practice what she taught us in the Novitiate ; I can truly say that I was edified by all that she said and did both in her life and at her death.

" Her death agony was calm, tranquil and patient From time to time she gave looks full of compassion on us at leaving her children.

" About ten minutes before her death she said in French : ' They are coming . . . . . ' and her eyes were fixed on a certain point. She did not move any more until she rendered up her beautiful soul to God."

Another member of the Community writes :

" She was a simple soul who knew how to find the bright side of everything. Although she allowed nothing extraordinary to appear on the outside, it was none the less true that in contact with this dear soul, one felt that the fire of divine love consumed her entirely. And precisely because this fire was as penetrating as it was invisible, because its flames were capable of warming all the souls that came in contact with her, without their knowing how or why, this furnished a convincing proof that her soul was burning with the love of God."

CHAPTER XIV

THE FOUR BRANCHES OF THE WORK OF INFINITE LOVE ARE FOUNDED UNDER THE PROTECTION OF THE HOLY SEE

Mother Louise Margaret was dead. The Community which she left was composed of two professed Sisters and four postulants. One of the professed Sisters was Sister Margaret. For ten years she had been closely associated with Mother Louise Margaret; she had been the daily witness of her heroic virtue, the travelling-companion given to her by the new Superioress of the Monastery of Parella on her journey to Rome, her assistant in the newly-founded Monastery of Vische, and her devoted nurse in her last illness. Mother Louise Margaret had told her beforehand of the role reserved for her, but in her humility, she could not understand what she meant till it actually came to pass. The little orphaned family instinctively turned to her to continue the work of Mother Louise Margaret and when she was unwilling, Pope Benedict XV, later on, insisted that it should be so. Monsignor Filipello, who was profoundly grieved by the early death of Mother Louise Margaret, appointed her to take charge of the Community and wrote to the Sacred Congregation for Religious for instructions at her urgent request.

Father Charrier wrote her the following letter on May 18th:

" The thoughts of God, which are not our thoughts, have reduced all our hopes to nothing. What shall the future bring? What shall become of the dear foundation? What shall be Rome's reply? I cannot believe that all is finished; rather is not the work to commence in earnest? In the meantime, I adore God's will and I pray for the saintly Mother Louise Margaret. I am plunged in grief but completely resigned. I will not give any advice because in the painful situation, it is not fitting that you should seek advice from any other than the Bishop of Ivrea; since he has written to Rome, let us await the reply of the Holy See. Let us have confidence and continue to pray."

The Holy See gave no decision on the case till about a year after the death of Mother Louise Margaret, and when it was given it was very definite; **it was that the foundation of the Monastery of Vische had been valid and legitimate, and that the Monastery was to continue.** Many things happened in the meantime. When, after the death of Mother Louise Margaret, the news got abroad that an application had been made to have the Monastery closed and the Sisters transferred to Parella, the laity, who regarded Mother Louise Margaret as a saint, would not hear of it, the parochial clergy of Vische, some dignitaries of the diocese and a number of priests appealed to Bishop Filipello to use his influence so that the Monastery should continue. None of these knew anything about Mother Louise Margaret except that she was a very holy Religious. Bishop Filipello had allowed the will of God to be manifested by events, and had merely asked the Holy See for instructions. It was at the urgent request of the members of his diocesan Curia and the priests of Vische that he decided to have recourse again to the Holy See.

In the meantime, Sister Margaret had gone to France to consult a friendly Visitation Monastery. The Sisters there encouraged her and advised her to hold out until the end of the war (which ended in 1918) and promised to get subjects for her.

When she returned to Vische, she found trouble waiting for her. An opinion expressed in Rome about the return of the Sisters to their Mother-house of Parella was misinterpreted, and the one professed Sister who had come from Parella at the time of the foundation, returned to that Monastery. Sister Margaret was left alone with the four postulants. Their only support was what the labour of their hands produced in the Monastery garden and alms from a few charitable friends. They waited patiently and confidently for the decision of the Holy See, and religious life went on with the fervour and regularity of a long-established Community.

BENEDICT XV PROTECTS THE LITTLE COMMUNITY

At Rome, the case was being studied carefully and thoroughly. In January, 1916, Monsignor Filipello, in reply to a request from the Holy See for all documents relative to the case, entrusted them to Sister Margaret and ordered her to proceed to Rome and deliver them to the Congregation for Religious. She did so. On her arrival at Rome, she was received in audience by His Holiness Pope Benedict XV and got a special blessing from him. A few days after she was summoned to meet Cardinal Cagliero, who in the meantime had studied the documents which she had presented. **He assured her that Vische was to remain, and that it was to be the first of many such Monasteries that were to be established all over the world " When everything about the foundation of Vische is settled," he said to her, " we shall then consider the establishment of the Priests' Universal Union," and he intimated to her that both the Monastery and the Priests'**

Universal Union were to be ultimately independent of the Visitation Order.

On the morning of February 7th she had the happiness of having a second audience with His Holiness Benedict XV, this time, a private one. He received her most cordially, made her sit down, questioned her about her case, assured her of his approval of the work, and when she told him of the great difficulties she had to contend with he replied : " I am quite pleased to hear about them, because they are usually the sign with which the works of God are marked."

He told her that the formalities of approval would take some time, invited her to remain at Rome as long as it would be necessary, and again gave her his Apostolic Blessing, with the promise that he would write as soon as the case was concluded.

" I believe," he said to her, " that you are, so to speak, the continuation of the soul of Mother Louise Margaret. Yours is a heavy responsibility, but pray fervently, my daughter, that the will of God may be manifested clearly." Subsequently, she had the further privilege of assisting at His Holiness's Mass.

While at Rome she met Cardinal Mercier, who became an enthusiastic advocate of the Priests' Universal Union of the Friends of the Sacred Heart.

On Holy Saturday, Cardinal Cagliero announced to Sister Margaret that her case was concluded at the Congregation and that official documents would follow in due course. On May 23rd Cardinal Cagliero met Monsignor Filipello at Turin, asked him to bear the message of His Holiness to Sister Margaret : that Pope Benedict XV wished the Monastery of Vische to continue, that Bishop Filipello was authorised to give it provisional approval and allow Sister Margaret to receive postulants ; and finally that the name of the Monastery was to be changed to " The Visitation of the Sacred Heart."

On the following July 17th, 1916, Cardinal Cagliero himself, accompanied by Bishop Filipello, visited the Monastery for the ceremony of the blessing of the bell. The little chapel was filled with priests from the diocese, and there was a large congregation of the laity outside waiting to receive the Cardinal and testify their joy that the Monastery was to continue. The Cardinal instructed Sister Margaret to send out letters asking for subscriptions to enable her to buy the house as soon as possible, and Bishop Filipello, addressing the little Community said : " The Pope wishes Vische to continue, you have the protection of a Cardinal, you have the support and precious advice of sure friends in high places, the whole authority of the diocese is with you, and your Bishop gives you his protection and his heart."

In his decree of erection Bishop Filipello said : " In answer to the wishes and prayers of our priests and faithful, and in order that the holy works of this Institute may remain for the greater good of our diocese, after laying certain doubts before the Holy See for greater certainty, and considering that Divine Providence has very frequently given manifest signs of Its special predilection to this Monastery by procuring for it in an admirable manner, gifts and help necessary for daily life, we confirm and approve this Monastery for women, founded with our approbation by Sister Louise Margaret Claret de la Touche, and in virtue of the faculties which have been granted to us by the intermediary of Cardinal Cagliero, we establish this Monastery of the Visitation under the title of *The Sacred Heart of Jesus* in order to obviate present and future difficulties and in order to respond to the wish expressed by the Sovereign Pontiff, who himself deigned to choose this title.

We prescribe for this Monastery the Rule drawn up according to the Spirit of St. Francis de Sales and approved by us, with the particular end already explained to the Sacred Congregation ; that the Sisters of this Monastery pray and offer up all their works to God for the Sovereign Pontiff and the whole Church, especially for priests in order that they may all live and exercise their holy functions according to the Sacred Heart of Jesus, and be worthy of their divine mission of diffusing the knowledge of Infinite Love."

New postulants, who had been awaiting the decision of the Holy See, soon arrived and were not long imbibing the spirit of the Foundress. Father Charrier, who, in obedience to his Superiors, had to remain aloof pending the decision of the Holy See, was invited to come on January 29th, 1917, for the ceremony of the renewal of vows of Sister Margaret—who on that occasion took the name of Sister Margaret of the Sacred Heart. In his letter of thanks to Bishop Filipello, he used these prophetic words which have since been realized :

" The frail shoot shall without doubt become a great tree, under whose shade many works shall be done for the greater good of our Holy Church, for the Catholic Priesthood, and through it, for the salvation of souls so dear to Our Lord Jesus Christ. May you be blessed a thousand times, for having so well corresponded with the designs of the Sacred Heart."

The four novices received the religious habit in the course of the year. There were indications that Providence had special designs over these postulants, and their fidelity to their vocation and their patience under the strain of poverty and uncertainty during the two and a half years that had elapsed since the death of the Foundress helped to confirm that conclusion.

THE SISTERS OF BETHANY OF THE SACRED HEART

One thing was still wanting to the young Community to enable it to carry out its mission without hindrance ; full freedom of action. They were still a branch of the Visitation Order and were under its control. Providence brought it about that they should retain the rule of St. Francis de Sales and at the same time become an independent Contemplative Sisterhood with a different habit and a different name. It came about in this way. The Sisters of the Visitation who, since the time of St. Margaret Mary Alacoque, rightly regarded themselves as having a special mission to propagate devotion to the Sacred Heart, made representations to the Holy See that the name "Visitation of the Sacred Heart" given to a single monastery was misleading, and requested that it should be changed. Pope Benedict XV, who was informed of the appeal, instructed the Congregation to deal with the matter in such a way that there should be no more trouble or misunderstanding. The Sacred Congregation, after mature consideration, decided that the Monastery of Vische should be formed into an independent Sisterhood with a special habit ; that their constitutions should be modified to adapt them to the mission which Mother Louise Margaret had received ; and that a name should be chosen for the new Religious Sisterhood which would express the work they were to do. Monsignor Filipello, who was entrusted with the carrying out of the order of the Holy See, on the advice of Father Charrier, decided that the title "Monastery of the Sacred Heart" given by His Holiness, Benedict XV, should be retained, and that the word 'Visitation' should be changed to 'Bethany.' Their title then was to be "Bethany of the Sacred Heart," which signified that the Sisters of that Institute should be for the Pope, bishops and priests of the Church what Bethany of Judea was for Our Divine Lord and His Apostles, a place entirely devoted to their interests. While the changes made in the constitutions of the new Institute make it more austere than the Visitation, the spirit remains the same, and what St. Francis de Sales said of the Visitation order : " that the life and all the exercises of the Sisters should be directed to unite them to God, to help Holy Church and to work for the salvation of souls," may be applied to Bethany of the Sacred Heart, with the modification that the Sisters of Bethany offer themselves as living holocausts for the sanctification of the clergy and for the extension of the reign of Infinite Love over the world.

The Institute of Bethany was born. Henceforth it was to continue to be the object of the special benevolence not only of its Bishop-Founder, but also of the Holy See. On repeated occasions, Benedict XV, whose authoritative intervention had been so opportune, showed himself a Father to the new Institute ; besides supporting it with his authority, he gave generous gifts to help the Sisters in their material needs. When he was informed that postulants were arriving from the various countries of Europe and that the " little house " could no longer contain them, he expressed his joy in a letter through his Cardinal Secretary to the Superioress, and sent the magnificent gift of 25,000 lire towards the construction of a new wing.

His successor, Pius XI, on several occasions sent encouragement ; he gave the Institute his Apostolic Blessing and manifested the greatest interest in its progress and development.

The following letter was sent to the Superioress of the Institute by Pope Pius XI, at the beginning of his reign through His Eminence, Cardinal Gasparri.

" The Vatican, January 31st, 1923
" Our Holy Father, Pope Pius XI, has been touched by the sentiments of profound devotedness and entire submission which you have recently expressed to him in an address of filial piety.

" This homage has been all the more pleasing to His Holiness, because it was accompanied by an artistic copy of the Rules of your Institute, the practical expression of the pious directions of your venerable Foundress.

" His Holiness congratulates you on devoting your lives to

God for the purpose of obtaining from God for the ministers of the altar in particular, all the graces which are necessary for them to be truly ' the salt of the earth and the light of the world.' As an earnest of the abundance of divine favours for the fullest realisation of this perfect life for yourselves and for the ministers of Jesus Christ, the Holy Father most gladly sends you and all the members of your Institute the Apostolic Benediction.

" Please accept, Very Reverend Superioress, the expression of my religious devotedness in Our Lord.

" P. C. Gasparri."

His present Holiness, Pius XII, who, while Cardinal Secretary of Pius XI, had written two letters on the Pope's behalf conveying messages of goodwill to the Rev. Superioress and Community of Bethany of the Sacred Heart, sent the following letter on His own behalf through His Secretary :

" Vatican,

" June 14th, 1945

" Reverend Superioress,

" His Holiness has welcomed with benevolent goodness the sentiments of fidelity and devotedness which you expressed to Him in your last letter. He thanks you for the prayers and sacrifices which you have so devotedly offered up for His intention.

" The Holy Father has been happy to learn that in spite of the war and of difficulties of every kind which have resulted from it, your young Community has continued to develop, and that you look forward to further increases in your numbers.

" His Holiness, while expressing the wish that your work should respond more and more to the designs of Divine Providence, most willingly sends to you, Rev. Superioress, and to all your Sisters, His Apostolic Blessing.

" Please accept, Rev. Superioress, the assurance of my devoted sentiments in Our Lord.

" J. B. Montini."

As the benevolence of successive Popes towards the new Institute became known, interest in, and sympathy for it, increased. The publication of the writings of Mother Louise Margaret removed prejudices that had existed in some quarters, and which were due solely to ignorance of the facts. Priests and Bishops in considerable numbers honoured the Institute with their visits. Vocations, which, even in the midst of the war, Providence had continued to send, increased during the succeeding years. At the time of writing, the Monastery of Vische had fifty-three professed Sisters and a large number of postulants and novices, representing nearly every country in Europe, all striving with one heart and one mind, by prayer and self immolation for the Church to diffuse the knowledge of Infinite Love to which they have consecrated themselves. Already a branch Convent has been established in France at St. Jean le Blanc Orleans, and applications for foundations have been received from many other countries.

The sufferings and self-immolation of Mother Louise Margaret have not been in vain ; they have given to the world a new Religious Sisterhood in which the religious life is practised with great perfection for the benefit of the universal Church.

ESTABLISHMENT OF THE FIRST BRANCH OF THE PRIESTS' UNIVERSAL UNION OF THE FRIENDS OF THE SACRED HEART

The foundation of the new Monastery, now firmly established, was the accessory, not the principal part of the Work ; its object was to provide a spiritual foundation of prayers and merits for the Priests' Universal Union, already approved by the Holy See. On account of the War, Monsignor Filipello found it necessary to postpone the foundation of this organisation, but he never lost sight of it.

On March 25th, 1913, he had for the first time given official approbation to the Statutes of the " Priests' Universal Union the Friends of the Sacred Heart." It was when presenting these Statutes to the Holy See on behalf of her Bishop and when speaking of the Priests' Universal Union, that Mother Louise Margaret had been invited to undertake the religious foundation. After her death, the different appeals to Rome to have the Monastery of Vische maintained brought out the fact that this house of prayer and immolation was necessary as a foundation for the Priests' Universal Union, so that the study of the two projects went on concurrently. When the Sacred Congregation gave its reply on January 25th, 1918, it was favourable to both projects alike.

Monsignor Filipello could then proceed with the official establishment of the Universal Union of the Friends of the Sacred Heart. At this time Father Charrier published a booklet entitled : " An appeal to Priests," in which he included the Statutes of the Priests' Universal Union as finally revised by Mother Louise Margaret and sanctioned by the Holy See. It was in this booklet that the word " Priests " was added ; henceforth this organisation was called " The Priests' Universal Union of the Friends of the Sacred Heart." At the end of this booklet, Father Charrier added the " Act of Adoration and Donation to Infinite Love " and a brief notice on the Sisters of Bethany of the Sacred Heart and on the affiliation of other Sisters and people in the world to Bethany of the Sacred Heart.

On his part, Monsignor Filipello judged that the time had come to act ; by a decree of June 16th, 1918, he erected the Priests' Universal Union officially and canonically. Thus, as Mother Louise Margaret had predicted, this organisation began its life in a foreign country, and not in France, where Father Charrier's booklet got a rather cold reception. Monsignor had this booklet translated into Italian and on October 10th, sent it to all the Bishops of Piedmont. The reception it met with this time was definitely favourable.

Since the diocese of Ivrea had founded the Priests' Universal Union, it was to have the first diocesan branch. The war, which detained a great number of priests in the armies, finally came to an end ; and towards the last days of May, 1919, most of the priests had returned to their parishes. Then, at the desire of Monsignor Filipello, a committee of priests was formed to found a diocesan branch of the Union and to adapt the general Statutes to the needs of the diocese.

This was no easy task. It required that a close study of the aim and origin of the Priests' Universal Union be made, in order to give an exact idea of it to the clergy of the diocese. Now with the exception of Monsignor Filipello, none of the priests who were entrusted with the mission was acquainted with either the writings of Mother Louise Margaret or the doctrine of Infinite Love as expounded by her, or the spiritual import, or the universality always demanded by her for the Priests' Union. Father Charrier was consulted and endeavoured to enlighten them on these subjects with untiring charity and devotedness ; in these days, he was really, as Mother Louise Margaret had predicted, " the Soul of the Work."

These labours lasted more than a year, and on September 12th, 1920, the diocesan branch of the Priests' Universal Union of Ivrea was officially founded. On October 1st of the same year, nine priests pronounced their Act of Consecration and Donation to Infinite Love before the Blessed Sacrament exposed in the chapel of Bethany of the Sacred Heart, and thus constituted the first branch of the Priests' Universal Union of the Friends of the Sacred Heart.

Much work and prayer was still necessary to arrive at a perfect understanding of all that the Priests' Universal Union stands for and to organise its extension abroad. The publication of the writings of Mother Louise Margaret, and of a more complete explanation of the origin and aim of this association, helped wonderfully to attain these objects. The seed was sown ; it was to grow up and increase silently and imperceptibly. The aim was not to get large numbers immediately, but to imbue priests' souls with the spirit and the doctrine of the Work ; this was the object which the pioneer members of the Union strove to attain in the numerous conferences which they held. A letter from the Holy See written on March 11th, on behalf of His Holiness, Pope Pius XI, gave well-timed encouragement to these early pioneers :

" In thanking the members of the Priests' Universal Union paternally for their filial address, His Holiness has been pleased to see in it, besides the homage and still more than the homage, one of the happiest and most welcome auspices for the supreme work of regeneration and salvation to which all the vital forces of the Church of Jesus Christ, under the guidance of the Supreme Pastor, should be assiduously and zealously consecrated.

" With the firm confidence that activity and good example, under the enlightened guidance of the promoter and chief, will correspond to the generous resolutions of the members of the Priests' Universal Union, His Holiness most gladly sends His Apostolic Blessing, and looks forward to fruits worthy of this noble apostolate."

TWO BRANCHES FOR ASSOCIATE MEMBERS

At the same time that the members of this first branch continued their study of the work and writings of Mother Louise Margaret and their efforts to put all her ideas into effect, the Bishop and his fellow-workers understood clearly that besides the two main branches, two other branches of the Work of Infinite Love were contemplated by her, instructions about which were found in her writings. In order to honour her wishes, these two branches were formed ; one for women was founded under the name of the " Faithful Friends of Bethany of the Sacred Heart," and another for men, under the name of the " Associates of the Priests' Universal Union." Thus were all the ideas of Mother Louise Margaret realised, and the Work of Infinite Love, which had such a modest beginning, attained the development of all its component parts ; the Priests' Universal Union for priests with its corresponding branch for laymen of the world and Religious Brothers, and Bethany of the Sacred Heart with the group of the Faithful Friends of Bethany.

DEVELOPMENT OF THE WORK OF INFINITE LOVE

On October 1st, 1930, Monsignor Filipello, in the following letter, gave an admirable resumé of the development of the Work of Infinite Love which was the fruit of ten years labour :

" To Our Venerable Confreres, and our dear children of both sexes, who have given their names for the Work of Infinite Love, salutation and blessing in the Lord.

" We have been filled with consolation by the progress of this Work which, we have reason to believe, has been suggested by God to the pious Sister Louise Margaret de la Touche and which, from humble beginnings, and almost in secret, has attained such an increase as we scarcely dared to hope for.

" It has caused us particular joy to observe that this Work, during the time that has elapsed since the beginning, has developed and is still developing according to the ideas and the plan formed by this pious Sister.

" All of you are aware that the Work of Infinite Love, commonly called the Sacerdotal Work, takes its origin, as can be seen from the writings of Sister Louise Margaret, from the special gift of the Sacred Heart of Jesus to priests, which gift will be the source of the following special graces for them :

" 1.—That they will be the first to come to a knowledge of Infinite Love by means of the Heart of Jesus, just as the beloved Disciple, by leaning His head on the Sacred Heart, attained to the most sublime heights of knowledge of the Divinity;

" 2.—That by this doctrine of Infinite Love they will so live that they will be truly one heart and one soul;

" 3.—That they will propagate this doctrine and explain it to all the faithful.

" It is to be borne in mind that the essence of the Work consists in the spirit and life drawn from the Heart of Jesus, diffused among the body of the priests, and through them among all men.

" Its principal exercise is love; love is the instrument by which to act upon souls.

" This work, like a flourishing tree, has cast its roots deep into the ground, and has put forth four vigorous branches which, as time goes on, grow out in every direction to the greater glory of God.

" **The first of these branches is the Priests' Universal Union of the Friends of the Sacred Heart,** whose functions are : (*a*) to make known to priests the special gift that has been prepared for them by the most Sacred Heart of Jesus : (*b*) to help the members of the Union themselves, so far as it is possible for them, to live the doctrine of Infinite Love, and to instruct others to do likewise.

" **The second branch consists of the Associates of the Priests' Universal Union,** and is composed of Religious Brothers and laymen of the world.   Their functions are (*a*) to become imbued with the spirit of the Work, and (*b*) by their prayers and good works, to co-operate with the priests of the Union to propagate the knowledge of Infinite Love.

" **The third branch is Bethany of the Sacred Heart.**   This Institute, founded by our decree of March 19th, 1914, may be justly called the root hidden in the ground, the home of the Work of Infinite Love.   The purpose of this new Sisterhood is (*a*) to consecrate their own lives to God the Father, Son and Holy Ghost, Infinite Love, in order that the Work of Infinite Love be accomplished in all souls by means of priests, and to work in co-operation with them towards this great end by prayer, self-immolation, and by diffusing around them the spirit of this Work; (*b*) by means of the contemplative life and by adoring in spirit and in truth Infinite Love of which the most Sacred Heart of Jesus is the living taber-nacle, to obtain superabundant graces for the Sovereign Pontiff, for the Church, for the Catholic Priesthood and above all for the Priests' Universal Union of the Friends of the Sacred Heart.

" **The fourth branch is The Faithful Friends of Bethany of the Sacred Heart.** These may be either women living in the world, or Sisters of other religious Orders who, united to Bethany of the Sacred Heart by a spiritual bond, purpose to live and act for the same end.

" These then are the four branches, all tending towards the same end and forming an admirable union of hearts and minds, an elite army combating to extend the reign of Infinite Love over the world.

" The Work of Infinite Love is spread over the five continents of the world : Europe, America, Africa, Asia and Australasia. Thus can be seen, in spite of the still relatively limited number of the members, that the Work has already realised this universality so much insisted on by Mother Louise Margaret."

The following letter from Monsignor Montini on behalf of Pope Pius XII shows the deep interest which His present Holiness takes in the propagation of the Priests' Universal Union and its remarkable progress in the Middle East :

Dal Vaticano,
November 15th, 1949

Segretaria di Stato
di Sua Santita,
Rev. Fr. Nazzareno Jacopozzi Alexandria

Rev. Father,
The Holy Father has accepted with paternal benevolence the presentation copy of your book on The Priests' Universal Union of the Friends of the Sacred Heart and instructs me to convey to you the expression of His deep gratitude.

The supernatural fruits of the Work of Infinite Love (The Priests' Universal Union and its three branches), for which you are the Delegate of the Central Council for the Middle East, are eminently precious, for its object is the sanctification of the clergy. His Holiness cannot therefore but rejoice at the news of the first development of the Priests' Universal Union in the Middle East, which has resulted in adding to its numbers

eight bishops, forty-five priests and six hundred associates representing all the rites of the Middle East.

Accordingly, the Holy Father gladly imparts to you for all the members and associates of the Priests' Universal Union His Apostolic Blessing, as a pledge of greater graces for the wider extension of the Work of Infinite Love and the greater fervour of its members.

While thanking you personally for the copy which you have so kindly sent to myself, I pray you, Rev. Father, to accept the assurance of my religious devotedness.

J. B. Montini.

The development of the Work goes on like a vital sap which gradually permeates the minds and hearts of the chosen ones and even of other pious associations. As has been made clear in the course of this volume, the object of the Priests' Universal Union and its allied Societies is not to substitute themselves for any other existing societies ; its object is to unite them for a common purpose while leaving them their individual characteristics and their liberty of action, and to infuse into them a new spirit of love and charity, drawn from the Sacred Heart of Jesus, the tabernacle of Infinite Love.   The Priests' Universal Union will help those clerical societies that become affiliated to it by adding a new powerful motive for priests to join these societies, and will unite them for the sublime purpose of working to establish the reign of Infinite Love in the world.   This has been fully recognised by the great sacerdotal associations of the Continent, and many other similar associations ; for example, the Apostolic Union of Secular Priests of the Sacred Heart, the Society of Priests of St. Francis de Sales, the Priest-Apostles of the Sacred Heart of Montmarte and many others have affiliated themselves to the Priests' Universal Union.   In the same manner, we find whole Communities of Sisters united to Bethany of the Sacred Heart by a spiritual bond of prayer and charity. Finally, while leaving it to each individual to judge from the evidence given in this volume, whether the Priests' Universal Union and all its details are directly inspired by Our Lord Jesus Christ Himself, we are safe in saying that it is His work, because it has been founded by the Holy See, His representative on earth, and blessed and encouraged by four successive Popes, and has as its object to realise the prayer of Our Lord after the Last Supper : " That they may be one as We also are." (John XVII, 11).

The tree is known by its fruits. She, who forty years ago wrote down for her Director the words of Our Lord which, she alleged, were addressed to her : " It is you who are to bear the overflowing torrents of My Love to priests, and through them to the extremities of the world," might have been mistaken for a proud or vain person. The events which have taken place since this was spoken, go to show, that she was indeed chosen by Our Lord to carry out his behests.

FIRST STEPS TAKEN TOWARDS BEATIFICATION OF MOTHER LOUISE MARGARET

On a Good Friday evening in the month of March, 1932, a silent funeral procession wound its way along the roads of Vische. A coffin was being brought back from the cemetery, and just as three o'clock was striking on the parish clock, it was entering the humble convent of Bethany of the Sacred Heart. It had left that convent seventeen years previously. The coffin was opened in presence of Bishop Filipello, twelve priests of the Priests' Universal Union, the civil authorities and doctors, all of whom were sworn. The body of Mother Louise Margaret lay there bathed in moisture, clad in her religious habit.

For two hours, those who were present could gaze with emotion on the venerable remains. The body, washed and clothed in a new Visitandine habit, was then placed in a new coffin and transferred to a vault prepared for it in the enclosure of the Monastery. Mother Louise Margaret had returned among her daughters to await the hour of the judgment which, no doubt, the supreme authority of the Church will one day pass on her.

On October 31st, 1933, His Excellency Monsignor Filipello set up the Ecclesiastical Tribunal to seek information for the cause of beatification of the servant of God, Sister Louise Margaret Claret de la Touche, and by a pastoral letter of December 8th of the same year he notified the priests and faithful of his diocese and the members of the Priests' Universal Union of this fact. This informative process has just been concluded.

May God, Who has begun and carried on His Work so magnificently, deign to complete it to the glory of His Infinite Love !

STATUTES OF THE PRIESTS' UNIVERSAL UNION OF THE FRIENDS OF THE SACRED HEART

(Composed by Mother Louise Margaret by order of Monsignor Filipello and sanctioned by the Holy See).

I. End of the Union : This Union which we call " The Priests' Universal Union of the Friends of the Sacred Heart "—in order to honour this saying of Jesus Christ to His Apostles : " I will not now call you servants ; for the servant knoweth not what his Lord doth, but I have called you friends " (John xv. 15)—has as its end : (*a*) to group together all the priests of the world around the adorable Heart of Our Saviour Jesus Christ in order to array them as an elite body against the errors and corruption of our epoch ; (*b*) to restore and develop the family spirit and the spirit of solidarity in the Sacerdotal Body, to make the same spirit circulate through it and to establish in it a more complete unity of views, a more uniform movement of action ; (*c*) to procure the personal sanctification of its members by a true and practical devotion to Our Lord Jesus Christ and His Sacred Heart, the tabernacle of Infinite Love, and to procure the sanctification of souls in general by the development and the good direction of the Apostolic spirit.

II. Spirit of the Union : Urged by the sublime impulse given by Pius X, the priests who form part of the Union undertake, under the guidance of their bishops and the directions of the Holy See, " to restore all things in Christ."

By their word, by their works, by their writing, especially by their example and their life entirely modelled on that of Jesus the Eternal Priest, they will fight courageously against everything which can injure the unity of the Church, its integrity and its glory. By the purity of their doctrine and their inviolable attachment to the Chair of St. Peter, by the regularity of their lives and the force of their virtue, the members of the Union will endeavour to be in truth," The light of the world and the salt of the earth " (Matt. v, 13-14). They will have but one heart and one soul among them, according to the words of Our Lord to His Heavenly Father : " That they be one as We are One " (John xvii, 22) ; and they will carefully guard the unity of faith in the bond of fraternal charity.

III. Organization of the Union : This Union has commenced humbly. If, encouraged and blessed by the Holy See, it spreads, and, according to its end, becomes world-wide, it would be proper that its headquarters should be at Rome, in order to extend its influence from there over the whole Catholic world.

As this Union is to be world-wide, as it must be adapted and conformed to all minds and to all places, it ought to be very simple and very broad in its organization. In each diocese the members of the Union will meet twice each year, if possible, under the presidency of their bishop. At the first meeting of the year, they will elect, according to their number, four or five or a larger number of their brethren, who during the year will be charged with helping, visiting, and assisting in their spiritual and temporal needs those of their brethren who have recourse to them. At their meetings, they will discuss everything which regards the spirit of the Union, and the secretary will make a report of all the interesting questions that have been brought up at the meeting.

IV. Conditions of admission : The priests who desire to become members of the Priest's Universal Union must address their petition to the diocesan Director, sending their surname, Christian name and address, mentioning whether they already form part of a Sacerdotal Union and if so, giving its name. They must not have incurred any censure for doctrine ; they must be of upright morals and of edifying life. They must be resolved, as far as possible, to be faithful to the practices of the Union.

V. Obligations : The priests of the Priests' Universal Union undertake : (a) to make, on the day of their entry, the total consecration of themselves to Infinite Love, in union with their brethren, according to the formula in use ; a consecration which they will renew on the First Friday of each month, and which they are advised to make each day at the end of their thanksgiving after Mass ; (b) to spread, each in his sphere of action, the knowledge of Jesus Christ, God and man, living in the Blessed Eucharist, of His Sacred Heart overflowing with love and mercy for souls ; (c) to assist at one at least of the two conferences of the year, unless prevented by serious reasons ; (d) to celebrate Holy Mass once a year for the deceased Confreres, and to give an intention each day in the Holy Sacrifice for the sanctification of the Clergy, and the extension of the religion of Jesus Christ ; (e) to make each evening an examination of the day, from the point of view of the conformity of the life of the priest with that of Our Lord Jesus Christ. (For that examen, they can use the formula given below) ; (f) to make each day, preferably in the morning, a meditation or spiritual reading from the same point of view. They can make use of the book *The Sacred Heart and the Priesthood* for that purpose.

N.B.—The employment of the morning in the ministry of Confession or in the visiting of the sick, dispenses from this meditation, as does an adoration of the Most Blessed Sacrament or any other time spent in prayer already imposed by another Sacerdotal Union.

Remark : Although this Union is specially destined for Priests of the secular clergy, Priests of Religious Orders can become members individually on the same conditions of admission.

These Statutes drawn up by Mother Louise Margaret and sanctioned by the Holy See were so composed as to be capable of being added to and adapted to the needs of the time and the circumstances of the country or diocese.

After years of experience the Central Council of the Priests' Universal Union has revised them and presented them in the following form. Each country and each diocesan branch is free to adapt them still further to its needs, but should submit changes made to the Central Council.

Statutes of the Priests' Universal Union of the Friends of the Sacred Heart

ARTICLE I—Definition. The Priests' Universal Union of the Friends of the Sacred Heart is an association whose purpose is to unite the priests of the entire world around the Sacred Heart of Jesus. The members pledge themselves to preach the doctrine of Infinite Love, to live that doctrine themselves and make others live by it as far as their influence extends ; they pledge themselves also to the closest union with the Holy Father, with their Bishop and with the other members.

ARTICLE II.—Means : To attain this end, the Priests' Universal Union makes use of the following means for the personal sanctification of the priest and for the diffusion of the knowledge of Infinite Love.

1) For their own sanctification :
   (a) Meditation on, and study of the doctrine of Infinite Love as set forth in the Sacred Scriptures, in the writings of the Fathers, in the various pious books both of ancient and modern times and especially in the writings of the Servant of God, Mother Louise Margaret.
   (b) Prayer having as its object to form a close and intimate friendship with Jesus through a lively faith and boundless confidence in His love and a constant endeavour to model one's own heart on the Heart of Jesus.
   (c) Imitation of the sacerdotal virtues of the Sacred Heart of Jesus (as explained in *The Sacred Heart and the Priesthood*) and above all of His loving abandonment to the will of His heavenly Father.
   (d) Love and esteem for the priesthood in their own person and holy joy and gratitude to God for having received such a great grace.
   (e) Special devotion to the Blessed Virgin, Mother and Queen of priests.
   (f) Friendly relations with the members of the Work of Infinite Love based on the love of God and zeal for His glory.
   (g) Days of spiritual recollection according to the spirit of the Work.
2) For souls :
   (a) In the first place, assistance to priests by prayer, self-sacrifice, good example, discreet and charitable advice and by material help when needed.

(b) Great respect for the priestly dignity: Members of the Priests' Universal Union should endeavour to diffuse the knowledge of Infinite Love and to promote union and peace among their brethren; they should endeavour also to avoid all unnecessary criticism and everything against the virtue of charity.

(c) Preaching the doctrine of Infinite Love by every means that their zeal suggests; by preaching, through the press, retreats and works of charity;

(d) Recruiting fervent members for the Work.

ARTICLE III—1) Who can be members of the Priests' Universal Union?
All priests throughout the world both secular and religious who are willing to make their lives conform to the spirit of the Work.
The members of the Priests' Universal Union are free to adopt any authorised form of spirituality which they judge to be most suited to their needs and their character; they are free also to belong to other sacerdotal unions or other spiritual movements; it is in fact desirable that they be already members of other unions.

2) Other sacerdotal associations can be affiliated (even if these associations are not formed for purely spiritual ends), provided they be willing to adopt the spirit of the Priests' Universal Union.
The sacerdotal associations which become affiliated to the Priests' Universal Union do not thereby become dependent on it or come under its authority, but form a simple bond of charity and co-operation—in other words they form a purely spiritual bond.
The Priests' Universal Union is not to be joined on to any particular religious Order or Congregation.

ARTICLE IV—Duties of Members.

1) (a) Priests, on the day of their entry into this organisation, are to make a total consecration of themselves to Infinite Love according to the established formula[1] and are to pledge themselves to employ faithfully the following means:

(b) To make each day, preferably in the morning, a meditation, or some spiritual reading meditated on, and in the evening to make an examination of conscience on the conformity of their lives with the life of Jesus Priest.

(c) To make a special memento in the Mass each day for the extension of the reign of Infinite Love: to make a memento for all priests, especially for their fellow-members and for the Associates and Faithful Friends, and a memento for all deceased members.

(d) To celebrate, or to have celebrated each year, a Mass for the deceased members.

1 See page 133.

2) Clerical associations which become affiliated to the Priests' Universal Union, should take their inspiration for their activities, even material, from the doctrine of Infinite Love, which is essentially a doctrine of charity.

A person who is a member of an association which is affiliated to the Priests' Universal Union does not thereby become a member of that Union. If he wishes to become a member, he must join in the ordinary way.

ARTICLE V—Organisation and Functioning.

1) The Priests' Universal Union has a Central Council and diocesan sections, directed respectively by a Central Council and a diocesan Council.

2) The Central Council is composed of a President, a Secretary and three or five Councillors. The Central Council can co-opt other Councillors in countries where this appears to be necessary.

3) At the present moment, the Centre is established in the Diocese of Ivrea in the Province of Turin. His Excellency Mgr. Rostagno, Bishop of Ivrea, the immediate successor of Mgr. Filipello, the Founder of the first branch of the Priests' Universal Union, is at the same time Head of the Work of Infinite Love and President of the Priests' Universal Union.

In the case of the death of the President, the Central Council elects another.

The Councillors, like the President, are elected for an indefinite period. Should any of them die, or resign, the President is to nominate another in his place.

4) The diocesan sections are under the General Centre, as are also general sacerdotal associations which have been affiliated, individual members and diocesan associations which have not yet an organised Section in their diocese. As soon as a diocesan Section is organised, individual members in the diocese come under it.

5) It is the duty of the Central Council to diffuse the doctrine of Infinite Love and the spirit of the Work.

6) The activity and vigilance of the Central Council extends over all the activities of the Priests' Universal Union (whether diocesan Sections or members not grouped in sections) and of the other branches of the Work of Infinite Love (Associates and Faithful Friends) in order that the spirit of the Work may remain unchanged.

7) *Diocesan Sections.*

In order to constitute a diocesan Section it is necessary:

    (1) that those who wish to organise it and to be members of it be already members of the Priests' Universal Union;

    (2) that the Ordinary approve of the Work in his diocese;

    (3) that the request to form it be made to the General Council which normally gives its consent when the first two conditions are fulfilled.

8) Diocesan Sections can add to the General Statutes of the Work a diocesan statute corresponding to the needs and to the particular character of their clergy. Every diocesan statute should be approved by the Central Council.

9) Each diocesan Section has its own Council composed of a President, a Secretary and three or five Councillors nominated by the Bishop (if he is a member).

It will be the duty of the members of the diocesan Council to help, to visit and to comfort the members of the branch in their temporal and spiritual needs.

10) The diocesan Section performs for its own diocese what the Central Council lays down for all the branches of the Work : it endeavours to see that the Statutes are observed and the spirit maintained.

11) A diocesan Section, as a rule, does not accept priests or associations that are outside the diocese. However it can facilitate communication with the General Council for them, especially in countries far from the Central Council.

12) The diocesan Sections will have all the more vitality if the members that compose it are well prepared. Therefore there should be no undue haste in setting up a diocesan Section. It is better that the members who are to compose it be well prepared, in order that they be thoroughly convinced and real apostles of the Work.

N.B.—In order to leave the diocesan Authority and the diocesan Clergy full freedom of action, those priests of Religious Orders who are members of the branch should not in ordinary circumstances be chosen as Directors of Sections or for official positions. They should rather be chosen to give conferences at meetings and act as spiritual guides.

Some considerations on the Priests' Universal Union.

A.—Advantages of this Union.

The Statutes of the Union given above show clearly that the priests who are members should study deeply the doctrine of God-Infinite Love and should live it and diffuse that doctrine in the world of souls.

A study of the books on the Work will show that there are incalculable advantages for the priest who performs faithfully this duty.

The principal of these advantages are : an increase of faith and love in the interior life of the priest ; greater generosity, more intense zeal, enthusiasm, confidence and holy joy in the exercise of the apostolate ; more cordial union and more active collaboration with his confreres ; more docile relations with, and closer attachment to his superiors. These are indeed great advantages, and the Priests' Universal Union has the right to think that it has accomplished its task if it succeeds in conferring them on its members.

B.—Utility of the Priests' Universal Union.

From what has been already said it is evident that immense benefits are to be derived from membership, but membership of the Priests' Universal Union for priests and of the other branches for persons other than priests, is of course a matter of counsel and not of precept.

On this question Father Louis Veseo writes :

" As an association, the Priests' Universal Union helps us to obtain more easily for ourselves and our brethren the treasures hidden in the rich deposit of our Faith.

" All associations formed under the authority of the Church are helps to gain the spiritual wealth of the Church but we do not say that they are indispensable. According to the order established for the sanctification and salvation of souls, three things suffice : the Gospel, the Sacraments, and the Catholic Church with its Priesthood.

" The Work of Infinite Love in its four branches helps its members to obtain for themselves these immense treasures deposited by Our Divine Saviour in the Gospel, the Sacraments, the Church and the Priesthood and to make these treasures available for those entrusted to their care."

C.—How are these precious fruits to be obtained by the members of the different branches ?

As in the case of all pious associations, it is not sufficient merely to have one's name inscribed as a member ; members must carry out faithfully the regulations of the association and live according to its spirit.

D.—Relations with other Clerical Associations.

The relations between the Priests' Universal Union and Clerical Unions which have been affiliated are dealt with in Articles III and IV of these Statutes.

We wish here to refer to the general relations which exist between the Priests' Universal Union and all other clerical associations.

The Priests' Universal Union has an aim, an object and a work to do different from all other existing Associations. The aim of the Union has been defined by Mother Louise Margaret as follows : " This Union which we call ' The Priests' Universal Union of the *Friends* of the Sacred Heart '—in order to honour the saying of Jesus Christ to His Apostles : ' I will not now call you servants ; for the servant knoweth not what his Lord doth, but I have called you *friends* ' (John xv, 15)—has as its end : (*a*) to group together all the priests of the world around the Adorable Heart of Our Saviour Jesus Christ, in order to array them as an elite body against the errors and corruption of our time ; (*b*) to restore and develop the family spirit and the spirit of solidarity in the sacerdotal body, to make the same spirit circulate through it, and to establish in it a more complete unity of views, a more uniform movement of action ; (*c*) to procure the personal sanctification of its members by a true and practical devotion to Our Lord Jesus Christ and His Sacred Heart, the Tabernacle of Infinite Love, and to procure the sanctification of souls in general by the development and good direction of the Apostolic spirit."

It is therefore in no sense a rival and in no way interferes with the work of other clerical Unions. On the contrary, it aims at assisting them and, so far from trying to take members away from them, its work will result in increasing their numbers. Members of other clerical Unions who join will still remain members of these unions and will be expected to become more zealous members; clerical associations which become affiliated will retain their identity and will receive valuable help. The Priests' Universal Union of the Friends of the Sacred Heart has much to offer. It provides priests of other societies with books specially suited for priests, which the Holy See has examined and has allowed to be published as private revelation containing a message from Our Lord to priests and directions for their priestly life and apostolic labours. It promotes unity and harmony between the members of the various clerical associations and between the members themselves, its motto being the prayer of Our Lord at the Last Supper for His apostles: " That they be one as We also are One." (John XVIII, 22).

The following quotations from the letters of Mother Louise Margaret show (1) the need for the Priests' Universal Union; (2) that it does not aim at supplanting other clerical associations; and (3) that it will help them by infusing new life and vigour without adding any heavy burden.

" It seems to me that Jesus wishes an organisation which will unite the good and faithful priests and group them around their bishops in each diocese, and that these dioceses be linked together and grouped around the Pope."

(Letter to Monsignor Filipello, Oct., 1910)

" For the past two or three years, and even this year, associations for priests have been formed in different dioceses; that makes for much diversity without however effecting the unity which Jesus demanded and still demands."

(Letter to Father Charrier, June, 1911)

" Indeed this Work of Love (The Priests' Universal Union), so long desired and demanded by the Divine Master, seems to me to consist in a Universal bond between priests based on the love which Jesus has for them, and which they ought to have for Jesus. This must necessarily begin in some diocese, but it must not be a diocesan work. It is something universal that Jesus wishes, something that can be accommodated to all places, all minds and all usages."

(Letter to Father Charrier, June 1911)

" Our Lord asks very specially of priests' obedience of spirit, dependence on the guidance of their bishops, love for Himself, the Divine Priest and love for souls that are so dear to Him."

(Letter to Monsignor Filipello, February, 1918)

" **I have shown the Work (the Priests' Universal Union) as a bond of universal charity destined to be, not indeed an extra work added to the other works which are already numerous, but an all-embracing bond uniting together all other associations and making complete fusion of all the priests of the world together."**

(Letter from Rome to Monsignor Filipello, December, 1913)

A.—Who can be members of the Priests' Universal Union?

All priests, both secular and religious, who are willing to live the doctrine of Infinite Love and diffuse it among those committed to their care. This demands, not indeed that the priest who proposes to enter should have arrived at the perfect practice of the duties of a member of the union, but that he should have a sincere determination to carry out his obligations.

A general idea of these obligations may be got (1) from the first Article of the Statutes drawn up by Mother Louise Margaret : " The end of this organisation . . . . . is to procure the personal sanctification of its members by a true and practical devotion to Our Lord Jesus Christ and His Sacred Heart, the Tabernacle of Infinite Love, and to labour for the sanctification of souls in general by the development and good direction of the apostolic spirit " ; and from a letter to Monsignor Filipello, March, 1909, in which she says : " The priests of this organisation (which will not be merely a work of prayer, like that of Father Eymard, but an active work) will labour in the spirit of the little book—*The Sacred Heart and the Priesthood*— to spread the knowledge of Infinite Love around them, and preach love for Jesus Christ, God and Man, and fidelity to the Church and the Pope."

Members of the Union will therefore take their priesthood seriously and will regard it as a duty to strive earnestly to arrive at that perfection which their state demands. They will be, however, humble and un-assuming and full of delicate consideration for their brethren in the priesthood.

B.—Preparation for making the act of Consecration and Donation to Infinite Love :

The mere recitation of the formula of the Act of Consecration and Donation to Infinite Love, which is the official act of entry into the Priests' Universal Union, will not make a priest a live member.

A period of serious preparation should precede the important step of consecrating oneself to Infinite Love. The priest who intends to become a member should read and meditate on the writings of Mother Louise Margaret. He will find in her *Life* an account of the origin and nature of the Priests' Universal Union and of the necessity for preparation for those who wish to become members. *The Sacred Heart and the Priesthood* will teach him the sacerdotal virtues which Our Lord expects him to cultivate and the zeal with which he should discharge his obligations as a priest. It will teach him also to have a tender devotion to the Sacred Heart of Jesus and the Immaculate Heart of Mary. In order to be thoroughly imbued with the spirit of the Work of Infinite Love and to be able to diffuse it around him, he should read the other writings of Mother Louise Margaret also, all of which are now available.

C.—How to become a Member.

If there is a diocesan branch, the priest who desires to become a member should inform the diocesan Director. When he has made sufficient preparation he can choose his own day to make his Act of Consecration and Donation according to the formula which is to be found at the end of *The Sacred Heart and the Priesthood* and in the other books on the Work of Infinite Love. This he should sign, giving his address and the date, and should send it to the diocesan Director.

If there is no diocesan Director, the priest who desires to become a member can do so by reciting his act of Consecration and Donation to Infinite Love according to the formula found in the books on the Work of Infinite Love. This he should sign giving the date and his address, and send it to :

> The Rev. Secretary,
> L'Alliance Sacerdotale,
> Vische Canavese,
> Torino,
> Italy.

No special solemnity or ceremony is insisted on for the recitation of the Act of Consecration and Donation. However, as there is question of taking on serious obligations (which however do not bind under pain of sin) it is fitting that this act should be surrounded with a certain amount of solemnity. It is advised that the priest should select some of the great Feast days of the year to serve as a landmark and to remind him of the yearly Mass for the deceased members. If possible, a short retreat or at least a day of recollection should be made as a proximate preparation. This is a matter of counsel, however, and the priest is free to choose any day he wishes.

He is recommended to renew his Act of Consecration and Donation to Infinite Love frequently ; if he renews it each day, preferably after Mass, besides the partial indulgence of 300 days, he will gain a plenary indulgence once a month.

D.—The Priest should live his Act of Consecration.

The beautiful formula composed by Mother Louise Margaret contains an epitome of the doctrine of Infinite Love, a prayer to the Blessed Trinity, a solemn promise to preach the doctrine of Infinite Love and ends with a prayer to our Blessed Lady. True devotion to the Sacred Heart of Jesus, the Tabernacle of Infinite Love, devotion to each of the three Persons of the Blessed Trinity strongly insisted on by Mother Louise Margaret, a spirit of zeal and self-sacrifice and a tender devotion to our Blessed Lady should characterise the daily life of the priest-member of the Work of Infinite Love.

E.—Diocesan Sections.

When in any diocese there are a number of members belonging to the central branch at Vische in Italy, or a number of priests who have finished their preparation, they should unite and form a diocesan section according to the rules laid down in Article V, Nos. 7-11. No definite number is specified, but Mother Louise Margaret mentioned six as sufficient to make a beginning.

F.—Activities of the Diocesan Sections.

The General Statutes composed by Mother Louise Margaret lay down that all members should attend at least one of the conferences of the Priests' Universal Union each year. If besides this, there are regional or national meetings, members of the diocesan sections should endeavour to attend.

Both Monsignor Filipello and Mother Louise Margaret recognised the difficulties for busy priests to arrange frequent meetings. When therefore, priests of the Universal Union belong to some other clerical Union, as will usually happen, they should be faithful in attending the days of recollection arranged by the President of their Union.

It is left to the initiative of the diocesan Sections to arrange more frequent meetings.

Mother Louise Margaret gives the following recommendations for more frequent meetings of neighbouring priests and the following suggestions for what should be done at these meetings:

" It would be desirable that the priests of each city or of each district meet once a month under the presidency of a priest delegated or nominated by the diocesan President. This priest himself will either give a conference or invite another priest, who may be either a member or not, to give a conference on some subject connected with the Union. *The Sacred Heart and the Priesthood* and the other writings of Mother Louise Margaret provide both suggestions and material for these conferences.

" This conference should be simple and apostolic ; and should aim at doing good, rather than at being learned or literary.

" There should be some exercise of devotion in honour of the Sacred Heart of Jesus during the reunion.

" The opening session should be held in the Church or Chapel. After it, the members should withdraw to the residence of the President or to some hall for familiar discussion on religious topics which would excite in them the love of Jesus and zeal for the souls He loves so much. Ideas about problems of missionary life could be exchanged and doubts solved.

" Young priests would get from these conferences directions for their works of zeal and their studies and ideas for their sermons.

" It would be the duty of the President to conduct the different exercises of the reunion according to the spirit of the Statutes. He should visit members in case of sickness or trouble and give spiritual consolation.

" As the object of the Priests' Universal Union is to provide a bond of union between the priests of the world, Presidents of branches should keep the Central Council informed about their activities and should welcome directions from it thus helping to foster unity of views and of action among the members."

These meetings while showing the vitality of the section will serve to foster that perfect union, that family spirit which is a guarantee of fruitfulness in the priests' apostolic labours and a pledge of the blessings of God.

"Behold how good it is for brethren to dwell together in unity." (Psalms CXXXII, 1).

EXAMINATION TO BE MADE EACH DAY

The Heart of Jesus, the divine Priest, was dominated all the days of His life by three sentiments : an ardent thirst for the glory of His Father, a passionate desire for the salvation of the souls of His brethren, an irresistible and constant need of self-sacrifice and immolation.

Have these three sentiments dominated my heart today ? What have I done today to glorify my heavenly Father ? What have I undertaken for the good of my brethren ? What sacrifices have I made in union with Jesus immolated ?

I. Jesus, the divine Priest, willingly accepted opprobrium and humiliations to repair the glory of God. Have I, today, humbled myself before God, recognising my nothingness and my miseries, and referring to Him the glory of the good which I have accomplished by His grace ? Have I received with joy the contempt and the outrages of men ?

II. Jesus, the divine Priest, never thought of Himself. He left all things, stripping Himself of everything and becoming poor, in order to give Himself completely to the salvation of His brethren. What have I done today for my brethren with my time, with my heart, with my goods ; if I have not given of my material goods, have I at least used my intellectual and spiritual gifts for them ?

III. Jesus, the divine Priest, having lived in a spirit of continual sacrifice, at the end offered Himself on the cross, immolating His own life by love. Have I manifested the spirit of sacrifice in my actions of this day ? What sacrifice have I made today of my satisfactions of heart, of my contentment of mind, of my strength, of my repose, of my life, for the love of Jesus, and for souls ?

Profound and sorrowful regrets for the shortcomings of this day. Offering to the Heart of Jesus of the good accomplished.

PRAYER FOR THE GLORIFICATION OF THE SERVANT OF GOD, MOTHER LOUISE MARGARET

O Infinite Love, living in the Heart of Jesus, make Thyself known to men, in order that they may love Thee as Thou wishes to be loved. And since it has pleased Thy divine goodness to make use of Mother

Louise Margaret Claret de la Touche to make better known to priests the abysses of Thy Love and of Thy Mercy, and to draw men toward the Christian Priesthood, deign, we beseech Thee, to crown Thy works by glorifying Thy humble Servant and, through her intercession, realise in the world, under the guidance of the Supreme Pastor and the Bishops of Thy Church, unity of mind and heart in the light of truth and in the peace of Charity. Amen.

Those who receive favours through the intercession of Mother Louise Margaret are asked to communicate them to :

> *The Monastery of Bethany of the Sacred Heart,*
> *Vische Canavese,*
> *Torino,*
> *Italy.*

THE WORKS BY AND ABOUT
MOTHER LOUISE MARGARET CLARET DE LA TOUCHE

The Sacred Heart and the Priesthood
The Book of Infinite Love
The Little Book of the Work of Infinite Love
The Love and Service of God, Infinite Love (Containing a Message from Our Divine Lord for the Clergy of the World)
The Life and Work of Mother Louise Margaret Claret de la Touche (Containing a Message from Our Divine Lord for the Clergy of the World)

With the publication of this volume in 1987, all five books have been returned to print by TAN Books and Publishers, Inc.

Today the "Work of Infinite Love" envisioned by Mother Louise Margaret Claret de la Touche has four branches:

1) The Priests' Alliance
   Via Lamarmora, 31
   10030 VISCHE (TO), ITALY

2) Sisters of Bethany of the Sacred Heart
   Betania del Sacro Cuore
   10030 VISCHE (TO), ITALY

3) Missionaries of Infinite Love (a secular institute for women)
   Soggiorno Caritas
   10010 CANDIA (TO), ITALY

4) Friends of Bethany (for lay people)
   Betania del Sacro Cuore
   10030 VISCHE (TO), ITALY

   The Sisters also have houses in France and Argentina.

The director of the Work of Infinite Love for the United States is:

Father Vergil Heier, C.M.M.
Mariannhill Missionaries
23715 Ann Arbor Trail
Dearborn Heights, Michigan 48127

If you have enjoyed this book, consider making your next selection from among the following...